Reversed Gaze

GAZE

An African Ethnography of American Anthropology

REVERSED

MWENDA NTARANGWI

UNIVERSITY OF ILLINOIS PRESS

Urbana, Chicago, and Springfield

∞ This book is printed on acid-free paper.

Library of Congress Cataloging-in-Publication Data
Ntarangwi, Mwenda.
Reversed gaze : an African ethnography
of American anthropology / Mwenda Ntarangwi.
p.   cm.
Includes bibliographical references and index.
ISBN 978-0-252-03579-1 (cloth : alk. paper)
ISBN 978-0-252-07769-2 (pbk. : alk. paper)
1. Anthropology—United States.
2. Anthropology—Africa.
3. Ntarangwi, Mwenda. I. Title.
GN17.3.U6N83   2010
301.0973—dc22   2010025589

Contents

Preface   vii

Acknowledgments   xv

1. Imagining Anthropology, Encountering America   1
2. Tripping on Race, Training Anthropologists   24
3. Of Monkeys, Africans, and the Pursuit of the Other   52
4. Remembering Home, Contrasting Experiences   78
5. Mega-Anthropology: The AAA Annual Meetings   101
6. A New Paradigm for Twenty-First-Century Anthropology?   126

Notes   153

Bibliography   165

Index   177

Preface

This book is a personal journey into the heart of anthropology; representing my own pathways as an African student entering American higher education in the early 1990s to study a discipline that I knew very little about. It is a story about my initial entry into an American academic space very different from my own experience in Kenya, where we followed a British system of education. It is also a story hemmed within a specific discourse and views about anthropology that can be best represented by remarks from fellow graduate students who wondered what I was doing in a "racist" discipline. This story, woven through a series of mini-stories, explores the practice of American anthropology at home and presents a side of American anthropology often absent in books and journals. When I started the journey into anthropology through which this story is woven, I was not conversant with American academic politics, especially the perceptions of anthropology held by other scholars and students. Consequently, I became quite disturbed by the "racist" label placed on anthropology by fellow graduate students in other disciplines, particularly those in sociology and political science. Troubled by this label, I consciously embarked on a journey to find out more about the discipline.

Other than the glimpse I got into the subject after reading an introductory textbook, I had little knowledge of anthropology as a discipline—how it worked, where it came from, or how it related to other disciplines with which I was familiar. Yet I knew that Jomo Kenyatta, the first president of Kenya, had had a brush with some form of anthropology that enabled him write his treatise titled *Facing Mount Kenya,* in which he chronicled the life of his

Kikuyu community. Renowned anthropologist Branislow Malinowski added legitimacy to Kenyatta's book with an affirming introduction that emphasized the value of "native" perspectives in anthropology. Malinowski's emphasis on "native" perspectives came at a time when anthropology was continually facing the paradoxes and contradictions that other social sciences had been dealing with. On the one hand, the discipline was following a rigorous scientific study of human societies and cultures, while on the other, the discipline was being used to advance notions of social Darwinism that regarded non-Western cultures as inferior. In this regard, Malinowski was championing the fact that Africans such as Kenyatta had something important to contribute to the discipline. Kenyatta's philosophy of self-governance and a respect for traditional cultural practices is not far from many anthropological principles that I have now come to embrace as a trained anthropologist. Interestingly, despite Kenyatta's book being one of the very first ethnographies written by an African in the colonial context, he did not promote anthropology as a discipline in Kenya even after becoming the country's first president.[1] My journey into anthropology was by all standards an adventure.

I entered into graduate school in America to study anthropology in the fall of 1992 and graduated in spring of 1998. Even though my anthropology department in graduate school followed the four-field approach (having cultural, linguistic, archaeology, and physical anthropology subdisciplines), I focused on cultural anthropology. Studying in such a context allowed me to acquire a richer understanding of the discipline. And now, in retrospect, I see that it gave me an advantage as a professor who was introducing undergraduate students to the discipline.

I was in graduate school at a very dynamic phase in the discipline of anthropology in general and in American anthropology in particular. Even though I took courses that allowed for a glimpse into the history of the discipline, I almost felt as though I were entering into a movie theater when the feature film had already been running for a while. How else could I explain having to read E. E. Evans-Pritchard and Meyer Fortes on the one hand and George Marcus, James Clifford, and Chandra Mohanty, Ann Russo, and Lourdes Torres on the other? I was reading about British social anthropology and its functionalist approaches while also reading about challenges directed at the authority of ethnographic representation of social reality or of White feminist projects' insensitivity to the plight of women of color.[2] It was a time of questioning the authority of the grand narratives that had shaped much of Western anthropology for the first six decades of the twentieth century. I was in graduate school during the postmodern phase in anthropology, where emphasis was more on the practice of representing culture and the process of conducting research than on the content of the research itself.

I chose to enter into anthropology while in Kenya when searching for a discipline that would allow me to understand popular culture from a holistic approach. Anthropology, my academic mentor and friend in Kenya told me, was the best academic field for me. I was at the time studying and teaching at Kenyatta University, one of the very first public institutions of higher education in Kenya, named after Jomo Kenyatta. My mentor mentioned that anthropology was the discipline that would accommodate my interest in people, their cultures, and even the various reasons they gave for their daily activities. By choosing the field of anthropology as a graduate student, therefore, I was hoping to expand my academic purview to include a holistic approach to lived experiences and the human condition through popular culture that I had come to enjoy as a subject of study. It came as a shock to me, then, that a number of my graduate school colleagues in America would be so critical of a discipline in which I was now cultivating a great interest. Yet at some level, I did appreciate the critiques made against anthropology, especially when I took them in the spirit of listening to my critics in order to polish up my trade.

Not everything I encountered about anthropology was negative. I found inspiration in a number of texts that I was reading in graduate school, including Kenyatta's book in which Branislow Malinowski states that "Anthropology begins at home" and that "we must start by knowing ourselves first, and only then proceed to the more exotic savageries."[3] The excitement that these words stirred in me gave way to a number of questions. If anthropology truly begins at home as Malinowski states, how come, as I had thus far observed, anthropology tended to focus on the "exotic"? How come only a small percentage of fieldwork and scholarship by Western anthropologists focused on their own cultures, and when they did, it was among individuals and communities in the peripheries, their own "exotics" such as those in extreme poverty, in gangs, and others outside mainstream culture? How come calls by well-known anthropologists such as Paul Rabinow to "anthropologize the West . . . [and] show how exotic its constitution of reality has been" seemed to have not brought forth much fruit?[4] Interestingly, Rabinow's own fieldwork took him to many parts of Africa, a continent that continues to be a popular location for anthropological research. He, however, never quite "anthropologized the West," even though his most recent work on reason and knowledge does look at things Western. In the absence of Western studies of their own cultures, anthropology seemed like a discipline shaped primarily by its focus on its object, an object based on some sense of alterity. Despite all my doubts, however, I was quite drawn to the discipline.

My graduate training in anthropology, therefore, became a two-pronged activity: on the one hand, I gained anthropological skills through courses offered in the department of anthropology as well as interactions with my professors, and on the other, I was determined to challenge the projection of anthropology as a profession that solely focused on the "exotic." To accomplish the latter, I planned on showing that I, as an African student of anthropology, was acquiring the same tools that Western anthropologists possess but was also keen to direct those tools not to the study of some exotic culture but to the urban and cosmopolitan culture of the Swahili. My doctoral research in anthropology focused on the Swahili popular music genre of taarab. Indeed the Swahili had stunned earlier European scholars of East Africa for their lack of the "tribal" identities that were used in the eighteenth and nineteenth centuries to characterize communities that Europeans had encountered during their numerous explorations of Africa. Despite this departure from the focus on the "exotic tribal" culture, however, my field of interest remained quite removed from the Western metropolis where anthropological theories and methodologies were framed.

Over the course of graduate school, I became more and more convinced that my own interactions and understanding of American anthropology provided a great opportunity to change this skewed pattern of anthropological study and apply an ethnographic lens on a Western culture. I became especially interested in the practice of American anthropology, within which I was already embedded. That is, my study of that subject had earlier been set in motion by the practice of journal writing that I had started the first day I left Kenya for America and had continued over the six years I was in graduate school. Inadvertently, I had started an anthropological study of anthropology by keeping records of my observations, interactions, participation, and studies of America. It was these field notes that allowed me to turn an anthropological lens on anthropology and anthropologists in America.

The content of this book constitutes a reversal of the ethnographic gaze that Western intellectuals have used to conventionally produce anthropological knowledge, especially about non-Western peoples. As an African anthropologist writing about American anthropology and anthropologists, I create an ethnography that represents a drastic role reversal especially because Africans and Africa have been among the quintessential objects of Western anthropological inquiry and writing for decades. The book enters into the growing anthropological conversation on representation and self-reflexivity that ethnographers have come to regard as standard anthropological practice—a participation that I believe will open up some new dialogues in the field by allowing anthropologists to see the role played by subjective positions in shaping knowledge production and consumption. Recognizing and acknowledging the cultural and racial biases that shape anthropological study in general, this book reveals the potential for multiple voices and views in shaping the discipline and consequently decentering it from what Faye Harrison has called the Anglo-French axis.[5]

I organize the book around six chapters that build a case for an ethnography of anthropology in which I am at times the observer and the observed—the participant-observer. Chapter 1 starts with a contextualization of ethnographic studies of the Other in Western anthropology and my own encounter with anthropology as a discipline. I then weave in the story of my arrival in America, framed within flashbacks of my own encounter with Americans and with anthropology while I was in my native country, Kenya. That story explores the impressions that my earlier encounters with Americans left in my mind and explains how they prepared me for anthropological training in America. I then share my methodological approach as I discuss the "crisis" in ethnographic writing that many cultural anthropologists have used to develop the more reflexive anthropology—a crisis into which my story also fits and one that had almost reached fever pitch when I was in graduate school.

In chapter 2, I argue—through a step-by-step account of an ethnographic research project in which I participated along with other graduate students—that it is hard for anthropologists to study their own communities because of inherent power dynamics and asymmetry. By extension, I argue that it is easier for Western anthropologists to work in non-Western cultures because of the asymmetrical power relations that advantage anthropologists over the local people. I show that even though the research process in our group project was a failure, we made a good public presentation of it, giving credence to those critics who have often regarded ethnographies as works of fiction.

In chapter 3, I turn the observation lens onto anthropologists and examine how they seek out and represent their research subject. I provide three different but related frameworks to see "anthropology in action" and to explain how this action is shaped or shapes the ethnographic project itself. I begin at the basic anthropological level with an analysis of an undergraduate anthropology association's meeting flyer and its hidden racialized imagery. I ask how anthropology students as members of the larger society bring to anthropology certain cultural habits and mental tendencies that "discreetly" creep into their mundane work. I then follow this analysis with a discussion of anthropology's quintessential romance with alterity by showing how some anthropologists—unable to conduct field research in Africa—never give up on their pursuit of Africans but rather follow them to the American metropolis. I end the chapter with an analysis of the ethnographic moment often favored by anthropologists, wondering how field notes that are twenty and thirty years old can be used to make comments about contemporary societies.

In chapter 4, I reflect on my own culture by using my anthropological training as I returned home to Kenya after two years in America. I seek to see how anthropology prepares one to study or "objectively" observe his or her culture by asking if indeed anthropology does equip one with a new set of lenses to view and critique one's own culture. I explore this issue by recording my reactions and observations of a culture that, because I was raised in it, I took for granted but am now able to look into it with a new set of eyes—a perception that I cultivated through anthropology and the experience of living in another and/or different culture. In this analysis, I focus on my own challenges in adjusting to my own culture, not as a product of a planned ethnographic study but as an individual trying to make sense of home after a few years of dislocation. I discuss the value of objectivity—the heightened sense of observation and analysis that comes from anthropological training and the changed social relations I found at home as well as from my observations of American culture upon my return from Kenya. In doing so, I enter the anthropological discourse on reflexivity and positionality, but I do so from two spatial locations.

In chapter 5, I provide an analysis of anthropological association annual meetings as symbolic sites that allow for an understanding of anthropology as an academic enterprise as well as a mirror of the history and practice of anthropology. By using my observations and my participation at the annual meetings of the American Anthropological Association, the Pan-Africa Anthropological Association, and the Association of Social Anthropology in the UK and the Commonwealth, I argue that just as America has become an economic and political empire, American anthropology has consolidated a lot of power and in the process has peripheralized other anthropologies, forcing them either to respond to its whims and hegemony or to lose their international presence and appeal. The American Anthropological Association (AAA), I argue, is an important cultural phenomenon that begs for an ethnographic analysis.

I conclude the book in chapter 6 by contextualizing my own academic identity within African studies by providing an analysis of some of the efforts that have been made by anthropologists, especially in Europe and North

America, to address the imbalance of power in the epistemology of and their own relationship to the anthropological subject. What is the relationship between anthropology and area studies— for instance, African studies? What lessons can anthropology learn from the experiences of African studies in an era of increased marginalization of area studies and heightened focus on global and transnational processes? I share examples of the kind of discussions going on within the AAA regarding possible strategies to engage with other anthropologies through collaboration and partnerships with organizations, departments, and individuals. As a discipline built on collaboration at the very basic frame of its operation, anthropology seems naturally suited for such collaboration and even charting the way forward in providing models of responding to global changes and area-specific academic practices. The recently launched programs on the World Council of Anthropology Associations (WCAA) network, the World Anthropology Network (WAN), and the Commission on World Anthropologies (CWA) network provide a good basis for this discussion. Using some examples of the practice of anthropology in contemporary Africa, I further argue for a systematic process of training and collaborating across national and continental boundaries in order to build world anthropologies. My hope is that anthropology has entered a new era that challenges the traditional focus on Otherness and alterity.

Acknowledgments

Support for writing this manuscript was generously provided by the Wenner-Gren Foundation for Anthropological Research, Inc., under the Hunt Postdoctoral Fellowship (Gr. 7532) to whom I am most sincerely grateful. My initial training as an anthropologist was also enhanced by support from Wenner-Gren Foundation for Anthropological Research, Inc., and I remain indebted to the organization's support of various phases of my life as an anthropologist. I would also like to thank Paul Robinson, Bill Martin, Njeri Bere, Owen Sichone, Maurice Amutabi, Andrea Freidus, and Aleksandar Bošković for all their comments on various parts of the manuscript. The initial proposal to seek funding for the manuscript had the good fortune of going through the keen eyes of Steve Hager whose comments are greatly appreciated.

As always my family has been very supportive of the work that I do as a scholar and I wish to thank my wife and friend, Margaret, our daughters Nkatha and Gatwiri for putting up with my constant work behind the computer. I am also very lucky to have a family that is genuinely interested in my academic writing and one that gives me critical perspectives regarding some of the issues that indirectly involve them and which I touch on in this work. I am also very grateful to two anonymous reviewers commissioned by the University of Illinois Press to read my entire manuscript. Their comments have greatly shaped this manuscript. Working with staff at the University of Illinois Press has been such a great joy not only throughout the work entailed in preparing this manuscript for publication but in my earlier book published by University of Illinois Press as well. I am especially indebted to Joan

Catapano, Angela Burton, and Copenhaver Cumpston, who have supported me through some of the intricate steps of getting my manuscript ready for publication. I am also grateful to Gayle Swanson for her careful reading and very insightful editing of the final draft of this book. I take responsibility for all ideas and positions represented in this book.

1

Imagining Anthropology, Encountering America

Introduction

Anthropologists' accounts of how they navigate their first moments in the field have given us clues to understanding the fieldwork enterprise.[1] In doing so, some anthropologists have often problematized their own subjectivity in the field (e.g., race, gender, class, or ethnicity) and the way it affects their process of data collection and analysis.[2] Following these "revelations" as well as various "crises" in the profession, some critiques of anthropology have come to regard ethnography as a contingent fiction that neatly packages otherwise disparate parts of culture and obscures the power relations and poetics of writing about a culture or cultures.[3] Such a critique may account for the move by some anthropologists to write against culture[4] or to share more about their subjectivity, struggles, and faults of the fieldwork process that produces ethnographies of various communities, peoples, and cultures.[5] Yet despite this subjective and reflexive turn in anthropology, few anthropological accounts tell us about matters such as how anthropologists conduct their lives at home; how they navigate race, class, and gender in their own institutions and communities;[6] or how they see those subjectivities playing out in their own fieldwork. Further, because "revelations" of the politics and poetics of Western ethnographies are predominantly provided by the Western anthropologists themselves by virtue of their preponderance in the discipline, readers of such ethnographic accounts or memoirs get to see only the parts that the authors choose to reveal or share. These "revelations" become "censored excerpts of the ethnographic enterprise" and, as a result, "rather than leading to the dismantling of canonical anthropologies, most critiques of the discipline have resulted—unwittingly—in the very reinvigoration and worldwide expansion of these standards through elite centers of anthropological production."[7] In a way, Western anthropologists end up "laughing" at themselves and the foibles of their fieldwork without really undermining their own authority and legitimacy as the default "representers" of the realities of the Other that they study. In other words, these representations of self as vulnerable and inadequate in the conducting of fieldwork do not in any way weaken the products of the fieldwork: the ethnographies.

Through an ethnography of anthropology, I present in this book an aspect of the "hidden/unrevealed" sides of Western anthropology that do not usually show up in the numerous accounts of field experiences that are present in the reflexive ethnographies and memoirs that are now a standard part of anthropological literature. I focus my analysis on anthropologists' subjectivities as they "practice" anthropology within academic departments, at professional meetings, in classrooms and lecture halls, and through ethnographic writing—all of which constitute the "other side" of anthropological practice that is often absent in scholarly papers, ethnographies, and memoirs. I embark on this project by asking a number of questions, including the following: (1) How different are anthropologists' lives at home in their own institutional and cultural contexts from their lives abroad while conducting the research that they subsequently share in their memoirs and ethnographies? (2) What part of the anthropologist's identity revealed in ethnographies is shaped by his or her own culture and how can it provide a window to an understanding of the general anthropological enterprise? (3) How do students of anthropology navigate the challenges of ethnography while undergoing training in their own institutions before they go "out" to the "field" to undertake their major ethnographic projects, and how might these projects inform each other? (4) Are "mini-ethnographies," conducted at home to fulfill research methods course requirements, symbolic representations of dissertation fieldwork carried out in any discipline? (5) How do anthropologists interact at annual professional meetings, and what does that interaction say about anthropology as a discipline within the larger terrain of academic practice? Is the annual meeting a ritual similar to the Balinese cockfight analyzed by Clifford Geertz, in which symbolic and interpretive analysis can decode meanings and lead to an understanding of an anthropological culture?[8] (6) Are anthropologists, as Melford Spiro has argued, alienated and hostile to their own Western culture so much that they compensate for it by idealizing other cultures through noble savagism?[9]

To answer these and other related questions I analyze American anthropology, anthropologists, and the "culture of anthropology," from a vantage point of a student of anthropology in training and later as a professional anthropologist teaching in America and sometimes Africa. I trace my own experiences and immersion into the culture of American anthropology mediated through textbooks, ethnographies, feedback, coursework, and professional meetings. My analysis encompasses my life before, during, and after graduate studies in anthropology—from the beginning, with my arrival from Kenya to start graduate studies in cultural anthropology in a large research university in the Midwest, to my subsequent transformation into a professor at a liberal arts college in the Northeast, teaching students in both the United States and sometimes Africa. This "African" ethnography of cultural anthropology continues the reflexive turn in ethnographic writing but also challenges some of the more unquestioned positions found in anthropological culture that have not promoted diverse participation and democratic decision-making procedures in the identity and praxis of the profession.[10]

Africa and Africans have been the subject and object of anthropological study for decades. And because anthropology as a discipline reflects the world-views and experiences of its practitioners, the image of Africa and Africans has often been shaped by specific Western notions of alterity. I seek to bring an African perspective into understanding anthropology, primarily endeavoring to use the tools of anthropology to decipher the underlying anthropological culture that has so much impacted the ways that Africans are studied and perceived. By using the term *Africans* here, I do not mean to generalize Africanity but rather to appreciate the shared history of Africans as being the object and subject of an anthropological inquiry that seems to be replicated irrespective of the particular African culture being studied. Using the same research tools that Western anthropologists have used to study Africans, I look at anthropology within the subjective positioning of being an African myself—or being what Faye Harrison has termed an "outsider within."[11] It is this subjectivity, this position of being African, that informs and allows for a specific perspective of an outsider looking into anthropology.

This book critiques dominant tenets of reflexivity, where issues of representation are reduced to anthropologists' writing style, methodological assumptions, and fieldwork locations—which in turn mask the inherent power differences that make it easier for anthropologists to study other people ("studying down") than to study themselves ("studying up"), as was envisaged by Laura Nader in her seminal essay on "studying up."[12] Through an ethnography of life on a university campus, of my interactions with anthropologists and students in anthropology, of my observations and participation at annual anthropology meetings, of my teaching anthropology courses to students, and of my reading anthropological accounts recorded in academic books and journals, I contextualize my analysis within larger debates in anthropology about race, class, power, epistemology, and the representation of the Other. I seek to continue the ongoing debates in and outside anthropology about representation, ethnography, and anthropological knowledge production that contributes to the process of "liberating the discipline from the constraints of its colonial legacy and post- or neocolonial predicament."[13] In this regard, I am particularly inspired by anthropologists whose works I had to find for myself in graduate school—such as St. Clair Drake and Faye Harrison[14]—and who have produced important ethnographies as well as important critiques of anthropology from the vantage of alternative epistemologies and standpoints.[15] Unlike most ethnographies, however, this current project focuses on lives of my fellow anthropologists in their own spatial locations and in the first language of the research subject. It is, therefore, an ethnography of anthropologists for anthropologists in ways that many ethnographies are not. It is a reversal of the anthropological gaze that presents anthropology as a cultural critique of both Western culture and the discipline itself (an anthropology of anthropology itself) as well as an effort toward, in Harrison's words, "'reworking' the field."[16]

Anthropology through the Back Door?

My own encounter with anthropology as an entity of intellectual curiosity came through a cultural anthropology textbook I read during my master's degree study at Kenyatta University in Kenya. My professor and mentor, Chacha Nyaigotti-Chacha, upon considering my desire to pursue a more holistic study of music, concluded that I would benefit from anthropological training and thus lent me a copy of Ember and Ember's introductory text, *Cultural Anthropology*. I read the work within a week—the fastest I had ever read any book, let alone a textbook. Its content intrigued me; it spoke directly to my own academic yearning for an approach that would incorporate multiple facets of life in an analysis of a cultural product like music. The authors talked about a holistic and contextual approach to culture in which the researcher assumes the position of a learner. Professor Nyaigotti-Chacha had himself started his doctoral studies at Yale in linguistics but was drawn to the anthropology department, to which he transferred with the support of Professor Keith Basso. Unfortunately, Professor Basso left Yale before Professor Nyaigotti-Chacha had finished his dissertation, but Professor John Middleton stepped in and worked with Professor Nyaigotti-Chacha to finish his degree. In both my undergraduate and graduate studies in Kenya, I had found Professor Nyaigotti-Chacha's teaching style and research very appealing and wondered if his training in anthropology had contributed to his having such a different pedagogical praxis. I wanted to be like Professor Nyaigotti-Chacha—to regard students not as dry sponges that were ready to soak up knowledge from the "sage on stage," as many of my other teachers in Kenya did, but as curious learners with opinions and insights that would also enhance the teacher's knowledge. He became my good friend and mentor and has continued to be so.

The effect that the Ember and Ember text had on me was so profound that I changed my graduate school focus from sociolinguistics to anthropology. I was at the time teaching Kiswahili language and literature at Kenyatta University and planning to pursue a doctoral degree in sociolinguistics. A year after reading Ember and Ember, I moved from Kenyatta University to Egerton University, where Professor Nyaigotti-Chacha had moved and already established a vibrant faculty of arts and social sciences. He was in the process of recruiting faculty members from various institutions in Kenya to build the newly instituted departments. I became one of his recruits and joined the Department of Languages and Linguistics to teach courses related to Swahili culture and linguistics. My research interests, however, continued to lean toward popular music, and I hoped that one day I would channel those interests into a doctoral program.

Previously, while pursuing my master's degree at Kenyatta University, I had carried out research on the popular music of Zairian-born Tanzania-based musician Ramathan Mtoro Ongala (commonly known as Remmy Ongala). I specifically analyzed themes of protest in his songs, seeking out texts that represented the needs and tribulations of the socially marginalized. Remmy's music was particularly attractive to me because I was (and still am) interested in the role that music plays not only in reflecting social reality but also in shaping that reality. In retrospect, I now know that I was also interested in social justice issues, which continue to be a dominant theme in my research and teaching. As a discipline, anthropology provides for me an important framework for understanding and engaging social justice. I had chosen Remmy's music because it represented a slice of music that stood up for the marginalized, and he was literally the "voice of the poor." His signature song, "Sauti ya Mnyonge" (Voice of the weak), for instance, continues to occupy an important place in the terrain of East Africa's repertoire of music with messages of social justice. During my investigation of Remmy's music lyrics, I realized that even though I was broadly interested in social justice, I needed to start cutting through its numerous layers of analyses and come up with a more manageable frame.

One such layer was the gendered way in which people encountered social injustice—the way that men and women experience life differently because of their gendered identities. In analyzing Remmy's songs, I was particularly drawn to a song titled "Fatuma," in which Remmy came to the defense of a woman who had seemingly succeeded economically in a male-dominated world despite various cultural and economic barriers. Remmy was using the song to challenge the demeaning position that society had created for the woman. This challenge aligned well with the anthropological explanation of gender as culturally constructed, which I had read about in the Ember and Ember textbook. It was yet another positive connection between my research interests and the discipline of anthropology. I started to see myself pursuing further studies in anthropology so that I could continue with these kinds of analyses within a discipline that seemed suited for multiple approaches to cultural practices.

While I was drawn to Remmy's excellent articulation and depiction of the social challenges facing women as marginalized members of their societies, I was also interested in finding women musicians who mobilized music to challenge their own culture's status quo. I wanted to know if women were themselves challenging the status quo or if it were male artists who, on their behalf, did so. I wanted to see women who represent themselves, so I started looking back at the music I knew from the past in search of appropriate examples. Luckily I recalled a few songs sung by women who challenged unequal gender realities. Some of those pieces were in the traditional songs genre while others were in the realm of popular music. I particularly remembered songs by Queen Jane (Jane Nyambura, a popular musician in Kenya who mostly sang in Kikuyu, which is the language of the largest ethnic group in Kenya) that had often found their way into the then state-owned radio station in Kenya. Many of her songs were about love and relationships, but a few had themes that articulated and castigated the oppressive behavior that men exercised toward women. Having majored in Swahili cultural studies in my undergraduate studies at Kenyatta University, however, I found myself more and more interested in songs by women that were sung in Swahili—or Kiswahili, as it is known.

In my undergraduate days at Kenyatta University, I had been captivated by Swahili poetry and was analytically drawn to taarab music and its literary value. For the most part, taarab is Swahili poetry that is sung with instrumental accompaniment. And even though it is a music genre mostly associated with the Swahili living along the East African coast and other urban areas in East Africa, it has found wider distribution through radio and commercial recordings.[17] I heard my first taarab song on radio when I was in high school. Later, after I had completed my graduate work at Kenyatta University and written my thesis on Remmy's music, I zeroed in on taarab music as my next research project, seeking to understand it more through a new framework that used gender as a unit of analysis. In making a choice to study taarab, I was able to find music that was sung in Kiswahili and also music performed by women that had messages of social protest. At the time of engaging this new academic adventure, I was aware of only two female taarab musicians—Zuhura Swaleh and Malika Mohammed (both based in Mombasa, Kenya, at the time). I was convinced that these two musicians provided a good enough starting base for my new research project but were within the realm of popular music with which I had already become acquainted.

As part of my research and analysis of Remmy's music, I had had some field experience, traveling to Dar es Salaam, Tanzania, interviewing Remmy about his music experiences, attending some live performances of his shows, and also consulting some secondary material at the Institute of Kiswahili Research at the University of Dar es Salaam. In retrospect I see that I was being prepared for my ultimate training in anthropology, where fieldwork was the expected rite of passage. Although much of the graduate students' research in my department at Kenyatta University entailed textual analysis, I was more interested in an analysis that sought data outside of the texts, to include the everyday life of the musicians and consumers of their music. This was to become the first of my many projects on popular music, especially the role it plays in representing social reality. My research interest in taarab was later rewarded when I received funding from the Organization for Social Science Research in Eastern Africa (OSSREA), based in Addis Ababa, Ethiopia. As it would turn out, that initial research project on taarab would later morph into my doctoral dissertation research as a cultural anthropology student in America.

When I finally decided to look into anthropology programs for graduate school admission in America, I had already been prepared for anthropology even though I did not realize it.[18] I had enjoyed a multidisciplinary background in my undergraduate training in Kenya, having majored in language education with a focus on Kiswahili and a minor in physical education. In terms of academic pursuits, I had become interested in popular music but never quite felt drawn to the research approaches that were current at the music department at Kenyatta University. I did not want to study traditional African instruments, or even learn to play any musical instruments, and did not want to learn how to read music either. I was interested in music as cultural texts—in what the music had to say about the everyday life of the people it targeted and reached. I wanted to know who listens to certain songs and what messages one derives from such songs. I wanted to know how recorded music differed from music performed at live shows. As a result of these interests, I felt constrained by the disciplinary boundaries that were overtly expressed not only by some of my teachers but also through our department philosophies. Many were the times when colleagues and teachers alike would ask me if my analysis of popular music texts constituted studies in literature or musicology. I had, for instance, to convince the graduate school board of the Faculty of Arts and Social Sciences at Kenyatta University that popular music was part of oral literature and that my study of Remmy Ongala's music was a legitimate topic of academic investigation in the Department of Kiswahili and African Languages.[19] I now believe that it is this multidisciplinary approach together with a holistic approach to research that led me to find an academic home in anthropology.

Moreover, my experiences at Kenyatta University were important in two ways: first, the core task of my department was to teach Swahili language and Swahili culture in a postcolonial education system where English language and literature dominated. As a student, I was introduced to Swahili culture and its contributions to the African intellectual world through world poetry and urban culture especially. Second, the department had an inherent interdisciplinarity in its approach to course content and analysis as well as a core of faculty members who were from different cultural backgrounds and were trained in different institutions and countries (such as Tanzania, Uganda, Kenya, the United States, and Germany). The perspectives and interactions that resulted from this amalgam of cultures and pedagogies prepared me, as Clifford Geertz so aptly put it, for my "academic identity and an ambition to connect just about everything with everything else and get, thereby, to the bottom of things."[20] Later my training in anthropology provided the opportunity for me to "get to the bottom of things" and identify myself as an anthropologist, but my initial preparations for anthropology came through my experiences and even frustrations in my Kenyan academic context.[21] What remained, it would seem, was formal validation of that anthropological identity by my joining an anthropology program.

Methodological and Theoretical Orientations

Entering anthropology with no formal training meant that I lacked the theoretical training I needed to analyze culture and society as anthropologists do. This theoretical training came not only when I studied under different professors in graduate school but also when I interacted with other students from all over the world. Even though I did not initially train as an anthropologist, I have always marveled at my initial unplanned decision to keep a "field" journal the first day I left Kenya. For the entire time I lived in America as a graduate student and later as a practicing anthropologist, I kept notes of my daily (and later, monthly) observations, thoughts, and interpretations of perceptions and experiences I had had in an American university context. I had found numerous opportunities to associate with students who were themselves undergoing training to be anthropologists within a department staffed by many anthropologists. Whenever possible, I took part in conversations with students and others not connected to the university as a way of getting to understand more of what I was observing and experiencing while living in America.

I was intrigued by many cultural practices that I witnessed and even participated in everyday experiences during my time in America. I remember, for instance, wondering once who had died in the city I was living in because I had noticed that many public buses and personal cars were displaying red ribbons. In Kenya, red ribbons on vehicles signify a funeral entourage. I had carried over that same symbolic meaning into my new location in America, and it is only when I saw the ribbons on vehicles for about two weeks that I gathered enough courage to ask one of my classmates what the ribbons signified. I was told that they signified the festive season of Christmas and other events around the fall and winter seasons. I took notes of such cross-cultural intrigues, of meetings and conversations in which I participated, and collected as much data as I could about anthropology, anthropologists, and America. I also remember a fellow graduate student in anthropology asking me if I had grown up with elephants in my backyard. I thought she was joking, but upon probing further, I realized she was serious. It is in the act of trying to understand these and other experiences and observations within a canvas of my own cultural orientation that I realized I was actually studying anthropology and America. I was reversing the anthropological gaze to focus on Western culture and on anthropologists in their own country as well as on myself and my culture both in and outside my country. I was able to collect enough ethnographic information to match what many ethnographers have been able to collect in their fieldwork in any location. I lived with Americans, read their books, interacted with them on many levels, and spoke their language; I became a participant-observer and recorded all of this information for a period of over ten years, culminating in almost nine hundred pages of hand-written notes in six notebooks.

Now as a trained anthropologist, however, I must say that what I present here is not the undiluted culture of America and of anthropologists but rather my understanding and interpretation of the ways and thoughts of individuals with whom I have interacted and of events that I have attended. It is an account of how Americans and anthropologists with whom I associated had constructed what I consider to be a relatively consistent and shared set of actions, thoughts, and beliefs that constitute a cultural logic that made sense to me. In the process, I encountered Americans and American anthropologists against the backdrop of my own culture, making this book as much about American anthropology as it is about my own cultural background; it is a conversation between two cultures and an analysis of key elements in the composition of that conversation within an anthropological frame.

I believe that my interactions with American anthropologists were events in which overarching cultural factors and elements were played out and manifested. For us as anthropologists, the difficulty is not in seeing this reality but in discerning the connections and influences of our own cultural orientation in our interpretations of observations and experiences and understanding the ways in which that orientation shapes the small expressions of everyday as well as the broader topics of ethnographic research. In retrospect I can say that even though I have tried to tease out the cultural differences that I think would enable a reader to see some common aspects of American anthropology, anthropologists, and their cultures, I am convinced that at the deeper level, we all are engaged in pursuing similar goals—seeking a higher quality of life, a clear understanding of our place in this world, some joy and happiness, and the ability to be accepted socially and emotionally. We are more similar to one another than we are different (even if anthropologists have often tried to focus solely on the differences), and it is in the (small) differences that we reflexively become aware of ourselves. How we do relate to others and our contexts and the meanings we attach to the pursuit of joy and happiness is what constitutes our cultural differences. Ethnographies are often made of these cultural differences, which I too highlight in this project. I look beyond common human traits by trying to understand another culture from the vantage point of my own. I, an African studying a Western culture through my training to become an anthropologist in America, constitute in this book a "reversed gaze." It is a gaze that I now realize was nurtured in a context quite amenable to anthropology while I was living in Kenya and later in America. My further experiences in Botswana, Britain, Cameroon, Ethiopia, Germany, Ghana, Liberia, Mozambique, Rwanda, Senegal, South Africa, Southern Sudan, Tanzania, Uganda, and Zimbabwe have also added to this cross-cultural frame that informs the writing of this project.

In the first two years of coursework in my anthropology doctoral program, I started to become interested in theoretical approaches that allowed me to develop a critical distance for understanding the new culture in which I was living and studying. I was particularly drawn to symbolic and interpretive analysis because when I joined the Department of Anthropology in the American university I attended, there were two professors under whom I took many courses and who embraced the reflexive turn in ethnographic writing. Both professors shared a style of ethnographic writing that emphasized multivocality, reflexivity, and a general discomfort with ethnographic authority. This symbolic and interpretive analysis is represented in the works of Edward Bruner, Clifford Geertz, Alma Gottlieb, Sherry Ortner, Edith Turner, and Victor Turner.[22] A symbolic and interpretive approach to anthropology would become an important analytical tool for my own research. In a general sense, this approach focuses on meanings manifested through people's actions and utterances that are themselves symbols representing social life. Symbolic and interpretive anthropology allows us "to access" a culture or community by using locally derived objects of representation. Within such a methodology, anthropologists analyze symbols and social texts (such as myth, stories, ritual, and performance) by which humans assign meanings in order to address fundamental questions about human social life.[23]

Following Clifford Geertz's interpretive approach I see culture as patterns embedded in a web of meanings that can be symbolically analyzed to give a better understanding of human aspirations, experiences, and practices. As Sherry Ortner has written, Geertz argued that "Culture is not something locked inside people's heads, but rather is embodied in public symbols, symbols through which the members of a society communicate their world-view, value-orientations, ethos, and all the rest to one another, to future generations—and to anthropologists."[24] In my own anthropological work, I have been particularly drawn to this idea of culture that Geertz favored as well as that of Victor Turner, who—as Ortner expresses it—saw symbols not as carriers of culture but as "operators in the social process, things that when put together in certain arrangements in certain contexts (especially rituals) produce essentially social transformations."[25]

Through the work of Geertz and Turner, I have come to regard culture as the shared ethos and world-view of a group or community that is constantly negotiated and reshaped through performance and process.[26] Even though the concept of culture has been greatly debated,[27] I find a combination of the theories propounded by these two anthropologists to be quite compelling. And the reason for its appeal to me is that the criticism leveled against Geertz's culture concept—by those who have seen it as a recipe for essentializing and reifying groups or communities as a distinct Other[28]—is subsequently addressed in Turner's ideas about "social dramas" that provide for schism and social change through "liminality" and "communitas."[29] Further, since my work is mostly in the realm of expressive culture, I find this culture concept useful in my analysis of the way in which participants in popular music, for instance, often use music and dance as political critiques and tools for cultural survival in a world in which there is an increased marginalization of indigenous cultures. I see music as texts that act as metasocial commentaries that the practitioners mobilize to talk about their cultures. In the same way, I see ethnographies, anthropology courses, professional meetings, and anthropology department meetings as texts that symbolize broader meanings. By analyzing them, I believe, I am privy to locally generated cultural tools for understanding local social realities as well as larger anthropological themes and practices. This approach, I believe, finds its strength in symbolic and interpretive anthropology.

In this regard, I share with Sherry Ortner—and other anthropologists who have an interpretive and constructivist proclivity—a specific understanding of culture that sees it as "shared by a group, part of their collective form of life, embodying their shared history and identity, worldview and ethos."[30] For me these symbols are located in expressive culture as products and producers of social realities. This is the theoretical orientation I have pursued in my research—especially in my focus on expressive culture[31]—because of my conviction that in every society creative expressions (music, art, dance, and so forth) provide much more than an expression of beauty, rhythm, or aesthetics; they also create and maintain social values in surprisingly profound ways. It is through the use of anthropological approaches of fieldwork and symbolic analysis that meanings embedded in the expressive genres can be accessed and understood. I bring this same approach to the current analysis of anthropology—looking at various cultural texts such as professional meetings, ethnographies, and classroom behavior—and regard them as rituals loaded with cultural meanings that are appropriated through a symbolic and interpretive approach.

Anthropology's Subject and Politics of Representation

Reading ethnographies and memoirs written by anthropologists opens up windows into other cultures, the lives of anthropologists, and anthropology itself. These ethnographies are, however, mostly coherent texts, telling seamless stories of a culture or community in ways that are not replicable in real life. In this way, ethnographic writing can be regarded as a cultural industry, a dynamic process of not only representing different cultures but also of selectively recording, authenticating, and making ethnography important by validating some of their aspects and not others, in order to reflect the ideal cultural images ethnographers seek. Anthropologists often use ethnographies to highlight and codify cultures into neat categories that exclude the complexities of the everyday that they try to represent.[32] Lives of the Other dominate storylines in ethnographies as Western or Western-trained anthropologists embark on living with, understanding, and examining cultures that are mostly non-Western.[33] This Otherness that is often objectified through ethnography creates almost unconscious desires, founded in Western ideology and epistemology, for a "Western gaze" a specific way of perceiving and experiencing the world that pits the West against the rest of the world in a top-down model constituted through power and exercised by the West.

This Western gaze is shaped both by the Western physical encounter with the Other as well as the imagined reality of the Other. Interestingly the Western gaze manifests itself also in the "Other's" perception and presentation of self so much that even when alone, the Other has this overwhelming desire to project self in a way that fits the West's construction of the Other. This is best exemplified in "Operation Dress-Up" in Tanzania, where the government forced the Maasai to dress up in Western clothes in order to look "presentable" and be "hygienic."[34] No one, in my knowledge, was directly asking the Tanzanian government to force its people to wear Western clothing. The government was intent on making sure the Maasai looked presentable, not to themselves but to an imagined Western audience—or at least so that the Maasai would fulfill an assumed national image of modernity.

Despite an overwhelming Western presence in the academy and especially in anthropology, the last four decades of academic anthropology have, however, been characterized by an epistemological and political shift, moving from these Western studies and representations of other cultures to an inquiry into the poetics and politics of ethnography.[35] "Other" voices have begun to appear in academia, illuminating the transformation of social reality from empiricism and positivism to reflexivity, constructivism, and interpretivism. Ethnographies are no longer considered objective accounts of culture recorded by detached anthropologists but, rather, accounts that incorporate the subjective positions of anthropologists. Yet a closer scrutiny into this epistemological and political shift reveals an interesting continuity: the bulk of anthropological inquiry remains focused on Other cultures.

When Western anthropologists study Western cultures, they tend—with a few exceptions—to concentrate on cultures on the "margins," such as ethnic/racial minorities, immigrants, communities of individuals with different sexual orientations, and the poor.[36] While studies of these cultures on the "margins" have contributed greatly to our understanding of the human condition, sociocultural anthropology primarily remains very much a Western enterprise that heavily focuses on the Other—despite attempts to portray it as a discipline no longer pursuing the "exotic."[37]

Since the 1970s (and even earlier), critiques of anthropology have emerged within and outside the discipline and have continued to this day. Some of the critiques came from non-Western anthropologists[38]—together with a small but important group of Western colleagues[39]—who found fault with the way anthropology presented its subject. These Western critiques of Western anthropology sought to "reinvent" the discipline of anthropology in response to changing sociopolitical relations in the world as well as to paradigmatic changes in academia that called for a different way of even imagining the ethnographic field site.

Critiques by non-Western anthropologists argue that this Other (non-Western) subject of inquiry is a construct of the Western gaze, subsumed in a dominant Western project of Othering that produces ethnographic accounts of passive and disempowered peoples and cultures. Such critiques demonstrated that many ethnographies are texts and representations of a very specific Eurocentric perspective of Others—one of authority, advantage, power, and analytical dominance. Other critiques have produced the notion of the cultural construction of reality and of place and people as exemplified in the "idea of Africa" that Zairian philosopher Valentine Mudimbe has so eloquently addressed.[40] Dominant ethnographic approaches place Western anthropologists somewhere on top of a mountain gazing into the Other, and as a result, the Other knows how to "pose" even when the Western anthropologist is physically absent, as I have exemplified above with the case of the Maasai in Tanzania.

This gazing, while having been perfected by Western anthropologists, has undergone a reversal. Non-Western anthropologists have steadily studied Western cultures and are continually writing about them.[41] Yet their numbers are still negligible compared to their Western counterparts studying non-Western cultures. John Ogbu's extensive work on race and access to education in some major American cities is one project that comes to mind.[42] His study of Western cultures pales in comparison, however, to the numerous studies conducted by Western anthropologists of non-Western culture and even of Ogbu's own cultures in Nigeria. Ogbu's research predominantly focused on what I refer to as cultures on the "margins," which hardly represent the cultures of the bulk of Western anthropologists. Ogbu's studies constitute, in a way, anthropology of a second category—a category of the Other not because there isn't value in such studies but because anthropology as a discipline was and continues to be shaped by what Faye Harrison calls the British, French and American axes that limit what can be studied, who can study it, and who becomes the "leading light" of the profession.[43]

Such disciplinary dominance has not deterred many determined anthropologists, who have persisted in producing monographs that "disturb" the status quo. I am here thinking of such scholars as Archie Mafeje, Ben Magubane, and St. Clair Drake, whose works and professional practice often found more acceptance in sociology than in anthropology. I am also thinking of other anthropologists such as Faye Harrison, Lee Baker, Maxwell Owusu, and Elliott Skinner, whose acceptance into the discipline of anthropology has paved the way for them to bring to it alternative epistemologies informed by their own subjectivities as anthropologists. Finally, there is another group of anthropologists represented by such individuals as Karen Sacks, Brett Williams, Pem Davidson Buck, Virginia Dominguez, John Hartigan, and Micaela Di Leonardo, whose research into various sectors of American culture transcends the Othering and "nativization" trends that are present in many of the works of the "leading lights" of the discipline. Moreover, many members of the Society for the Anthropology of North America (SANA) have built their careers studying various aspects of North American cultures and practices and form a critical part of this growing number of Western anthropologists studying their own cultures.[44]

These inroads into mainstream anthropology are important for the growth of the discipline. However, even though these anthropologists have "disturbed" mainstream anthropological work by virtue of their racial or gendered identity (either as African, African American, or women in a discipline that was for a long time dominated by White males), they are not a monolithic category. Despite their shared racial and gendered identities, these anthropologists have tended to occupy unequal and different spaces in the anthropological hierarchy. Elliott Skinner and Maxwell Owusu, for instance, are among anthropologists whose works occupy a higher social ground in the eyes of many mainstream American anthropologists compared to St. Claire Drake and Archie Mafeje, even though the four are African and/or African American anthropologists. Owusu's essay "Ethnography of Africa: The Usefulness of the Useless" is considered a classic in anthropological writing—at least, as it was rated in a survey sent out to a hundred international scholars by Roy Grinker and Christopher Steiner before they put together their monograph on scholarly perspectives on Africa.[45] Elliott Skinner's position as Franz Boas Professor of Anthropology at Columbia University also is a reflection of his high standing in the discipline, as is Virginia Dominguez's election as president of the AAA in 2007, taking on its leadership in 2009 after an outstanding service to anthropology as editor of the *Ethnologist*. Yolanda T. Moses is another example of an anthropologist of color who ascended to the presidency of the AAA, leading it between 1995 and 1997, while in 2008 Johnnetta Cole was the AAA's Distinguished Lecturer, adding another feather to an otherwise scantly adorned minorities-in-anthropology hat. Yet, although these strides of inclusion in anthropology are laudable, there is more work to be done— especially in defining what constitutes anthropological citizenship. Who belongs at the center of anthropology's canon? Which texts get selected for core courses for both anthropology's graduate and undergraduate programs, and who is seen as the theorist who must be read by anyone planning on becoming an anthropologist?

These are important questions because the art of training in anthropology is much a process of establishing boundaries and standards of what constitutes anthropological knowledge. And race and gender are insidious factors that shape the production and consumption of the underlying epistemologies that construct anthropological knowledge. I learned about these academic politics of knowledge production early in my training as an anthropologist when I had the good fortune of meeting Glenn Jordan. He had been a graduate student in my department but abandoned the program before he earned his PhD. The summer when I met Glenn, he had come back to the United States from Britain, where he had relocated, and was trying to get all his belongings from his former office at the Black Culture House on campus. He asked for my help in cleaning up the storage room and putting his belongings together—and even invited me to take as much as I wanted from the many piles of anthropological texts and papers that he had. This was the first time I had come across the work of St. Clair Drake. Glenn had numerous articles and manuscripts by Drake that specifically spoke to the role and experience of African Americans in and with the discipline of anthropology. As I marveled at this newfound dimension of anthropology, I wondered how I had missed these important perspectives on the discipline. Glenn mentioned that he had been frustrated by marginalization of African American voices in the discipline and had made Britain his home because he felt the British were more accommodating of racial differences and had fewer charged racial politics than Americans. As I reflected on my training in anthropology up to that point, I realized that there were no theoretical perspectives in the discipline that were attributed to Africans or African Americans. I asked Glenn if I could keep some of St. Clair Drake's manuscripts, and he told me to take as many I wanted. I took them to my apartment that evening and started reading some portions of Drake's essay "Anthropology and the Black Experience." I quickly learned another dimension of anthropology that I soon came to realize I would not get in my department: the politics of race and racialized knowledge production in anthropology. Clearly there were hierarchies in the discipline, and these hierarchies had a lot to do with race.

Despite this glaring absence of a corpus of literature engaging race and knowledge production in anthropology, at least in my graduate school curriculum at the time, I came to learn of other inconsistencies in the discipline's reflexivity. I found that having a self-reflexive practice did not change certain paradigms established in the discipline. There existed hierarchies, and these hierarchies were very much present in different places and took on different shapes and realities. Indeed, as I came to learn, hierarchy within anthropology extended beyond race and gender. And such hierarchy was often reproduced in very intricate and intimate ways within the academy as certain students got into certain schools that were taught by certain professors who assigned certain texts that ended up becoming central in the discipline—with the result that there are numerous anthropologists from multiple subjective positions and racial/ethnic identities who are marginalized because they did not graduate from one of the "prestigious" universities in America. Graduating from a "not-known university" tends to affect one's chances of getting jobs at "prestigious" institutions or even at relatively non-prestigious universities.

In the summer of 2009, I carried out a small search concerning the anthropology faculty at Washington University in St. Louis, Princeton University, the University of Michigan, and the University of Chicago. I was surprised by the high percentage of faculty in these institutions who had received their doctoral degrees from only a handful of institutions: Out of 28 faculty at Washington University, for instance, 9 (32 percent) were trained either at the University of Chicago; Harvard University; the University of California, Berkeley; or University of Michigan. Out of 11 faculty at Princeton, 8 (73 percent) were trained either at the University of Chicago; Harvard University; or the University of California, Berkeley. Out of 49 faculty at University of Michigan, 23 (47 percent) were trained either at the University of Chicago; Harvard University; the University of California, Berkeley; or the University of Michigan. And out of 36 faculty at University of Chicago, 14 (39 percent) were trained either at the University of Chicago; Harvard University; the University of California, Berkeley; or the University of Chicago.[46] This academic endogamy guarantees that only a few members of the discipline get to occupy the high seats of prestige because they are the ones who accrue social status and visibility in the discipline. Such visibility may be reflected in academic citations, in invitations to give lectures, in who edits special journal volumes and books, or who takes an endowed chair at a highly visible institution. When these "stars" in the discipline recommend their students for consideration to be hired in other equally prestigious schools, their word carries more weight than the actual abilities of these students. It is not uncommon to hear people refer to new PhD graduates as having been students of so-and-so. The fact that they were taught by professor so-and-so is proof enough of their excellence as anthropologists. Granted, there are truly remarkable anthropologists in the so-called prestigious schools. But there are a whole lot of not-very-good professors in the same institutions as well.

Given such interesting trends in the hiring of anthropologists in different institutions, it is prudent to say that when these anthropologists enter into these "prestigious" institutions—which also happen to have more resources for research and teaching than other universities—their careers will continue to flourish as they are given more and more time and funds to carry out research and write. However, this is a disparity that affects all anthropologists across the board, irrespective of their racial or gendered identities—even though I must add that for women and anthropologists of color, there is a sense of being twice removed from the canon or center of anthropology. How can a discipline with such inconsistencies and hierarchies claim to be self-reflexive and changing, as has been intimated in the postmodern turn in the discipline? Or is postmodernism in anthropology, as Faye Harrison, puts it "an intellectual response largely by Western White males to the challenges of Western hegemony and White supremacy in a world marked by the ascendance of postcolonial nationalisms, Japanese capitalism, and feminism"?[47] In other words, is postmodernism a decoy by mainstream anthropologists to show they are concerned about their hegemony but not quite committed to transforming and decolonizing it?

omg yes.

The difference in the hierarchies discussed above brings me back to the issue of the anthropologists who "disturb" the "canon." If the discipline has these internal challenges, what real impact do these disturbances have on the way the discipline is organized and mobilized as a social science? Can anthropology really change from the inside out and become a discipline in which all voices and perspectives have equal presence and prestige? To use Gayatri Spivak's words, can the subaltern anthropologist speak and reshape the discipline or conceive of the West as a subject or object of anthropological inquiry?[48] Or are we to remain, as Faye Harrison has clearly stated, "outsiders within"?[49]

There now seems to be an increase in the number of American and Western anthropologists working "at home" who might contribute to a reversing of the canon by shaking the pillars of anthropology as the science of the Other. However, this turn toward home may not be a voluntary gesture on the part of anthropologists but rather a phenomenon that may be attributable to a number of unseen factors. One factor that I think is critical in this regard is the noticeable change and shift in focus that has occurred in Western anthropology. This is the kind of shift that comes from the permanent crisis of Western sociocultural anthropology noted by Clifford Geertz. This crisis points to specific important changes in the field that have affected the way Western anthropologists carry out their work. According to Geertz, these changes include the rise of indigenous anthropology; the transformation and/or the disappearance of the subject matter of sociocultural anthropology—namely "primitive" and "tribal" societies—through globalization and the use of fieldwork in other academic disciplines; and the popularity of the hermeneutical-semiotical perspectives in opposition to scientific positivist perspectives in the study of culture and society.[50] These changes require new ways of representing the cultures and communities that anthropologists study. Stories packaged in ethnographies are also increasingly open to critiques from the "source" with possible recasting of these ethnographies in local lore as the Other increasingly gets a hold of anthropological literature written about them.

Anthropological collaborations with local interlocutors in ethnographic projects is another example of this change in the way anthropologists think about and represent their subject. As we see more and more of the people we study writing about their own cultures and challenging our representations of their lives, we have to reconsider the standard anthropological practice that often presents ethnography as an anthropologist's show that is singularly constructed and performed. We can no longer write for a limited audience that excludes the people and communities that we often write about. I consider myself a very conscientious writer and often write my ethnographies with the hope that the people I write about will have a chance to read my work. I was, for instance, particularly excited to read a presentation by Ali A. Mazrui—Albert Schweitzer Professor in the Humanities and director of the Institute of Global Cultural Studies at SUNY Binghamton—in which he favorably cited my work on Swahili gender relations in Mombasa, Kenya, especially given that he is both Swahili and a Muslim from Mombasa.[51] Such attentiveness to our research interlocutors or subjects as direct consumers of our ethnographies makes for an important turn in ethnographic writing as matters of representation become all the more contestable.

Irrespective of the audience for our ethnographies, however, accurate representation of whatever culture an anthropologist writes about is important for any anthropological project, and this immediacy of ethnographic feedback from anthropology's "subjects" calls for a new paradigm of representation— a paradigm that recognizes ethnographies as partial, rather than complete, renditions of a people's culture.[52] This decentering of the authority of the researcher—in this case, the anthropologist as the agent of representing a culture, community, or another person—sustains the anthropologist's subjective position of humility and self-doubt that is often present during fieldwork in which the informant has more "power" over the ethnographer in so far as the ethnographer depends on the informant/interlocutor for information about the subject of inquiry. Without the informant, the local language teacher, or contact in the field, the ethnographer is clearly incapacitated unless he or she is studying his or her own culture or community. This shift in how we create our subject, how we relate to our field respondents, and how we report our field experiences also means that we have to be both transformed by our field experience as well as by our process of writing ethnography.

For me, this transformation occurred in almost reverse order: first of all, I came from Africa to study anthropology in a process that allowed me to deal with my own close cultural encounter with a society that has continued to produce and train numerous anthropologists who study Africa each year. Second, over the years during and after my anthropological training, I have had a chance to read and conduct ethnographic research in my own country and to deal with the challenges of representing "other" cultures.

As an anthropologist I, therefore, straddle these two worlds of being gazed at and at the same time doing the gazing. What I bring to bear in this book is the surprising benefits of contrasting these two gazes and the meanings that emerge in their respective locations and perspectives. Rather than represent the experiences of one location individually and the perspectives that may accrue from it (as is common in many ethnographies), I bring my experiences in America and in Africa onto the same platform, using ethnography both as my frame of reference and as my point of entry. These two locations and perspectives interact and dialogue with each other on equal terms, producing an ethnography of American anthropology through an African cultural framework and training. Consequently, I am able to show that anthropology is about a set of specific tools that one acquires to use in engaging and analyzing cultural phenomena—a tool that says as much about the study population as it does about the anthropologist. What is different in this book is that these worlds are overtly presented rather than implied.

Straddling Between Cultures

As you read this book, I hope you will see the value of using anthropological eyes to look at the life of others and ours as well. There is value in the anthropological framework of cross-cultural comparison that allows us to understand other cultures because it illuminates our own. It is a process of straddling two cultures, both objectively and subjectively. I use my own experiences as an entry into understanding American anthropology as a cultural phenomenon while at the same time using my experiences in America as a window to understand my own culture and myself. It is in this kind of approach that, following George Marcus and Michael Fischer, I see "anthropology as cultural critique."[53]

My own cultural analyses underwent gradual transformation throughout my time in graduate school as I was socialized into the values and sensibilities of anthropology as a discipline. I attempt to create meaning from various texts, interactions, and experiences, even as prior socialization and cultural experiences influence the choice of topics I have included in this book. Overall, this is a record of slices of my life, the bulk of which reflect my time as a graduate student in anthropology in a large public university in America. With a student population of over 36,000, representing cultures and practices from many states in America and countries of the world, this field site was a gold mine of information for a budding anthropologist. But more than anything else, this book is a record of the process of knowing another culture and knowing self.

Now as a trained anthropologist writing about my own "fieldwork" when I was just getting introduced to the discipline, I identify with some of the flaws in ethnography emphasized by critiques against the anthropological enterprise of ethnographic writing. Yet I want to believe with Raymonde Carroll when she asserts:

> We are often intimidated by the idea of attempting such a foray into the cultural imaginary of the other, of confidently propelling ourselves into cultural analysis, because we are convinced, deep down, that this constitutes an act of arrogance on our part. Indeed, how can I claim to understand Japanese and German culture if I cannot really understand my neighbor, my parents, my children? Nevertheless, cultural analysis is not an act of arrogance but, quite the contrary, an act of humility by which I temporarily try to forget my way of seeing the world (the only way I have learned to consider valid) and briefly replace it with another way of conceiving this world, a way which by definition I cannot adopt (even if I want to) but the validity of which I assert by this act.[54]

It is in the process of this forgetting of my own way of seeing the world and attempting to adopt another that anthropology begins to make sense to me. Yet this forgetting is temporal and only instrumental in my attempt to illuminate the object of my study. It is an attempt that follows Beatrice Medicine's process of "Learning to Be an Anthropologist and Remaining a 'Native,'" [55] even though I turn my own gaze on Western anthropology and anthropologists who have traditionally studied me and others like me. How much this project is a product of my own cultural orientation as an anthropologist, my theoretical training, or information gathered on the ground, is a matter best decided by critics and analysts of the product.

The process of cross-cultural interactions and straddling that I had experienced throughout graduate school allowed me to gain some degree of reflexivity and transformation. I became much more aware of my own cultural biases and developed a deep empathy for students studying abroad. Let me share an example. When I completed my doctoral training in cultural anthropology in 1998, I returned to Kenya and worked for a study abroad program in Nairobi, where I taught a field-based course in anthropology and acted as a cultural broker for undergraduate students encountering Africa for the first time. Having spent six years living in America and armed with relatively good training in anthropology, I was intrigued at how my life as a student in America was relatively comparable to that of my students on a study-abroad program in Kenya but also definitely dissimilar from theirs because of our different racial and socioeconomic identities. Granted, as they had more power to relate to Africa than I had in relating to America, on the surface I could see myself in their experience—the self that knew very little about the people or the place my study focused on and yet was drawn to them by the stereotypical images I had encountered in the popular media. They, like me, had encountered their location of study (Kenya and Africa as a whole) through friends, parents, some academic courses, and the popular media.[56] They, like me, came knowing very little about their study location and culture(s) and ended up learning a lot and loving the place to an extent that, for different reasons, they returned independently. Indeed, many of my students on the program in Kenya made return trips or traveled elsewhere in Africa, following the fire that was ignited in them by their first encounter with the continent of Africa and the country of Kenya in particular through that program. I, like them, have returned to America where I now teach anthropology after five years of working in Kenya as an anthropologist. I have, as it is often said, come full circle. So that I can trace that circle, I will share in this book some of the few topics that my anthropological journey highlighted, starting with the ever-present, but least debated notion, of race in anthropology.

2

Tripping on Race,
Training Anthropologists

Why does the bulk of anthropological research entail studying other people, especially those in non-Western worlds? Are anthropologists genuinely interested in other cultures, or do other cultures provide convenient subjects for anthropological study? Why go through the kinds of agony and challenges of fieldwork that have been recorded by many anthropologists in their fieldwork memoirs? Is fieldwork an adventure that, once completed, allows one to enter a new social status and that therefore offers a justifiable end for an excruciating process? Is studying others a consequence of the ease that might generally come with one's finding and working with local non-Western research subjects? Are anthropologists able to work with other cultures because those cultures are subordinate to anthropologists and therefore are more "welcoming" and "accepting" of anthropologists? Or is anthropology, as the late Archie Mafeje has argued, ontologically derived "from historically-determined white racism"?[1] While there may be no hard conclusions to be drawn regarding answers to these and other related questions, my argument is that anthropological work has predominantly been shaped by the asymmetrical relationships that attend between the anthropologist and his or her subject as framed within race.

Many parts of the non-Western world studied by anthropologists happen to be former colonies that continue to receive Westerners in new superior roles as development czars, bilateral aid managers, volunteers, and investors. Many of the nationals in these post-colonial locales have never seen Westerners in subordinate positions and especially under local authority. When

Western anthropologists enter into these non-Western field locations for research, such hierarchy and asymmetry "assist" their cause in ways often obscured by much of the ethnographic rhetoric found in anthropological literature focusing on reflexivity. It is this "research advantage," I argue, that makes Western anthropologists choose "other" field sites than those in their own communities. Moreover, even research funding for fieldwork tends to be dominated by these structures of an asymmetry that favor studies of the Other. In an attempt to demonstrate how difficult it is for anthropologists to study in their own communities, I share in this chapter a step-by-step account of a research project on race in which I participated with four other graduate students as part of a course. Using this project as a window into how anthropologists work in the field and how race shapes such work, I conclude that the power dynamics attendant in anthropologists' own cultures present fieldwork challenges that in turn may make research in "other" locations more tenable.[2]

When our group for the course project chose to study race in a relatively poor neighborhood inhabited by Blacks living close to our university and consequently allowed me to actively participate in planning and implementing the research project, I was excited. Moreover, I became privy to the logistical and personal challenges that anthropologists face in the field as a result of their subject positions marked by race. Such subjectivity may, however, not have equal parlance in locations where anthropologists carry out their fieldwork abroad as compared to those where anthropologists carry out research and work in their own societies—especially in America, with its highly marked racial ontology.[3]

After only a few months of my stay in America, I came to recognize the enormous centrality of racial politics in public and private discourses. This revelation was quite interesting to me—especially given the fact that, prior to my arrival in America, I had not quite had an opportunity to see how important race was in defining America's socioeconomic, political, and economic landscape. Witnessing the omnipresence of race in America, I wanted to learn more about it: how race manifested itself in all aspects of American life, what its current and historical discourses were, and what the everyday processes of dealing with race were, especially on a university campus. Further, up to that point, I had not had a chance to talk to African Americans who lived in the community that we had selected to focus on in our research, even though I had become aware, within my first semester in graduate school in America, of the absence of African Americans in the university generally and in graduate school specifically. Interestingly, African Americans had been overwhelmingly present in my initial images of America—those I had acquired in Kenya, as mediated through music and films to which I had access.

The research project seemed like a promising avenue for me to explore these curiosities in a systematic way and still get academic credit for it. Initially, I was interested in the issue of equal opportunities at the university. As I read numerous job advertisements and statements of history about the university, I kept seeing the phrase "the University is an equal opportunity employer." When this opportunity to carry out research on race became available through our field methods course, I jumped at the chance. It did not matter that I did not have an idea of the existence of a place called the north end, where we would focus our research. As it would turn out, this was my first fieldwork experience in anthropology or as an anthropologist in training.

Fieldwork Ritual: A Group Research Project on Race

When we got together as a group to plan how we would carry out research for our class project, it was clear that each one of us had his or her own perspective on what to focus on and the kind of data to collect. In an attempt to find a common thread for the project, we decided that each of us would make an outline of our goals for the project and share them with the rest of the group. After that initial exercise, we came up with a number of goals.

April, a Chinese female student, said that her interest in the topic was shaped by the fact that during the Los Angeles riots in 1992, she noticed that African Americans seemed to target Chinese stores. Mildred, a White female student, said that she grew up in a city in the South where she would see Blacks living on the other side of her neighborhood. The Blacks, she said, lived in a poor neighborhood compared to her own, and she had always wondered about their everyday social experiences. Her story was very similar to that of Ruth Frankenberg, who grew up in an all-White suburb, and when driving with her family to the city, she mostly saw poorer neighborhoods that were inhabited by people of color.[4] Freda, another White female student, said she had always wanted to know something about the Black people she saw as she rode her bike around her neighborhood in the city in which our university is located. She, like Mildred, had had no substantive interactions with Blacks.

Mike, a White male student and the only non-anthropology student in the group, said he was curious to understand why there existed two cities with two different administrative structures in one geographical area. He was interested in the planning of those cities—in what had led to the need for their separate administrative structures and how race might have played a role in such planning. As an African male student, I was generally interested in race relations in America and in understanding how anthropologists approach the issue. I saw the group project as an opportunity to study how race played out on a small scale. I had realized that race, as a subject, had been studied by African American scholars and by other disciplines such as sociology and cultural studies, and I wanted to see how our racially mixed group (dominated by anthropologists in training) would deal with the topic.

We started the research with the following three broad research questions:

1. What form does neighborhood segregation take in the area? Is it economic, social, some combination of these, or some other factors altogether?

2. Does the segregated living pattern discernible between the area and the surrounding neighborhoods reflect itself in other interactions between residents and nonresidents of the entire community? How does it manifest itself? Is it an attitudinal/perceptual, physical phenomenon, or something else?

3. How does gender play a role in the perception of segregation?

We consulted official city documents to get a picture of the research area, the place referred to as the north end. Besides giving us the physical boundaries of the area, the official 1979 literature also stated that the north end had the greatest concentration of minority population of any neighborhood in the city and was regarded as having the lowest income and highest unemployment rates in the county. Further, some of the specific needs for the area identified by the city planners included housing, capital improvement, environmental, and commercial development. Thirteen years later, in 1992, the city initiated what was called the "Neighborhood Wellness Action Plan," which aimed at emphasizing a new approach to the delivery of city services. The plan centered in the livability of all neighborhoods—housing would be decent, safe, and affordable; private yards and public spaces would be well maintained; crime rates would be low; streets and other public facilities would be in sound condition; and residents would be actively engaged in neighborhood affairs.

In the plan, which was said to represent the first full-scale citywide neighborhood planning effort in the city's history, the north end was categorized as a restoration neighborhood. This restoration was, however, concentrated

around physical structures and did not include strategies for addressing issues of poverty, unemployment, education, family support, and affordable
housing. Later, when talking to some of the local residents, I found out that
these issues were relevant to a number of residents and may have shaped
participation in the neighborhood's wellness efforts initiated by the city. It
seemed as though the city planners knew the needs of the community but
had deliberately chosen to ignore them in favor of their own planning needs.
I wondered if other sectors of the city-planning department operated in the
same way.

On the first day of our project, we met to discuss how to integrate our
views into a single project. The consensus was that each of us find some background information on the project. Mike was to look at official information
recorded about the research area in books and other records; Freda said she
would call up a friend and get some contacts in the area; I said I would take
a walk or ride around the area and do a "visual survey"; April said she would
talk to an African American woman who worked in the building where our
department was located; and Mildred said she would go through the phone
book and see if she could make a few contacts by calling up local institutions
like the church.

In the Field

To fulfill my part of the project, I took a bus through the area that I thought
would constitute the north end but did not notice anything out of the ordinary. Granted, there were a few neglected houses and numerous African
American residents present around the houses. Having lived only in houses
close to the university that tended to be large apartment buildings with many
tenants living closely together, I saw nothing that struck me as out of the
ordinary about the houses in the north end, which were mostly single-family
houses. Later, an African American friend in graduate school gave me a ride
around the area and, although she came from another state, she mentioned
that there was a tendency for Blacks to live in the poor areas of most cities.
On paying closer attention to the proximity of the houses to one another, the
state of the streets, general cleanliness of the area, and my friend's comments
on the poverty of the residents, I did start to notice differences between these
houses and the apartments that were closer to the university. By American
standards (at least the parts I was familiar with), the north end was poor—
though by Kenyan standards, those houses looked much better than many
I had seen and lived in myself. The neighborhood seemed to be close to

factories and big manufacturing plants. There were children playing outside (jumping rope, playing catch, or just wrestling) and some youths hanging out around the houses. There were a few women cooking outside in groups. This second trip to the north end proved to be my first lesson in fieldwork—learning to see reality from the "native's" point of view.

I went back home after my preliminary "physical survey" and talked to my roommate, who knew about my research project. I was surprised when he told me, "The north end is a dangerous place. You will get shot. Do not bring any informants in here. What will the fieldwork reveal about racial segregation that is not known already? Do you need fieldwork to establish that there is segregation?" His questions could have been motivated by his own identity as a White male from a middle-class background, but the fact that he was an anthropologist also baffled me. His questions set me thinking about what my colleagues and I would do, what questions we would ask, and what the study would accomplish. Why did we choose the north end? Weren't we acknowledging a constructed notion of the project? Could we really confess to having a clean slate and an objective approach to this study? And if we "already know about racial segregation," what is the value of fieldwork? My roommate's questions also revealed an attitude that I eventually noticed among many of the other White students with whom I interacted—an unspoken fear of Blacks and an assumption that the majority of them were "bad" people.

Our next research project meeting was at Dan's Café on campus. We went through the project plan, and Mike took charge of directing the way the project would proceed. We had a summary of our expectations and our individual reasons for conducting research for the project. Freda and Mildred were wondering how we would present ourselves to the people we wanted to talk to. Freda mentioned that she did not want to commit herself so much because she felt the project was superficial—even though a few weeks earlier when we were making plans for the topic, she was the most excited about "doing some fieldwork." Mildred talked of how the north end was "different," adding that we knew that the difference was there but we did not have concrete points to prove it. It was a gut feeling, she said. Freda wanted to go to church with me, but unfortunately that weekend I was going to visit my friends out of town. I, however, made sure I introduced her to my friend's wife, who was willing to go with her to an African American Baptist church that I had earlier attended. I guessed Freda did not mind going to the church even though it was not in the north end. She may have been interested in going to an African American church and did not care where it was located—

something that made me wonder if she had ever been to that kind of church. We divided up our duties further, and I took the part of writing up what we expected to find out in our project. On top of that, we had to come up with two books that we thought were relevant for our study.

Reading ethnographies had taught me that one could find leads to research from some very unlikely places. A few days into our project, such a lead became available when I went to have lunch at a café on campus that served vegetarian dishes. I sat next to two women—one Black and one White—who were having lunch together. We got talking, and in the process, Janet, the African American woman, asked me if I could find someone to play the piano at her church (since I had mentioned that I was interested in studying music). Janet gave me her office phone number so that I could call her in case I got someone to play music at her church. I also told her that I was involved in a project on the north end and asked if she would be willing to share her thoughts on the topic. She agreed but asked that we set up an appointment to meet later. When we met later at her office, I explained to Janet my interest in the project and told her the sort of things I wanted to learn from her. I mentioned that I was particularly interested in how race influenced the everyday experiences of people around the university and especially those in the north end.

Janet mentioned that the north end included specific street boundaries located close to the rail tracks, which made property cheaper but unattractive to many. She also said that there were a number of factories in the area and that it was a poor people's area, the majority of them Black. She said that some of the problems in the area were social—there were early pregnancies, negative changes in family values, and the tendency for many people to become involved in criminal activities in search of quick and easy money. She felt that the people who lived in the north end did not necessarily want to stay there forever, and she suggested that if they made enough money to allow them live elsewhere, they would move. She said there were differences in the social and economic status among Blacks in the north end, as some lived in public housing while others had their own homes. Toward the end of our meeting, Janet told me that she, her family, and some friends usually met every week for coffee and that if I had time, I could join them and maybe get their perspective on my project too. I agreed, and she said she would pick me up later that week to take me to their next meeting.

On the day we agreed to meet, Janet came to pick me from the anthropology department, and we drove in her car to a mall in the downtown area that had a coffee shop, where we were joined by three other members of her family. We talked for almost two hours, sharing different views regarding race, class, and education. And since I did not have a systematic questionnaire to follow, I highlighted for the group a few of the things I found relevant for my project. My "respondents" agreed that a portion of the people living on the north end, especially those in the "projects" were on welfare, were low-income earners, and were dealing in drugs. Those on drugs would seek the company of other drug dealers, just as Christians tend to interact with other Christians. Everyone also concurred that crime was prevalent in areas with high levels of drug use—and they were quick to add that the same was true of White neighborhoods.

As if she anticipated my next question about representing crime on television, Janet's sister said, "You know crime by Blacks gets sensationalized, while White crime is swept under the rug. You know what I mean?" "Yeah," I said in agreement. "There is fear among Whites about Blacks," Janet added. "They do not want to know about us. They are just afraid of us." I was reminded of my own roommate and his own racialized fear of people from the north end. Crystal, who was introduced as Janet's cousin, said that some of the people in the north end were lazy and did not want to work, that they just wanted easy money. "Why do you think that was happening?" I asked. "They have forgotten the strict rules instilled in them when they were growing up," she said. "Can you imagine? There is no more spanking of kids," she said inquisitively, almost inferring that a rise in crime and drug use could directly be linked to poor child-rearing practices. There ensued a short discussion between Janet and Crystal regarding the role of poverty in shaping the "culture" Crystal had observed about Blacks in the north end. I sat and listened to both sides of the exchange.

From the ensuing conversation, I learned that in the 1960s, there were White people who lived in the north end, but they had moved out during the infamous "White flight" after desegregation because they did not want to live with Blacks. Crystal remembered that in the '60s the housing projects were well maintained and had a good community. There were screening and background checks before tenants could get into any of the houses, and occupancy seemed to be more family-oriented. Nowadays it was mainly single-parent families—"children having children"—which was a result of loose morals, she said. Crystal also said that the problems of the north end were economic, social, and racial and that there were various ways of limiting racial and class integration. "They do not want us to live in their neighborhood," she said referring to Whites, adding that there was discrimination in the sale of property by real estate agents, who were reluctant to sell homes in White neighborhoods to Black buyers.⁵ At the end of it all, I felt that my perceptions of the north end were broadening and that this African American family's perception of the area had also been shaped by their experiences and identity, especially their social class and educational background. Their voice, I concluded, was one voice among many.

Our conversation on the north end expanded our discussion to include Black-White relations, and some examples were shared regarding how a number of White people thought that Blacks are inferior. Crystal mentioned a time when she was not allowed to charge a washing machine to her credit card in a store at the local mall. Determined to make the purchase, she went to the bank and got the cash and returned to the store and purchased the machine, to the utter dismay of the White salesperson. Another example concerned a White woman who was shocked that her Black colleague was earning more than she did, even if she were more qualified than the White woman. Overall, our conversation went very well, and Janet's family seemed genuinely happy to have spent time with me and to be able to address issues so close to them, especially to someone conducting an ethnographic study. They had many other examples of racial discrimination that they had personally experienced, but my time was running out and I had to excuse myself and leave. I thanked them as they offered to pay for my coffee and went to the bus stop to catch a bus back to my house, which was close to the campus.

The following Sunday, I decided to visit the church in the north end that I had been invited to by one of the church elders, whose name Janet had given me. I got into the church building—located on Main Street in the north end—and asked an usher where I would find Mrs. Mulder. I was directed to a Sunday school class for advanced grades. Upon seeing me at the door, Mrs. Mulder came out of her classroom. She said she was expecting me. She then introduced me to the pastor, who was in his office just next door to Mrs. Mulder's room. I lingered in the church building until Sunday school was over and then went into the sanctuary for the service.

The choir, which was impressive, was largely comprised of women (out of a total of twenty-six members, there were only six men), and only one of the women was White. However, the pastor—a middle-aged Black man with an infectious smile—was surrounded by men. They were sitting on both sides of the pulpit. Most of the women with notable positions in the church were ushers. A clear gender divide was apparent. The sermon was relevant to the community where the church was located. Its focus was on finding a few good men for God. The pastor mentioned that the African American male was an "endangered species" and that it was up to the women to try and bring the men to God because without faith, there would be no end to crime and sexual harassment.

I felt welcome at the church and enjoyed my time there immensely. This particular Sunday was a day for men's fellowship, and there was to be a men's day service in the afternoon. I met Gail, an African American woman whom I had seen in the Foreign Languages Building on campus, and asked if I could talk to her later in the week about our research project on the north end. Gail agreed and gave me her office phone number. As more and more opportunities availed themselves to me for my research, I found myself in some dilemma. Could I be objective enough to study the people in the north end, including those who attended that church, or should I have kept my distance? Would my study require that I stop attending the church when I had received all the data I needed for my project? What questions would I ask, and how would I keep my own curiosity about an African American church service separate from the research project? At the time, I had not been introduced to reflexive ethnography, and I now realize I was being too cautious, assuming that there was a need, and even the possibility, to separate "research" from "real life."

After the service, I talked to Mrs. Mulder and her husband, who invited me to lunch. We went to a restaurant not too far away from the church (I later learned it was famous for its lunch buffets). As we had our lunch, we talked about many things regarding life in the north end and the church. I felt a little weird conducting research in a restaurant with informants who paid for my food. In many of the ethnographies I had read, anthropologists were the ones who paid for the services entailed in their research. Moreover, money and payments made for or during fieldwork has always been a sticky issue in ethnography. Indeed, the absence of any serious analyses of power relations in the field as mediated through exchange or use of money in the field is quite telling of the history and practice of Western anthropology.[6]

The Mulders said that the church was started in 1969. They themselves had come to the general area in 1947 and settled in the north end in 1950. Mrs. Mulder said she liked her neighborhood and would not move to another place. She was proud to mention that her church had never been broken into despite break-ins happening to other churches in adjacent neighborhoods. She added that it was not an area for Blacks only—there were White students who lived in the north end, in the government housing just behind her church. I wished I could have a chance to talk to those White students and get their perceptions of the neighborhood as well. She said that White men also frequented the neighborhood, looking for Black women. Regarding her connection to the community, she said that she was running two day-care centers that she considered crucial for her community.

I asked her about Black and White relations in the community, now that she mentioned that some White students lived in the public housing there. She responded by giving me a case of a gang that she had managed to break up after she found out who was masterminding it. She said that a White man had been using Black kids as delivery boys for drugs, and she felt she had to do something about it. She kept seeing the man in the neighborhood and noted down his car's registration number and reported it to the police. When she realized the local police were not quick to take action, she threatened to report it to the federal government in Washington, D.C., and that is when the man was "removed from the area." That was in the '50s, and for a while, the neighborhood had no more drug problems. But sadly, she said, the problems came back. She, like Janet, mentioned that in earlier times, Whites and Blacks lived in the area, but gradually the Whites started moving out, and the Blacks kept dispersing "all over the place."

I was getting good data on the course project and on my larger project on America. I started to feel like a "real" ethnographer. "How is the relationship between the members of the community?" I asked her. In response she mentioned that it all depended on how hard people were willing to work for their communities, adding that what many of the young people in the "housing projects" needed was positive role models and people who could hold them accountable for their actions. This message resonated both with the sermon I had heard at her church earlier and with the conclusions drawn by social scientists who worked among the urban poor.[7] Mrs. Mulder also mentioned that sometimes she managed to enlist some of the young people, who were idle and who could have easily connected to crime, to do some chores for the community. Engaging idle youth in such projects, she said, allows them to see the community in positive light and foster better relations.

Schism in the Group

After our initial individual research on the topic, we had a group meeting in the department's computer lab to put together a final research proposal that we would present to our class the following day. A discussion ensued about the trajectory the project was to take. We spent some time on the different parts of the proposal and the role to be played by each participant. Mike and Freda were more active than the rest of us at the meeting. Mildred looked ambivalent—at times, distant. April was quiet and left no room to interpret what she was thinking. I was not much help either. I sat there and just observed. Mildred and Mike typed the proposal as we served as consultants on sentences and phrases. After the proposal was complete, three of us were assigned different parts to present to the rest of the class. Tension developed at the end of the meeting when we discovered that, in sharing out the parts of the project, we had left April out of the presentation. She was upset by this exclusion and left the room. Mike, who had not expected this turn of events, asked Freda to intervene and cool April down.

The next day, we met to review questions that would guide us in the interviews we planned to conduct, but we ended up abandoning the idea after it was clear we could not agree on the kind of data we needed to gather. Freda suggested that we just go ahead and each "do our own stuff" and then staple it together and present it. Mike, Mildred, and I felt that we could still work on a group project since we had an umbrella theme, and we could each pursue our own specific questions but then keep meeting regularly to make our findings fit into our topic. April said that she had doubts about the validity of Mike's archival work as fieldwork. To me, she seemed to be suggesting that Mike was taking an easy option to the project given the sensitivity of the research topic. I found her argument quite valid, even though I could tell she didn't really like Mike's role in the group. Before we dispersed from this meeting, we decided to state what each one of us would do for the next week. Mike would do archival work, looking for official records (police and city plans). Mildred would go to the African Methodist church and try and link up with some people there. She mentioned that she would also listen to the sermon with an analytical ear. Freda would brainstorm some twenty or so questions that she would work on and also try to get into schools and talk to some people. I said I would continue interviewing random people as opportunities availed themselves and added that I had conducted three interviews already. April said she would talk to an African American woman at the Media and Instruction Center within the building in which our department was located.

Despite these important attempts to focus our specific parts of the research to the main topic of study, it was pretty obvious that our own individual interests were taking precedence and that the web of "communitas" that had kept us together in the initial stages was slowly weakening. Mike, who seemed happy with his part in the project, mentioned that it was not safe to go to the north end alone, prompting Freda to ask why. He responded by saying that it was because we were new to the area. Mildred said that going to church was not dangerous, even though she wondered how it would feel to be the only

White person in church. I told her it did not matter, but she seemed a little disconcerted. April said she needed to pair up with someone else because she found it odd to go "out there" and try to meet people with whom to talk. I kept wondering to myself if what I was witnessing were issues specific to our project or issues common in fieldwork in general. Since I had not read an ethnography written about anthropologists' experiences working in groups, I assumed that the emerging issues were shaped by the amorphous nature of our group. Moreover, our group was desperately trying to stay unified. Yet I had this gut feeling that the issues we were facing were also present in fieldwork and that anthropologists either ignored them or experienced them differently because of their race, class, gender, and field location.

Our struggles in the project were not reflected in our proposal presentation to the entire class the next day. Indeed, no one would have noticed that there had been "fireworks" between Mike and April the previous day. How easy it is to compromise for purposes of public impression! I realized how hard it was to gauge the process and quality of the field experience by just looking at the final product, which leaves out a lot. In that respect, it almost gives a perfect image of culture and of ethnography itself. This presentation of perfect cultures and ethnographies, as I have stated in chapter 1, may be why many like Lila Abu-Lughod talk about "writing against culture" and also why James Clifford and Clifford Geertz liken ethnography to fiction.[8]

After observing these initial group dynamics, I got interested in studying the group members, hoping that our different assumptions and interests in the project would give me a worthwhile inkling into how anthropologists generally conduct research. We had all taken the course on ethnographic research methods because we were preparing to go out in the field and conduct our pre-dissertation research. Even though I understood the limitations of this project in approximating what a year-long fieldwork project would be in anthropology, I was attracted to the prospect of that it would be able to offer a small window into race relations and the subtle realities of ethnographic research. Interestingly, all the students in the course had expressed research interests in sites outside America. Participating in the research project with these students provided for me a golden opportunity to observe some anthropologists working in their own society, since they all had not yet carried out any research abroad.

As part of the course grade in our research project, we had to write short reports individually and turn them in to the professor. After reading many of our reports, the professor noted that we were having internal problems and asked that we meet with him as a group to address the schism. The group meeting took place at the coffee shop on campus where we had met before. The professor addressed the common issues that were raised in the papers and assured us that if we saw that the project was not manageable, we could cut it down to something that we could handle. The meeting focused on some complaints about group dynamics, and the professor tried to address all our concerns, making sure that each group member stated the importance of his or her role in the project. Personally, I felt much better about the project and my role in it after that meeting. Mike, however, did not seem to have enjoyed the meeting. He said that he had thought that we were meeting to go over some of the "technical" issues the professor had raised about our proposal and added that we "should have focused more on the project than our personal issues."

Interestingly, I found myself agreeing with him on that as well. I felt that we needed not only to resolve the personal tensions in the group but also to chart our way forward for the sake of making the project successful and meeting our initial goals. By the end of the meeting, however, we had still not addressed our project goals. Freda was especially interested in the process and not the product of the research, and it was easy to see why: she was the only one who had done little, if anything, of what we all had promised to do for the project. As we compared notes, it turned out that I had done the most in terms of finding people in the north end to interview. No one else in the group had any field information from the north end to share. I decided to carry on with this line of research, regardless of what my colleagues had—or had not—accomplished. I knew that I had gathered enough data to contribute to the project, and at that point, I was determined to find more information to buttress my existing data.

Where Is the Field?

Anthropologists have written about redefinitions of the classic notion of the field that have been formulated.[9] We no longer have the luxury of finding a well-bounded field site. The shifting nature and fluidity of my field site in our class project became apparent one day while I was having lunch at about three o'clock in the afternoon at a McDonald's restaurant on campus. I met there an older African American man who started talking to me when I was on the queue waiting to place an order for my food. We ended up sitting together for a while. Our conversation initially focused on the rain that had been coming down heavily that day, and then we slowly began to touch on some issues regarding the American political system (with which I was barely familiar). I kept wondering why this stranger was sharing so much information with me, when all I had managed to say was "yes" and "uhuh." He changed topics and talked about Somalia, and that is when I mentioned I was from a neighboring country, increasing his interest in our conversation even more. We talked about how kids nowadays were sensitized about current affairs because of improved technology. He also said that improved communication had made the world smaller and that people were now traveling all over the world. I could tell he was well informed on the issues that he chose to talk about. He spoke about the Bible and said that some of the things mentioned in it were now being fulfilled. On a matter that was closer to my research, he talked about the social system. The Negro, he said, had been used by the system—as in the case of the army. I was a little surprised he used the word "Negro" instead of African American. He said that Africans and African Americans had been divided and made to hate each other to the advantage of the system. It became apparent to me that the old man was going to be useful to my study, even though I had not met him in the "field." I had to find a way to talk to him about my group's research project on race in the north end. We even talked about the care of old people in my native country, which made me guess he wanted to see what happens to older people like him in other cultures.

I had to leave to go to do some homework, but before I did, I formally introduced myself to him and asked him where he lived. He told me that his name was Mathews and that he "lived in the heart of the ghetto," six blocks north of where we were sitting. This was my day. Here was a man who seemed conversant with some of the issues I was hoping to address in the research project, and he lived in the north end. I mentioned to him that I was conducting a project on the north end and asked if he would be interested in talking to me about it. He said he would be glad to do so and gave me his business card. I was feeling very good about myself at that point. While my group members seemed to be struggling to find a single African American to interview, I had already found many. Reflecting on the fact that I had never taken an anthropology course prior to joining my graduate anthropology program in America, it became clear why I was delighted by my work in the project thus far. The project was proof that I had made the right choice in selecting to become an anthropologist, and my data-collection abilities for our project were further proof that I was going to be good at it.

There were a number of reasons working to my advantage, though. My skin color may have endeared me more to the people I was making contact with—besides the fact that I was a foreigner. Since there were very few Af-

ricans and people of African descent in and around the university, it was
easy for us to notice, and even connect with, one another. Moreover, as John
Ogbu has shown, being a foreigner can allow an ethnographer to ask the most
mundane questions such as "why do you go to school?"[10]— questions that a
native ethnographer may not even think to ask in his or her own community.
Claire Sterk also found that being from a European city where prostitution
was legal made her initial entry into her urban field site to study prostitution
in America a little less difficult.[11] I am sure that being a foreigner to America
was an advantage for me, but I also found it generally easy to strike up a
conversation with a stranger. Moreover, as a foreigner, I was not part of the
dynamic of race relations in the American academy and, as a result, may
have been more welcome in a conversation with African Americans about
race than my White colleagues would have been. Is this condition of being
an "outsider" or a foreigner an advantage when it comes to fieldwork? Is this
what makes anthropologists more at ease and even successful in foreign field
sites? Does being a foreigner mean I was easily included in such configura-
tions as we had in our research project?

Cracks and Faults

While working in the computer lab in the anthropology department, I realized that my foreign "advantage" was short-lived. Freda, April, and I were
chatting about our upcoming project meeting, which was scheduled at our
usual coffee shop venue on campus. Freda said that the women in the group—
just the three of them, minus the men—wanted to meet at 8.15 P.M. alone,
before our 8:30 P.M. group meeting. I sensed something might have been
cooking and jokingly asked if it was the "gender thing." Freda said, as April
laughed, that they just wanted to plan to go to the same church together.
"Why can't you call each other up and plan that?" I asked them, sensing
that there was more going on than they were willing to divulge. Was I now
located outside the group? No further information was forthcoming from
Freda or April about their "secret" meeting. Was I being excluded because
I was male? At about 8:20 P.M., we left the computer lab and walked to the
coffee shop, leaving a note for Mike telling him where to find us.

Freda said that she felt that Mike was assertive and was dominating the
group. She asked for my opinion. I said I did not think that he was dominating the group but that he tended to be more interested in keeping us on task,
which often could come out as being assertive. Freda suggested that each
of us share what we had written in our individual papers for the course. I

started the process by saying that I had met and interviewed a couple from the church that I attended, had met the family of a university employee, and had met an older man who agreed to an interview. I said that I was getting a lot of information about the north end. April said that she felt segregated from the group and that it all seemed to go back to Mike—although I did not know if I was involved too and she would not tell me to my face. Mildred said she had spoken with all the members of our group, except me, about what they seemed to be interested in. She did not know what my interests were in the project. Freda said that she had talked about commitment and the struggles we were experiencing in the group and that she was more interested in the process than in the product of the project. I was right after all. Freda had, in my view, done nothing to contribute her part to the project so she had taken the easy way out.

After sharing our reports, we talked about the process through which we would present our field notes in class. Mike had not showed up yet, and the question seemed to be what would happen if he wanted to make a presentation in class. We reached a consensus: only Mildred, April, and I would present our field notes in class. It seemed to me that there was some fear of Mike's prevailing over the presentation despite his absence in the meeting that night. April, Mildred, and Freda were all uncomfortable with him and his role in the group project thus far. Mike had become this power that no one was ready to challenge, and even as we talked, the other group members were constantly looking toward the door to see if Mike was coming.

The discussion then turned to me. Freda said she thought that I felt superior, that I felt I was an outsider looking at things from the outside, from above. This comment made me understand why they had wanted to hold a separate meeting for the three of them before the larger group meeting where Mike and I were present. It is true that I did feel a little more productive than the rest of the group because they had not gathered as much information as they had initially promised. All they had were notes of the process of our group project. None of them had had any "real" contact with someone from the north end, or at least none had made any report of such contact. Why then would I be in the same category if I had already done three interviews and visited the area? It became clear that there was a schism developing in the group, and unfortunately it was taking on a gendered dimension. This revelation would affect my relationship with the group from then on. I did not know if I would relate the same way with the group members despite Freda's statement that she didn't care if I agreed with her or not. I said that I had a personal commitment to the project and that I did not care what shape the project took, because I would still pursue those interests. I told her that they, as members of the group, did not seem to have done much of what they promised to do anyway. We dispersed and agreed to meet again in class.

Mike did not come to the class. I mentioned to the group that I was going to talk about the project in class that day and that, overall, I was focusing my study of the group dynamics, besides the earlier-stated goals of the project. The professor informed the group that Mike had dropped the class and that it seemed as though he had been disturbed by the meeting we had had with the professor earlier on, when each member had addressed personal issues rather than the project per se. April said she felt guilty that she had contributed to Mike's dropping the course. The professor said he felt responsible for it too and promised to telephone Mike. Mildred asked that we be notified of what Mike said. What would happen to the group now? Would I be further alienated too, or would I become more integrated into it, now that Mike was gone? I convinced myself that at this point in our project, it did not really matter which way the dice rolled. I had started to collect good material for the project and felt that I could gather enough to write my final paper on the original objectives of the project. I promised to follow through with my part of the project.

The Problem of Studying Up

Our group project had proceeded a bit slowly the last few weeks of the semester. We had been able to read each other's notes once—except for Freda's. Given the schism in the group, and especially because I was on the opposite side of the three other students, I was uncertain about whether the other members had been deprived of Freda's notes as well. As it turned out, although Freda had been very vocal about the research project at our weekly meetings, she was not able to follow that enthusiasm with field data for her part in the project. We were supposed to meet at 9:00 P.M. a week before our class presentation, but Freda called to tell me that we may not have a lot of material to discuss and that it was better to postpone our group meeting till the following Wednesday at 9:00 P.M. at the coffee shop.

As I went through the field notes written by my colleagues, I was riveted by the comment that Mildred had made about my role in the project: "I must admit that in Mwenda's case, his goals are still not clear to me. He seems to be struggling with his notion of being the outsider, the native studying Western culture." This was an interesting observation. Maybe I did not have to look too far to see the same things that we had addressed in some of the readings in the class about fieldwork. Mildred's lack of understanding with regard to my goals in the project seemed to have led her to the conclusion that I was struggling with being the outsider, the "non-native" studying Western culture (not segregation in the north end). Yes, I was interested in the group dynamics, as I had mentioned to the group earlier, but Mildred's notes seemed to say more than she had shared with us. Her observations reminded me of Christine Obbo, a Ugandan anthropologist who describes a scenario in which her Western colleagues were desperate to see her field notes and had become quite uneasy on realizing she might have been studying them along with their culture. Obbo says, "Westerners, both academics and others, have responded to my fieldwork in their home countries in ways that reveal their discomfort when the accustomed power relationships between anthropologist and 'native' are reversed. The fieldnotes of a non-Westerner studying Americans upsets and makes them anxious because they feel that their culture is on the line."[12]

My silence and seemingly noncommittal attitude to our project might have caused Mildred to feel anxiety. Since she could not access my thoughts about the project, she seems to have experienced the same discomfort that Obbo mentions. Reflecting on this subject now as an anthropology professor, I am reminded of the anxiety—and, at times, the hostility—I often see in my American students when they realize that Horace Miner's classic essay "Body Ritual among the Nacirema" is about their own culture.[13] I usually make copies of the essay and bring them to class just after we have spent time reading an ethnography of a remote village in West Africa. I ask my students to read Miner's essay carefully, and individually, during that class. I then ask them if they would consider living in such a society. Students who are reading the essay for the first time feel tricked and often insist that Miner's work is dated and does not represent the contemporary world. I usually sense, however, an awkwardness when students realize that their own culture can appear as bizarre when placed under an ethnographic gaze.

What happens when one's culture becomes the focus of scrutiny by an outsider? Freda shared Mildred's view of my "mysterious" role in the project. The dynamics that were emerging among the group members were turning out to be truly exciting for me as an anthropologist in training. I wondered how the local people that anthropologists studied felt about the prospect of being observed and studied by an outsider for a long time. Do they conceal information from the anthropologists, or do they try to present an ideal picture of that culture? Do they just tolerate the anthropologist, or do they truly accept and embrace him or her? My own experience working in the field later revealed that informants tend to describe ideal cultural practices in certain circumstances, especially if they know that the outcome of fieldwork will be made public in the form of a book or journal paper.[14]

Let Me Climb My Own Tree

The schism in our group did not restrict my own contribution to the research at all. If anything, my work got even better. Wednesday afternoon the following week I went to Mr. Mathews's office in the downtown area as promised. Before I started my interview, he asked if I had carried a tape recorder to preserve the interview. It seemed as though he did not mind being recorded when expressing his views on the north end. I told him I did not bring a recorder but had carried a notebook instead. He said it would suffice. I was warming up inside. This was my first "real interview" for the project where the respondent was as enthusiastic about the project as I was. We got down to business and I started to ask questions. "What is your idea of segregation in the north end?" I asked Mr. Mathews. "If I go to the lumber yard and buy a pound of nails, I can put the nails in a shed house or a $300,000 house, and it won't make any difference to the nails. But the red-taping of the realty people will not let you do that," he said in response. To me, this was a very interesting reading of the issue of segregation in the north end. I realized that I was not just getting information but also wisdom. Mr. Mathews's responses reminded me of some older people in my own community back home in Kenya who were fond of explaining issues through metaphors, proverbs, and short stories.

Mr. Mathews said he was now eighty-one years old and had moved to the area in 1914. At one point, his family had moved to Indianapolis, where his father had a job and his mother, who was ailing, could receive better medical care. They had moved back to the area in 1919, living in a house on Ellis Avenue that was owned by a Black man. The neighborhood was mixed, and even his school, Lincoln School, was "salt and pepper," as he put it. He said that there was no prejudice then—unlike the way it was now. "So what went wrong?" I asked. According to Mathews, segregation was built on a number of things, including federal grants, state grants, real estate companies, the judicial system, zoning boards, and children and family services. "This is deep. White folk don't think no nigger know that," he remarked with a sense of contentment. I was surprised at his use of the word "nigger" and wondered if he would use it when speaking with a White interviewer. He continued to explain that in the past, there were few Blacks in the north end and they were servants. Only the YMCA was there to integrate people, and it was located at the university. "In the '20s, there were few Black-owned businesses," he added.

He said that physically the north end was a geographical fact, but it was now classified as a bad area, and the term *north end* was a moral rather than a geographical reference. "And this is because of dope," he said. "White people use the dope and bring it to the area in order to find violations of the law in Black neighborhoods, leaving their own neighborhoods suitable for increased government support. Dope is run by the police department; they deliver it and then use the silly people to peddle it. Where do you think these people get the dope from?" he asked. He went on, "It is a class conspiracy. It is like the game of tennis. The Black people are the net where the ball goes over. They do not want us to be better. The judicial system is bad; it is the worst in the country. If you want to get away with murder, come to our county. The judicial system can be bought." "How was it in the past?" I asked as I became more and more intrigued by his social critique. "Families were together in the old days. They have destroyed our families by introducing laws against disciplining kids." This information seemed to echo what I had heard from Mrs. Mulder and Crystal. I wondered whether it was confirmation of the reality or a reflection of generational values. Mr. Mathews said he wished he could tell the government that he knew all about its wicked plans, but then he mused that even if the government knew, it would not do anything. "They got Kennedy, they got Martin Luther King Jr., and they got Lincoln. If you are good, they will get you," he said in resignation.

"Are Black people racist too?" I asked him trying to see if he was one-sided on the issue. "Everybody is prejudiced. You are prejudiced and I am prejudiced. You cause it by taking from someone else. You create boundaries. We should be talking of giving people equal opportunities, not segregation. Let each man stand in his shoes, let every woman wear her dress, and let me climb my own tree. Equalize opportunities. Whites are taking from Blacks, Blacks are taking from Whites," he said. A feeling like this one needed to be concretized: I asked, "What should be done in order to bridge the gap between Blacks and Whites?" He seemed as though he was expecting the question. He said, "We should not be talking about bridging the gap. We should be talking about giving people opportunities. Each human being wants to be with his own. You have to leave them alone. You interfere with them, then you brew trouble. We need to clean up the judicial system and the family and the child services department. America does not care about human beings. It cares about money. There is glory in money, and one will do anything to make money. If you don't make money, you are sad. And instead of going to your family, you commit suicide. You make money and you are happy—you are successful."

I was impressed by Mr. Mathews's analysis. He sounded like some of the intellectuals I had read, only without the professional jargon. I was curious, however, about his insinuation that segregation was natural, as people "want to be with their own." I asked him if he thought that Blacks and Whites should stay in separate places. He said that when people have equal opportunities, they would soon sort themselves out and live wherever they wanted. It would be back to "salt and pepper" as in the old days when Mr. Mathews's family moved to the area. I could not but agree with his analysis. Once structural and systemic issues of discrimination were minimized, it was easier to develop a more vibrant and diverse community.

Before completing our interview, I told him, "I have other members in my group who are interested in this issue. Would you like to have another interview with them and me?" "Yes, tell the other Black men to come and listen to what I have to say," he quickly offered. "The other members are not Black," I informed him. He changed his posture a little, leaned forward, and then said, "No. Just keep quiet and see if they will come up with facts. They will wait and see what you'll find out. They will just be looking for dope. They know the facts and we know the facts, but they don't think we know the facts." He seemed to have some sort of psychic insight into the nature of our group project—except for the part on looking for dope. I found myself wondering how as an African American he would have responded to a request by one of the White members of our group to participate in an interview on race relations in the north end. Would he agree to it? What kind of information would he give them compared to what he shared with me? How does this play into the question of Western anthropologists studying their own societies? At the end of our interview, Mr. Mathews said, with a broad smile on his face, that he was happy about our meeting because these were issues he liked talking about. I thanked him and told him I would seek him out again as the need arose. As I left his office, I could not help but think, "this man seems to know what was going on in our group." My group members had not come up with any field data almost two months into the project. As he walked me to the elevator, he mentioned that he would introduce me to a friend of his named Doris, who he thought had insights into the issues my project was seeking to highlight.

Our next group meeting was scheduled for 9:00 P.M. at the coffee shop. I arrived seven minutes late, but no one from the group was there yet. I stayed for a half an hour and left, only to learn later that no one had actually come to the meeting. The other members of the group were all aware that there would be no meeting, except me. Maybe I should have seen it coming and braced myself for isolation. The other group members must have e-mailed or called each other to cancel the meeting and decided to leave me out of it. The next day when we met, April said she was interested in taking pictures for our project. No one else seemed enthusiastic about taking pictures. It appeared as though she just wanted to take pictures to enhance our presentation. I wondered if pictures were really necessary. How much data had we gathered so far to necessitate pictures? I personally was not interested in taking photographs for this project. I saw pictures as a way of framing and controlling people, especially if they were not part of my social world. Taking some random photos of African Americans in the north end was to me a kind of objectification. I told her I was opposed to the idea.

As promised, Mr. Mathews set up a meeting for me and Doris. I called her up, and she gave me directions to her house on the east side of town. She had a very impressive house, and from the kind of stuff in her house as well as the neighborhood it was in, I could tell she was middle class. When I told her about our research project, she mentioned that she was part of a community group that met regularly to discuss racial issues and that I was welcome to attend one such meeting that was coming up in the middle of the month.[15] I told her I would be more than happy to attend if my schedule allowed. Meanwhile, she said, she was ready to answer any questions I had about race relations in the north end. I started the interview by asking her to give me her overall impression on racial segregation in the north end. She said that no matter how bad Black people were to each other, they liked being together. "They may fight or kill each other, but they still like staying together," she said. But once they get an education, they tend to move upwards and go into other areas. She said that she had lived in the area for three years and at her current address for a year. She had originally come from Mississippi. Her grandmother had bought a house here, which meant she did not need to look for a place to live when she was ready to go to school. She had earned a BA and now taught at a local high school. Earlier, she had had plans of going to law school, but her priorities had since changed. She had just returned from Senegal that summer and shared with me some of her experiences there—especially the fact that for the first time she was in a context where the majority of the people were Black.

Her grandmother was the first Black person to buy a house on First and Church streets. Initially, the area was Black and White, but when the Whites moved out, the value of property had depreciated, and more Blacks came into the area. She said that prejudice went both ways: Whites fear Blacks, and Blacks hate Whites. There had been crime in the White neighborhoods too, but since the Whites were not lumped together like the Blacks were, it had been easy for White crime to go unnoticed. This seemed to be a common feeling among the people I interviewed for this project. After a few more minutes of discussion, I begged to leave and thanked Doris for her time and input, promising to return and join her in a meeting to discuss race, which she had mentioned would take place later in the month. At that point, I had gathered enough data to build a story for our project. I was also getting comfortable with my mini-ethnography and felt that my preparation as an anthropologist was bearing fruit. I only hoped that our final class presentation would not be marred by our internal strife.

All Is Well

Despite the tensions and schism in the group, we were determined to make the project work. We had been planning to go to the American Legion, which Freda had suggested we visit in order to "experience the life of African Americans." But Mildred felt we should not go if Freda had not made any prior arrangements for our arrival there. She also felt that I was more involved in the project than anyone else and asked what I wanted to do. And she did not know whether she wanted to go to a Black church or not because she thought she might look ridiculous. What would they think of her? Would she stand out? Interestingly enough, Freda expressed the same concerns. She, first of all, wanted to know how I felt about going with the group to the American Legion. Were they concerned I might not want to go with them, given the emerging negative chemistry within the group? But I said I was ready to accompany them to the club, and we set a date when we would all go together.

The American Legion was on Hickory, two blocks south of Main Street, which meant it was in the north end. When we arrived, we found an all-Black patronage. We had gone in early (around 9:00 P.M.) and noticed that there were few people. More people only started coming in as we were getting ready to leave (at around 10:00 P.M.). We had spent about an hour in the club, and things did not seem to be going too well. There was this drunk man who started hitting on Mildred, pestering her to dance with him, and she was losing her nerve. She told him that she was with me and was not interested in him and that he should leave her alone. It was quite clear from her face and body language that she was not comfortable with the whole encounter.

She looked a little scared too, and her face turned red. He did not make the situation any better when he told her that he had shot people. I was not sure why he said that to her, and I too started getting a little uncomfortable in that club. After a while, I avoided any eye contact with the other patrons, lest they would be encouraged to come and put a claim on the women in my group. I did not want any scene to be created if someone insisted on dancing with one of my colleagues. After a while, things took on a more relaxed turn as the drunk realized he was not very welcome anyway. I am sure Freda would have handled the situation "better" than Mildred if she were the one whom the drunk had approached. We left at 10.00 P.M. and promised each other to go back—although I had doubts that Mildred would be keen on a return trip.

Nobody really discussed our experience at the American Legion when we met the following day to talk about the format for our final presentation. Freda felt that we had learned nothing about segregation in our group project but that the process and group dynamics had been very interesting and we should concentrate on that aspect of it in our formal presentation. I felt bad because I knew that my final paper would have data related to the initial focus of the group project on race relations in the north end. I wondered if I should give my colleagues my notes to use in their own write-up. Would it even be useful to them? I decided against it and went along with the suggestion to talk about the group dynamics in our formal class presentation.

At the end of the semester, we all put together different parts of the project and presented it to the class and then wrote individual papers that had to incorporate the contribution of all group members. In the class presentation of our project, we stayed away from "hard" data and discussed more the group dynamics and the challenges of finding people to interview. We touched on how race was a major factor in how much we were able or unable to accomplish the goals of our project in terms of finding research participants to interview. We also talked about how our individual interests in the research had weighed heavily on the project, leading to a lack of a coherent discussion of the issues at hand. In my final paper, I incorporated a number of the interviews I was able to conduct and argued that the experience was critical in preparing me for the challenges of actual research for my dissertation. As far as I could tell, we all got an A in the course. The question that lingered, however, was what I had learned about race and anthropology's approach to race as a social reality and as an analytical category. Clearly, race was an almost-taboo topic—as I later undeniably learned in one course I took in which we were assigned a text specifically focusing on race.

Race as a Topic of Classroom Discussion

Race as a topic of anthropological inquiry has been glaringly absent in America, despite the discipline's prominence as trope.[16] This absence extends into the classroom, where many students find it hard to discuss topics related to race. After the "failed" class research project on race relations in the north end, I became interested in seeing how race played out in classroom contexts. There is a certain level of discomfort that the issue of race brings into an American classroom context—a fact that became apparent to me in a course I was taking in cultural anthropology. One of the texts assigned for discussion in the course was Ruth Frankenberg's *White Women, Race Matters.* I enjoyed reading the book and was looking forward to our class discussion because I had found her symbolic and interpretive analysis of the popular discourse surrounding race particularly interesting. Moreover, I found some of her points resonating with what I had observed in my own short sojourn in America.

When I responded to a flyer put out by undergraduate students in the department— which I discuss in the next chapter—I remarked on its insensitivity. Many of my fellow graduate students who were willing to discuss it with me talked about how innocent and unintentional they thought the students who prepared the flyer had been. In response to such a scenario, Frankenberg says, "Whereas earlier, seeing race meant being racist and being racist being 'bad,' causation here is reversed: a person who is good cannot by definition be racist. . . . This is an important moment in the color- and power-evasive repertoire, for this is the logic that undergirds legislative and judicial approaches to both workplace race discrimination and hate crime, placing the burden of proof on the intent of the perpetrator rather than on the effects of an event or situation on its victim(s)."[17]

To render racism to intention—as did a number of those who shared their opinions with me—is completely to misread symbolic practices connected to race. The structural and cultural embeddedness of race in American society reveals the culpability of Whites, as the dominant social group, in the existing asymmetrical power relations that favors them because they are "already in power through multiple formal and informal processes."[18] It is this analytical reality that made me find Frankenberg's book quite intriguing to me, and I was looking forward to a lively discussion in class.

I was, however, shocked that there was utter silence in class on the day we were supposed to discuss Frankenberg's book. I too was guilty of not saying anything in the class, but I was hoping to take notes on what other students would say about the book. From their body language, I could tell that some of the students did not like the book and later learned from other students that the professor did not particularly like the book either. This "cold" response to an assigned reading was not typical of my fellow students, many of whom I had taken other courses with. For instance, when we read Baudrillard's *Simulacra and Simulation* (1994), in which he critiques American culture, many of the same students criticized the author for "generalizing about America." I was, therefore, surprised at the silence that emerged in connection with Frankenberg's book. I figured here was a book about an issue that permeated every aspect of American life, but not a student had a critique to share. Many just commented that Frankenberg's book was "interesting" and then went on to critique her methodology, saying that she should have limited her study to a particular group and that she was "heavy handed" in her analysis. Others commented that she did not interview any of the various women in these particular women's lives and that it was an ambitious project, seeking to grasp a topic that is so broad and complex. I personally found her analysis very telling and quite comparable to what I had observed about race around the city in which I was living at the time.

Interestingly, other foreign students in the class did not say a word either— at least until one White female student said, after our break, that the book was about the White students in the class. She said that Whites were so trapped in their own "Whiteness" that they took the book personally and could not objectively critique it. I later learned that one foreign student in the class had asked the White female student to bring up this point about "Whiteness" because she wanted the critique to come from an American. Another female foreign student said that we had glossed over the chapter on interracial relationships while the majority of the people in the class either were or had been in such relationships. Some of the White students concluded that the text would be useful for an introductory course and not a graduate-level course. Another one mentioned that she did not think that the book was talking about the White women in the class.

I felt so angry in that class. Reflectively I might have been angry at myself for thinking that our class would have some honest conversations about race. I had expected more about anthropology and race, and I did not get it—making it even worse for me because I was ready to get the "other" side of race issues from fellow anthropology students, who were seldom compelled to be sensitive to their racialized subjectivity. Yes despite this turn of events in our classroom, I learned something about academic anthropology books and the responses one gets from the "natives" who read those books. I wondered if what I was witnessing was an indication of what happens when the object of anthropological study gets a hold of ethnography about itself. Were the students too greatly implicated in the study that the only way to deal with the data was to dismiss it? Was I expecting something more than was common practice in an anthropology classroom?

3

Of Monkeys, Africans, and the Pursuit of the Other

My participation in a group project on race opened my eyes to other avenues of understanding the dynamics of race in the classroom and beyond. I soon found myself quite drawn to sociocultural texts that allowed for a deeper understanding of race. My next opportunity to analyze race came not in the form of a book but through student activities within the department as I looked not only at classroom behavior but also at some of the strategies used to bring students together. Interestingly, anthropology—no matter what level—seems to be fixated with alterity. Whether it is in the undergraduate anthropology meeting, in a research project in West Africa, or in scholarship and theory making, Africans and people of African descent seem to not only occupy a "special" place in anthropology but also tend to bring out anthropology's proverbial "dirty linen."

Student life in a university is a multilayered engagement that compels many to respond to multiple activities and expectations from both the academic and the extracurricular domains. Amid all these demands, students also form not only personal but academic identities. Academic identity outside the classroom can be enhanced through discipline-specific clubs. In my department, there were two such clubs—one for undergraduate students, the Undergraduate Association for Student Anthropologists (UGASA), and the other for graduate students, the Graduate Anthropology Student Association (GASA). Given students' demands for participation in other activities outside the classroom, these academic clubs often struggled to maintain a sizeable attendance at meetings. In the department's attempt to contend with this apathy and bring students to the meetings, free food and drinks were offered as bait. This was the case on a beautiful fall day, two years into my doctoral program, when UGASA put out a flyer to announce one of its meetings.

I was in the department of anthropology to check my mail at about 10:30 A.M., when I saw the UGASA flyer on the department's bulletin board, located next to the students' lounge. At the time, I had a tendency to read all announcements posted on the board to get a sense of what was going on in the department as well as among students. This particular flyer was an announcement of a "new course" in experimental primatology (Primatology 304—the same course as Kinesiology 009). In reality, though, there was no such course offering in the department; the flyer was just a creative gimmick meant to catch undergraduate students' attention and entice them to attend the advertised UGASA meeting. The flyer announced that some of the topics to be covered in the "course" were tree climbing, brachiating, and termite fishing—all probable anthropological topics that could fit into the physical anthropology subfield.

The "course" also included mandatory all-expense-paid field trips to Ecuador, Kenya, and Sumatra, making me realize that the students who put together the announcement were quite familiar with the department because at the time there were graduate students as well as faculty whose fieldwork took them to the specific locations mentioned. Below the "course" announcement were two images—one was Michael Jordan in his legendary scissors leap in the air and the other of a monkey hanging on a tree staring at the observer. Under the two images were the words "maybe you'd have known if you'd shown up to the last UGASA meeting." The announcement ended with a reminder of the upcoming event in which one of the students would talk about UGASA field trips. From my conversations with undergraduate students, I knew that their field trips were local or within the state, and I doubted that the club was planning any trips to Ecuador, Kenya, or Sumatra. The flyer was simply playing on the exoticism of the discipline to draw students to the meeting.

What was interesting to me upon seeing and reading this flyer was the juxtaposition of Michael Jordan and a monkey. I considered a number of possible interpretations of the images: Michael could have represented a recognizable popular cultural icon that would have captured the attention of the reader. Maybe he represented kinesiology and the monkey represented primatology—the two "courses" announced in the flyer. Yet I could not help but wonder if what I was witnessing was a play with symbols. What was the flyer signifying? Why did the club choose those specific images and words?

Was this another of those moments of anthropology's dance with alterity, especially where Africans and people of African descent are concerned? My symbolic-interpretive mind was in motion. Because I did not want to overreact, I went upstairs to the office of a fellow graduate student whose opinion I respected and asked him what he thought of the flyer. I needed a sober assessment of the message in the flyer. Besides being a person who was not afraid to speak his mind, even regarding contentious issues in the department, my colleague was a White American—a fact that, I felt, positioned him a little differently than I was and that would provide him with a different read from mine. When he saw the flyer, he said that it was inappropriate and offensive, and he offered to sign a petition, should I wish to notify the chair of our department about it. I had not thought about a petition and was not actually sure I wanted to involve the chair of the department in my interpretations of a flyer. I decided the best way to respond was to write a commentary and post it next to the initial flyer. That way, I thought, I would not make a big deal of it, and both pieces could create some kind of "dialogue." When I went downstairs to the hall where some of the flyers had been posted, I found that someone had scribbled on one of them "racist! get a life." I was relieved that I was not the only one interpreting the flyer as offensive and that after all I was not overreacting.

I wrote a commentary and placed it alongside the original flyer. I stated that words and images are powerful symbols that signify much more than meets the eye and cited anthropologist Combs-Schilling, whose 1989 book *Sacred Performance: Islam, Sexuality, and Sacrifice* I had been reading. Combs-Schilling argues that some things are almost subconscious and people may do them without consciously intending to and yet project a certain message that can offend others. I went to class that morning after posting my "rejoinder" and came back after an hour, only to find that all the flyers had been removed. I saw a White female student placing another flyer on the bulletin board and recognized her from one of the undergraduate courses I was taking to fulfill my anthropology requirements. I thought she might have been responsible for putting up the first flyer, but I did not ask her. A fellow graduate student asked me to give a copy of my comments to the chair of department, which I did, by placing one in the chair's mailbox.

Upon reading my response, a professor in the department told me that it had actually inspired him to write something intelligent. After a short while, all copies of my response to the flyer disappeared as well, and in their place came a new flyer from UGASA apologizing for "an unintended slur." The apology stated that UGASA wanted to apologize to individuals of African descent who may have been offended by the initial flyer. I wondered why the apology singled out people of African descent when most of my colleagues who found the flyer offensive were not of African descent. Was this singling-out related to the fact that I, as an African, had responded to the flyer? Coincidentally, two weeks earlier there were racist flyers in the mailboxes of Black and Jewish students in the university's law school. The flyers had sketches of monkeys with captions comparing the students to primates.

The UGASA flyer took on a very public presence on campus, prompting the chair of the anthropology department to respond to it in the student newspaper. I even learned later that some Black faculty on campus had discussed the flyer in one of their meetings and that one professor had shared her opinion about the flyer with her students, who then wanted to call the anthropology department and complain about the racist nature of the flyer. I felt sorry for the students who had put together the flyer because I surely believed they did not deliberately plan to demean anyone, and I felt bad that I had set the process in motion. Yet I wanted to make sure we, as anthropologists, questioned the underlying deep structures that reproduce unintended messages because of how we are socialized. I hoped that America, as a deeply racialized society, could benefit from an anthropological critique of its taken-for-granted social sensibilities that show up in unintended places such as the UGASA flyer.

I wanted anthropologists to critically interrogate how our students and we ourselves present our discipline, which—as I mentioned earlier—was not the most adored among some of my friends in other departments. After the flyer issue had seemingly subsided, an African American administrator asked me how many Black faculty were in the anthropology department. When I told her there were none, she said that anthropology had all along been criticized for being racist and patronizing, and it was amazing how little had changed over the years, as the flyer had proved. I was perplexed. I had really liked the anthropological methods to which I was being introduced in graduate school and had been drawn to the discipline by what I thought it could do for me and the study of themes and topics I deemed important. I had indeed applied anthropological tools to critique the UGASA flyer, clearly showing that the discipline was vigilant in accurately representing others.

I did not have enough of a grasp of the discipline at the time to give an appropriate rejoinder to the negative projections I had heard about anthropology, but I planned on going deep into the history of the discipline to gain a better sense of its place within the academy. I was drawn to the discipline because of its promise to equip me to respond to such intricate social and cultural matters. Indeed, I later came to learn that my sentiments about the discipline were not isolated. Faye Harrison shares a similar story of her own journey into anthropology, stating that "among people of color, in the United States and in some other parts of the world, it [anthropology] has a reputation for being racist and colonial."[1] While I chose anthropology because of its methodological approach to culture (especially the holistic and comparative approach), for Harrison it was "curiosity about race and racism—a curiosity borne not only from an intellectual exercise but from the social suffering and outrage of a people subjected to oppression—[that] prompted me to raise serious questions that in later years I would realize were most amenable to anthropological inquiry with its comparative ethnographic lens."[2] Thus, despite being separated by time and space, Harrison and I were both drawn to the discipline for similar reasons. Moreover, Beatrice Medicine—a Native American anthropologist—had also chosen anthropology to "make living more fulfilling for Native Americans."[3] Had we made mistakes by choosing to become anthropologists? I think not. We were just entering into a discipline that like many others has its own challenges, some of which are often addressed by anthropologists in different forums.

When the African studies faculty at the university had a discussion on the flyer, for instance, an anthropologist at the discussion responded and said that the flyer was shocking not only for its racist slur but for the fact that it came out of anthropology, a discipline that was teaching students to be culturally sensitive. Later in the week, a friend of mine who worked as an administrator in the university said that he did not think that enough was done following the UGASA flyer because even though the "perpetrators" had apologized, they did not admit that their action was racist: they had said only that the flyer had been interpreted as racist, meaning that their original mission was not guilty but that the interpretation made it so. My friend felt that the students should have been made to realize that their action was racist in the first place; otherwise, it would end up looking like they were forced to apologize for something they did not do.

When I talked to a friend from the sociology department about the flyer, he said that it was reminiscent of "the primate problem" that pervades anthropology. He suggested that the department of anthropology hold workshops and develop a specific curriculum to sensitize people on the scientific racism that anthropology carries out, especially in the images of Africa that it promotes and in the problems that belie such representation. He further stated that the problem lies in the "secular missionary syndrome" that anthropologists have, whereby they think that Africans are different from Westerners and that it is the anthropologists who can interpret and make sense of African lives for Western audiences as well as for Africans themselves. His critiques were starting to reflect some of the texts I had read in some of the courses I was taking in the department.[4] Clearly anthropology was aware of this challenge and was responding to it, or so I hoped.

I found myself searching for strategies to get anthropology to move away from this caricaturing. I did not want the discipline—which I had truly grown to like and admire—to be representing *itself* so poorly, and yet the challenges were seemingly larger than I had realized. I soon understood, however, that negative representation of Africans and people of African descent was not just an "anthropology problem." It had permeated the corporate world as well, and I wondered if that fact were a direct result of anthropology's pursuance of alterity. In October 1993, for example, an advertisement in *Focus,* an AT&T employee magazine, featured the company's long-distance telephone coverage over the entire world. While all other continents were represented by humans, Africa was represented by a monkey,[5] making me wonder if many Americans viewed Africans as monkeys. Was this the "primate problem" that my friend in sociology had mentioned? How had academia and anthropology contributed to this representation? Or was it actually the manifestation of subliminal American cultural perceptions of Africa?

Hidden behind this seemingly bizarre representation of Africa is the notion of race, a dynamic that complicates America's stated ideals of equality expressed in the Constitution and the reality of social hierarchy and the bigotry that pervades both the public and private social space.[6] Race has presented an even greater challenge for anthropology in the form of accusations leveled against the discipline for its complacency and even for its abetting racism through physical anthropology. While Franz Boas has often been hailed as the anthropologist who challenged racism in America, a reread of his work may reveal a different understanding of anthropology's engagement with race as a social construct.

In a thought-provoking article on the role of race and culture within anthropology, Kamala Visweswaran actually challenges received wisdom in anthropology that often regards Boas as antiracist and states: "I suggest the disturbing possibility that the attempt to expunge race from social science by assigning it to biology, as Boas and his students did, helped legitimate the scientific study of race, thereby fueling the machine of scientific racism." Visweswaran further argues that it is this act of moving the study of race from social science to biology that has led to anthropology's "failure . . . to be in the vanguard of debates . . . on race, racism, multiculturalism, or revising the canon." Debate on race has thus been left in the hands of the emerging fields of multiculturalism and cultural studies "that radically foreground race and racial identity precisely because the modern anthropological notion of culture cannot do so."[7]

This reality of anthropology's relationship to culture, as George Marcus notes, is "supremely ironic that anthropology in the United States, so long identified with the concept of culture, has had so little to do, until very recently, with the emergence of the lively interdisciplinary arena of research, discussion, and thought now known as cultural studies."[8] In trying to understand this "absence" of race as a topic of discussion in anthropology, I wondered if it were more about the classroom as a space that stifled real conversations or if American graduate school seminars were structured to fail at any attempts at discussing race. To place these issues within a larger subcultural terrain, I now focus on the typical classroom experiences I had in my anthropology seminars in America.

In the Classroom

Besides the expected seminar discussions that occurred in class, professors required research and response papers that allowed for an evaluation of how well students had learned the course material. In my first semester of graduate training in anthropology, I was surprised that I had been awarded a B in a research paper that I had done research for and had taken time to write. I had expected at least an A-. When I asked the professor, after class, what I should have worked on to make it a better paper, he said that I received a B partially because I had placed a lot of emphasis on specific issues of the book instead of focusing on the big picture. As I pondered the professor's response, I wondered if my earlier educational culture was inadequate in my new setting in America. Was I a victim of my own training in literary studies, where I was used to having lengthy papers that focused on and analyzed a single text or idea? If that was the case, how about the texts written by anthropologists that I had read, which tended to be full of stories that could be interpreted from various perspectives to derive different meanings?

I talked to an American student in the department and asked if she would read my paper and tell me why I received a B. She graciously agreed and came back to me after a day with some very useful comments that made me aware of some of the weak points of the paper. Since she had taken many anthropology courses, including the same one that I had taken, she was able to guide me toward an understanding of what a good paper in anthropology entailed.

She mentioned, for instance, that my paper was too wordy and needed to focus on some specific anthropological issues such as structuralism, functionalism, agency, and change—which were pertinent to the texts assigned for the course, especially those dealing with British social anthropology. She also cautioned me not to take the "regular" meanings attached to these terms but rather to use them as did the anthropologists. This was an important cultural lesson. I also learned that a B in America was very different from a B in Kenya. In Kenya, at least when I was a graduate student in the late 1980s and early 1990s, a student needed to score 70 percent to make an A, while in America, I realized, an A needed a score of at least 93 percent. Getting a B meant that I needed to work harder, especially since I was in the initial stages of my graduate training in anthropology. At the end of the semester, I had improved my writing and received an A in the course.

What intrigued me even further in my experiences in the American graduate school courses was the amount of reading I was supposed to cover in one class and in such a short period of time. It seemed as though we were reading a book a week for each of the courses I was taking, which kept me wondering how long I could sustain such a load. Interestingly, when the professor came into the classroom to discuss the 300-page text we had read, he or she would go through it in an hour-and-a-half or less. How can one go through a 300-page book in such a short time? Was this "the big picture" phenomenon that I seemed to have missed in my first seminar paper? When this practice repeatedly occurred in almost all my courses, I was convinced I was witnessing an American style of academic analysis that I myself needed to acquire if I were to be successful in my graduate studies in anthropology. Compared to my academic training in Kenya prior to my enrolling in graduate school in America, I could see some notable differences in the two education systems. In Kenya, there was a tendency for a student to do a close reading of the text, analyze every small detail of it, and then write a lengthy paper that expanded on one of the common themes identified in the text. This approach was not going to work in the cultural anthropology graduate program in America. I had to adapt quickly. I subsequently learned from my fellow anthropology students that what we were doing in the one-and-a-half hours that we devoted to a 300-page text was a "critique" of the text. The goal was to target the main anthropological issues raised in the text, especially as they related to other similar issues relevant in the discipline or academy. These texts were part of other "academic conversations" that I seemed unaware of at the time. Yet race did not seem to be part of the larger anthropology conversation, and indeed, it was a topic rarely discussed, even outside of the anthropology classroom. Were anthropology seminars mirror images of larger cultural discourses and practices? What exactly went on in casual conversations between Americans, and how were these conversations reflected in the classroom?

Discussing race—as I show in the previous chapter—is difficult, but figuring out how graduate school seminars work is not. After a while, I started seeing patterns in those seminars and could almost predict what would happen in the subsequent sessions: the professor would come into the classroom and say, "So what do you think of this work?" or "What are the main issues?" Then someone in the class would start a discussion by talking about this and that, often using some very sophisticated language. Many times I found myself asking, "What book is this student talking about?" "Did they read the same book I read?" "What part of the book deals with the notion of anti-structure and hegemony the student is talking about?" Surprisingly, the professor would be impressed by the student's comments, make some more comments of his or her own and move on to someone else. Sometimes I felt as if I were watching a dialogue between two actors who knew their roles well. After a while, I too learned the trick and was sometimes able to say a lot about a text without really saying much.

Moral philosopher Harry Frankfurt has captured well what I think was happening in many of those classrooms sessions. He would call them "bullshit sessions"—occasions punctuated with very little substantive material despite the often seemingly heated discussions that ensued. How else would one describe a case in which a fellow student walked into a classroom after confessing to a group of us in the hallway that she had not read the text for the day and yet went on to give a "superb" critique of the text in a way that shaped the rest of the conversation in the classroom? Clearly the student had mastered enough lingo and jargon that she tossed around during the discussion and convinced everyone that she had something intelligent to say about the reading. Frankfurt says that "bullshit is unavoidable whenever circumstances require someone to talk without knowing what he is talking about."[9] In this case, the student knew what she was talking about because many anthropology texts tended to share some common themes and style; they were part of the same conversation. Yet she did not quite know the content of the book we were discussing.

Much later, I narrated this classroom experience to a colleague from another department. She said that she, too, had had very similar experiences in graduate school at an elite university in the Midwest. A fellow seminar student asked her what the reading for the day was and then walked into the seminar without having read the texts. When asked to start the discussion on one of the assigned texts, the fellow student looked at the book cover for a moment and went on to give a very "articulate" critique of its contents—an analysis that set the tone for the rest of the seminar discussion, even though the student had not read the assigned text. Such experiences made me wonder if graduate school seminars were presented in such a manner that they required participants to sound intelligent without giving much thought to the actual content of the texts. My graduate school experiences, especially in seminars, were dominated more by how one sounded and not what one said. Was this a practice shaped by the reality that out of a large pool of applicants, only a few students got into graduate school and that these few had to constantly impress their professors and peers so as to remind them of their legitimate claims to belonging in the department and the discipline? Is obscurity part of our academic club membership?

Now, as I look back at my experiences, I am convinced that academic culture in America has almost equated intelligence and scholarly excellence with obscurity. It has also created a divide between theory and praxis where, as Catherine Lutz argues, theory is considered impenetrable, abstruse, and hard to understand.[10] By placing theory on such a high pedestal, anthropologists often miss the rich analytical and interpretive frames hidden in story, metaphor, fiction, and proverbs, which are often used by the subaltern to critique dominant anthropological narratives.[11] The more we cannot understand what a scholar is saying, the more impressed we are with him or her. English professor Gerald Graff regards obscurity thus: "One of the most pervasive beliefs in our culture—shared by academic and nonacademics alike—is that the concerns of the intellectual world are so difficult that only a small minority can understand them."[12] If a text is rated highly because it can be understood only by a few, can we truly become public intellectuals and bring anthropological knowledge to the masses? I remember struggling to make sense of V. Y. Mudimbe's books on Africa, especially at a time when all reviewers of his books seemed to praise the books' intellectual worth in Africanist circles—at least during my graduate school days in the 1990s. Why were his books so highly rated? Was it because only a few could "understand" them? If I could not make sense of the main arguments in such texts, was it my fault as a reader or that of the writer for failing to communicate?

Things were also a little different in the undergraduate classroom in the '90s, as I found out through my experiences in a course in folklore that I was taking with a number of upper-class undergraduate students. One day when we received our examination papers back, I noted that many of the undergraduate students in the class wanted to know the questions that would be in the next examination. When they realized that the professor would not give them the questions, they asked her to give them the specific areas in the course content that they needed to focus on. I was quite surprised by this behavior—and especially the fact that the professor did not find it odd. I thought that the students just wanted to get a good grade and not really learn a thing. I wondered why a professor would give an examination and narrow the scope of the examination to fit the demands of the students. Cora Du Bois explained this phenomenon in the mid-1950s when she argued that "In the American context the link between conformity, effort-optimism, and material well-being leads inevitably to mass education with the emphasis on the common man rather than the uncommon man, to its technical and practical cast to what seems to observers its low standards."[13]

In the undergraduate class I was taking, the students knew that the exam was a means to an end and that mastering the means assured one of a good end. The professor asked the students to read specific areas of the course material, but the students insisted they wanted to be told what to concentrate on. There was one particular female student who insisted she wanted to know what the professor wanted in her answers because, as she said, she did not seem to get them right. Apparently there were options to do something else for extra credit in the class, but the student had not taken advantage of them and was now panicking because her grade was not looking too good and it was almost the end of the semester. I wondered what kind of education laid so much emphasis on examinations and the reproduction of specific material for the professor.

Where was the depth? Where was the thinking? Why undertake something for extra credit? And was that extra credit meant to test one's knowledge of the concepts one had not grasped for the examination, or was it just to help one get a better grade? I found this practice of offering extra credit quite intriguing, and I am sure there must be some logic to it. Part of this logic could be the corporatization of higher education that has turned colleges and universities into commercial centers. Consequently, students have become clients whose success is based on how well they master the new corporate culture. The undergraduate student probably wants to pass the tests, get good grades, and be accepted into graduate school. The graduate student wants to sound intelligent and impress professors and become accepted into the academic club. Could this explain the lack of discussion that ensued in one of my seminar classes when we were scheduled to discuss race and no one had anything substantive to say? Or is it just an isolated case? Is American education, as Du Bois sees it, "a means to make more men more effective workers and better citizens"[14] and less focused on depth and the critical development of the intellect? → DOES IT EVEN MAKE THEM BETTER WORKERS?

A friend of mine who was an exchange student from France once told me that he thought it was very easy to study in America because all one needed to do was read and then "vomit" it out on paper. One did not have to think. "Americans do not think," he said, adding, "In France, you have to think. You have to convince your teacher that you know what you are being tested in." Though this comment is spiced with ethnocentrism, I thought he did have a point—especially given my own experiences in the undergraduate classroom, where students were overwhelmingly focused on grades. While I could not pretend to come from a particularly "thinking" tradition in Kenya, I did not constantly ask my lecturers to tell me what would be covered in the examinations. In fact, we took examinations at the end of a year, not after the short five or six weeks that I saw happening in the American university. We had to know and remember a lot of material, and our teachers told us to study everything we had covered in the year. In my experiences in America, however, I realized that by the time the semester was over, students could hardly remember what they covered in the first few weeks of the semester, maybe because they had done well in the tests that covered those weeks' readings—and that was all that mattered.

Does this difference in education systems have anything to do with the fact that most of the scholars who are considered the big thinkers and theorists in various disciplines are foreign or foreign-born and trained? Many such scholars are French, British, German, Polish, African, or Indian. Karl Marx, Max Weber, Jean Baudrillard, Pierre Bourdieu, Michel Foucault, Gayatri Spivak, Homi Bhabha, Jacques Derrida, V. Y. Mudimbe, Edward Said—all come from outside of America. A fellow graduate student once mentioned to me casually that Americans are anti-intellectual and that they tend to look at people from France and Britain as snobs because Americans pride themselves in practical knowledge and street-smartness. But as the world's most powerful nation militarily and economically, what good does intellectualism bring to America? As Jack Nachbar and Kevin Lause say, "Anti-intellectualism reflects the faith Americans have in common sense and immediate experience as the best guide to effective living and the virtue we find in a view of human nature which finds the soul nearer the heart than the head."[15]

This focus on practical knowledge is not all bad, and I personally find it appropriate for anthropology in particular. One of the sources of frustrations for me when I was being trained in anthropology was the lack—at least in

my department at the time—of a specific program in applied or practice anthropology. Where was the practical application of all the "head knowledge" I
was gaining? Where were the anthropology equivalents of social workers and
psychologists who spent most of their professional time focusing on social
and individual problems? Could the absence of such anthropologists be a
reflection of why so many anthropologists tended to focus on cultures other
than their own and thus not have a "real" investment in the local political,
cultural, and economic problems? Diane Lewis argues that an anthropologist working in his or her own community or country could not "justify a
lack of commitment [to local problems] while deriving professional benefits
from his research among people who are in a position to make enforceable
demands on his sense of responsibility to them."[16]

Working with communities at home seems to compel anthropologists to
attend not only to theoretical matters but also to praxis, as often happens
among applied anthropologists. But can we say that theoretical and applied
anthropology are incompatible, or do they simply occupy different spaces in
the academic world? This implied difference between applied and theoretical
anthropology seems to be the case in both British and American brands of
anthropology. In the mid-1970s, for instance, Ruth Landman interviewed
sixty British applied anthropologists and found overwhelming evidence of
their sense of inferiority compared to the rest of the profession.[17] In America,
the Society for Applied Anthropology (SfAA) parted ways with the American
Anthropological Association (AAA) in the late 1940s and holds its annual
meetings separate from those of the AAA. Central to the mission of SfAA is
"to promote the integration of anthropological perspectives and methods in
solving human problems throughout the world."[18] Maybe this separation was
necessitated by a focus on theory by one (the AAA) and praxis by the other
(the SfAA), as often happened in British social anthropology. It is telling how
applied anthropological work tends to have less clout in the academy compared to anthropology that is considered theoretical. In a sense, it seems like
a division of labor where "smart" anthropologists do theory and "ordinary"
anthropologists do praxis. Hidden in such a division of labor is a hierarchy
that degrades works produced from the "margins," while also evading critical
analysis of race, gender, and class that pervade the Western societies within
which most anthropologists train and work. Indeed, as I came to learn while
in graduate school in America, social class is an important analytical frame
for understanding anthropology and American culture, and it plays out itself
quite creatively in the classroom.

Social Class in the Classroom

American higher education, even though often presented as open to the masses (at least compared to the European elitist education system), has its own hidden class dynamics. One's social class often determines the quality of one's education because high-cost private colleges tend to attract students from high-income social brackets. Students attending large universities for graduate training in anthropology often come from these private colleges. When such class dynamics interact with a neo-liberal market structure of education where students become customers, a unique cultural practice emerges inside the classroom.

Now as a professor with experience teaching undergraduate students in small liberal arts colleges, I argue that these students, most of whom come from middle- and upper-class backgrounds, present their unique social-class identity in various ways—one of which is remaining largely silent in class. They hardly participate in classroom discussion, and often expect me (the professor) to make the most effort to teach them. Many students come from an American subculture where personal status and respect cannot be gained or improved through the verbal prowess identified by bell hooks as critical for African Americans growing up in poor and working-class backgrounds.[19] Rather, many of these liberal arts college students have been socialized to expect similar or even higher standards of living than their parents, and they believe that the best way to "earn" it is to conform to the system. Such conformity may often be manifested through classroom behavior, where students remain quiet and subdued until "motivated" to actively participate in their learning. Professors like me, who are trained in several different educational systems, are compelled to do all we can to find the "right" method to teach such students and to meet their expectations. Moreover, given the numerous institutions available for students to choose, many colleges—trying to enroll as many students as possible—have turned to the same strategies used to market consumer products. As federal and state funding for higher education diminishes, many tuition-dependent schools are compelled to aggressively market themselves to prospective and current students in order to remain operational. As a result, students start to see themselves as customers with a right to the best product, and we, as their teachers, are expected to deliver that product to them in the most attractive package that we can. This customer-service model of higher education, which Faye Harrison ties to "a postcolonial corporate hegemony," is leading to the marginalization of the subaltern intellectuals who are unwilling to conform to these market forces.[20]

This commoditization of higher education also leads to more hierarchy in the classroom as lower-class students tend to have less sense of entitlement and may be less "successful" in such institutions. Indeed, some lower-class students may develop a cultural attitude that is counter to the one that makes middle-class students successful.[21] Interestingly enough, we anthropologists have not been as active as one would expect in our study of this phenomenon, despite the readily accessible data at the institutions where we teach and conduct research.[22] And there is yet another consequence of this corporatization of higher education and the sense of entitlement that students, as customers, bring to the classroom: the heavy reliance on student evaluations of instructors by an institution in determining which faculty members "fit" the college and deserve to be granted tenure.[23] Faculty who do not "fit" the prevailing culture of teaching in these institutions end up losing out.[24]

How different would a college experience be if each student believed from the onset that he or she was individually responsible for making the classroom learning a success? Likening education in liberal arts colleges to a menu or to shopping at a store with variety of items from which to choose, in a 2005 report to his faculty Grant Cornwell (a dean at St. Lawrence University at the time) examines students' sense of entitlement. He asserts:

> Lacking seriousness of purpose, four years [in college] can, in the worst case, be another manifestation of the vulgar excess of the privileged in advanced capitalism. I am always wary of the commodification of "collegiate experiences," nervous that students, without meaning to, but because they are products of our culture, make their way through [college] as mildly bored consumers, selecting in the aisles—stocked with options—their "collegiate experiences." One, two, maybe three aisles of these experiences are stocked with academic choices.... choices [that] are not organized by any clear sense of purpose. Lacking this purpose, there is a leveling effect between their multiple commitments and activities, so that their academic pursuits are just one set competing among others, rather than the organizing central purpose of their being [in school].[25]

The threat of this kind of approach to education is that students will look at college as another experience on their way to experiencing life in a culture filled with brief events that are the markers of prosperity. When we add to this "experience" students' expectations that faculty will motivate them to learn, we end up with apathetic students whose college experience entails, for the most part, a process of just going through the motions. What can anthropology tell us about such a culture—one that anthropologists teaching in both public and private academic institutions confront on a daily basis? How can anthropology discern the embedded class dynamism reflected in this consumer-like behavior among students?

The predominant focus that many American anthropologists have on cultures other than their own has made them inactive in studying classroom culture as well as social class in America. This absence of anthropological focus on social class may have led Raymond Smith to declare that "the concept of social class is relatively new to anthropological theory."[26] In the absence of a spirited focus on social class by anthropologists, much of the research on class has been conducted by scholars in sociology and cultural studies. Sherry Ortner confirms this fact when she writes: "The first thing that strikes an anthropologist reading the ethnographic literature on America, written by both sociologists and anthropologists, is the centrality of 'class' in sociological research and its marginality in anthropological studies."[27]

Consequently, we often have to turn to sociologists to get a glimpse of a discourse on American social class structure. Herbert J. Gans, for instance, argues that "The upper middle-class world, stressing as it does individuality, is a highly competitive one. In the typically upper middle-class occupations such as advertising, publishing, university teaching, law, and the arts, individual achievement is the main key to success, status, and security."[28]

This desire for security, success, and status may explain the classroom culture I mention above, which leads many middle-class students to be conformers, often following a set of rules and adapting to institutions' expectations. Ortner also notes the presence of high levels of anxiety among children of middle-class backgrounds over their ability to maintain their parents' social status.[29] Most students from such middle-class backgrounds—often socialized to see education as their ticket to a similar or better lifestyle than that of their parents—tend to focus more on grades and less on the process of learning itself. Parents too know that for their children to have a middle-class life, their best bet is education. Such parents tend to be quite involved in the daily educational experiences of their children, often calling or visiting their children's institutions—especially if course grades are not reflective of parents' expectations.

Given this anxiety to maintain or even surpass their parents' social class and the connection between "good" grades and success after college, many students from middle-class backgrounds come to class and try to figure out the best way to succeed in that situation. For many of them, coming to class is where their obligation to their education ends. As long as they are in class, it is up to the professor to teach them and make them learn. Professors are then pushed to meet these student "needs," often by being encouraged to use multimedia, group discussions, and short projects that will keep the student "entertained" in order to learn. Without disparaging the efficacy of these strategies in contributing to student learning, my argument is that even the growing literature on the scholarship of teaching and learning in America tends to focus on what the professor needs to do to enhance student learning, and little is said about the student's active role in that learning process. It is as if these scholars would be overstepping their bounds if they were to write about the need for students to make some effort that would contribute to their own learning. When an education system turns to commercial models of success, students become customers, and as the adage goes, "the customer is always right." An example from one of the colleges where I was a member of faculty may suffice here.

I went to a meeting for first-year faculty members and sat through a session that was meant to help us become better teachers. A faculty member, who was known for her success as a teacher but had been asked to take up an administrative role in the institution, was leading the meeting. What I remember most from that meeting was the time and effort we spent going through the evaluation process that students undertake in gauging the teaching effectiveness of their professors. The evaluation protocol entirely involved what students thought of their instructors and nothing at all about students' own contribution to their learning. All that the students had to do, it seemed, was show up in class, and the teacher would motivate them, keep them interested, and make them learn. Because of the value I saw placed on student evaluations and the students' awareness of the power their evaluations had in shaping instruction, I started to understand the anxiety I often sensed among many untenured colleagues, who constantly worried about their teaching and the way their student evaluations would turn out each semester. Many such colleagues seemed to be teaching to the evaluations, and I often heard them say that they did not want to do anything "bad" in the classroom, lest it jeopardize their tenure process. I am not aware of any anthropological study of this culture of the academy—especially one surrounding the politics of student evaluations and tenure—and I would surely want to read an ethnography on the topic. As I observed my colleagues through all the ordeal of tenure, I could not help but truly see students as customers whose evaluations of instruction were really customer-satisfaction surveys. I make these critiques not because I am a bad teacher hiding behind the inappropriate burden placed upon me by student evaluations or their apathy in the classroom, but because I see in this subject an important field of anthropological inquiry.[30]

This customer mentality that I mention here seems to be a middle-class attitude to life that asserts, "I am paying for it, and as the consumer, I want you to do all the background work and bring the product to me so I can consume it in the easiest way possible." Maybe this attitude explains certain practices I have observed among professors who "bribe" their students just before the evaluations by bringing cookies and candy to class or inviting students to their homes for dinner. Such behavior by faculty often heightens students' sense of entitlement even more, especially if they come from wealthy backgrounds. Sherry Ortner regards these practices as all "about money."[31] Indeed, as bell hooks notes,

> money . . . shaped values, attitudes, social relations, and the biases that in-formed the way knowledge would be given and received. . . . Although no one ever directly stated the rules that would govern our conduct [in college], it was taught by example and reinforced by a system of rewards. As silence and obedience to authority were most rewarded, students learned that this was the appropriate demeanor in the classroom. Loudness, anger, emotional outbursts, and even something as seemingly innocent as unrestrained laughter were deemed unacceptable, vulgar disruptions of classroom social order.[32]

Being loud and talkative especially in class, as hooks explains, is associated with the lower class or with people who do not have middle-class values, making it hard for many institutions to be truly welcoming to students from diverse economic and racial backgrounds.

These middle-class values, as Ortner argues, are mobilized through a dominant ideology of ownership of the means of production, discrimination, and cultural hegemony that become frames of reference for meanings and behavior of groups and individuals.[33] When people from different social backgrounds come together in an institution of higher education governed by middle-class values, a paradox results: either the "outsiders" conform to the middle-class values or they get excluded. Invariably professors, as agents of these middle-class values themselves, tend to act as the "socializing agents" in the classroom, and students soon learn to appropriate or copy such behavior as a means of "success." As Peter MacLaren has noted, classrooms "constitute cultural arenas in which. . . . the fundamental conflicts within the larger society" are played out.[34]

Looking back at my graduate school seminars and the absence of a concrete discussion of race and class, I see a picture that makes sense within this framework of the classroom as a cultural arena representing the larger society. By virtue of the social privilege bestowed on them by Whiteness, most of my fellow students were unable to disengage themselves from their racially constituted identities and to discuss objectively an ethnography that directly interrogated their social reality. It was hard for these students to analyze their privileged positions through an objective critique of Whiteness, which in turn was also tied to social class. It soon dawned on me that the experiences I had had in the classroom, both in the graduate seminar as a student and the undergraduate classroom as a professor, were critical in unlocking an important puzzle about ethnographic fieldwork. Unable to study up—that is, to interrogate their own social class and racial identities— anthropologists thus consistently pursue alterity and otherness in order to remain relevant within the academy. Otherwise, why is it that even though many anthropologists spend the majority of their career in the classroom where research data is easily available, compared to fieldwork abroad, there are few scholars focusing on the classroom and the university as a research site? With all the ample topics and fields of research available to Western anthropologists in institutions of higher learning, one can only see their insistence on studying the Other as reflecting the discipline's modus operandi. As I show in the next section, anthropologists' pursuance of the Other, even where there are other options for study, confirms the discipline's fascination with difference. This fascination recurs in different contexts even when the Other is only the anthropologist's frame of reference.

In Pursuit of the Other

Studying "others," or what Alcida Ramos calls the pursuit of the exotic, has constituted anthropology's distinctiveness from other related disciplines such as sociology, cultural studies, and history. [35] Even in cases where there is concerted effort to make anthropology "exotic no more,"[36] and anthropologists continue to conduct fieldwork "at home," anthropology's pursuit of the Other persists even into the big Western metropolis, creating some form of spatial incarceration where "others" are pursued in specific spaces and for specific purposes. One can sit at annual AAA meetings and hear anthropologists joke about how certain research topics, especially those involving the Other, are more sexy than, say, studying a Western corporation. Numerous reasons can be given for this lingering pursuit for the "exotic," including its development as a colonial science;[37] its competition for Western research subjects with such disciplines as sociology and cultural studies; and the continued construction of anthropology as a discipline defined by its object. The centrality of the object in the organization and operation of anthropology's episteme and praxis makes it much harder for an American anthropologist, for instance, to just appear in an American suburb, rent a house, and study the local people.[38] It is not that such a project is not possible but rather that it is less common and often complicated by anthropology's definitive procedure of participant observation that would make it hard for a stranger to just come into a community and start asking questions about the people's livelihood—what they eat, why they eat it, what they do for a living, how much they make, and so forth—as is common in fieldwork locations in non-Western societies.

During my graduate school days, I did come across numerous examples of work by anthropologists that specifically focused on their own cultures, but I also noted that such works often followed from successful careers studying non-Western cultures.[39] My assumption was that these anthropologists had already made a name for themselves and could "risk" studying up. Orvar Löfgren explains it well in concluding that "anthropology at home functions as training ground for students . . . [or] part of a retirement scheme [for] scholars who have been out there 'doing the real thing.'"[40] Not everyone can do the "real thing," as I came to see when I found a few examples of anthropologists who had initially planned to conduct research abroad but for various reasons had to abandon such plans for fieldwork in their own society. Interestingly enough, however, these anthropologists chose to focus on the Other, or the "exotic," even when conducting fieldwork in their own societies. This pursuit of the Other became apparent when a fellow student in my department, who had planned on conducting his research in Africa, switched his field to a metropolis in the United States. The student had initially visited his field site in Africa one summer with funding from the department, but for personal reasons decided to switch his field site to Washington, D.C. He, however, retained his interest in Africans and zeroed in on kinship and gender among African immigrants in Washington. In a way, this switch reflected a situation where the field research was about different sites but the research object remained the same.

Another anthropologist who seemed to have switched her field site from Africa to America but still focused on the Other is JoAnn D'Alisera. Initially she conducted her ethnographic work in West Africa but ended up in Washington, D.C., still pursuing the Other—the African immigrant. Admittedly, ethnographic fieldwork is no longer limited to a spatial location rooted in geography, but anthropology's object of study remains the same, making me wonder if Africans, irrespective of where they are located, will always constitute the exotic and the Other of anthropology. Maybe pursuit for the Other is persistent because as anthropologists our research projects are shaped by the whims of funding agencies that tend to define what we should study and leave us little wiggle room to define our research focus. Or maybe we do not want to start a new theoretical project after we have invested so much in the one that did not materialize. These possible scenarios did not seem to apply in the case of D'Alisera.

JoAnn D'Alisera did not receive any funding for her research when she switched field sites from West Africa to Washington, D.C., and as she says, "I had never been trained to do fieldwork in an urban environment, and it was unclear to me how I should proceed."[41] Given these circumstances, she could have studied any group in any American metropolis, but she did not—probably because of the inherent challenges in studying up. Maybe she was looking ahead at her career and felt compelled to prepare herself as a postmodern scholar studying transnational culture with a specific focus on African immigrants. Reading about her research process and experiences as documented in her doctoral dissertation, I was puzzled by her object of study and the reasons she gave for switching research subject and field sites. Was the object of research based on the alterity of the African that did not change, regardless of place?

The title of her dissertation, "The Transnational Search for Muslim Identity: Sierra Leoneans in America's Capital," makes for an interesting analysis as well. Granted, it would be interesting to know how Sierra Leonean Muslims adjust to life in America, yet I want to believe that there is more going on here. As I read this work, I struggled to see its rationale beyond the implicit pursuit of the exotic. Not satisfied with such a conclusion, however, I looked for other explanations. Could the topic of Islam be D'Alisera's pull into this study, and therefore the shift in field locations may have given her a better opportunity to study Muslims? If it were the topic and not the object that was driving her study, couldn't she have studied Muslim realities in Washington, D.C., among any cultural group? Or maybe it was because she had contacts there whom she could use to generate a number of interviewees for her research. Again as she shows, Washington was not so new to her; she had visited the city as a child and as a college student and had certain memories of the place.[42] It seems that perhaps she had not planned on studying Africans in America but that, because of hardships in the field in Africa, she decided to follow Africans to America.

In 1990, the Liberian civil war spilled over to Sierra Leone just when D'Alisera was trying to start her research project in Sierra Leone. In 1989, after a feasibility study, she had decided to study the Susu, but deteriorating political conditions made that impossible for her to do. Instead of abandoning her study and ethnic group all together, she decided to follow the Susu to America, where some of them had relocated. This is what she says of her frustration leaving Sierra Leone unable to accomplish her initial research project: "Back home [America], caught between my ambition to be an anthropologist who worked in a small village in Africa and my disappointment at the obstacles that made this impossible, I turned to friends and teachers for advice on how to salvage my project. My advisor suggested I look into research that was being carried out with Francophone West Africans in New York City."[43]

Anthropologist Paul Stoller was at the time conducting research on West African street traders in New York.[44] He, unlike D'Alisera, had spent many years in West Africa studying the Songhai of Niger. He had published a good number of articles and books on the Songhai and was now on his "retirement scheme" scholarship that Löfgren mentions above.[45] D'Alisera's breakthrough in her research dilemma came in the form of a phone call to a friend, as she explains: "Now as I dialed Simeon's Washington phone number after my disastrous second trip to Sierra Leone, I wondered if he could be disappointed in me and my inability to conduct fieldwork in his country."[46] I found this statement quite interesting because it seemed to suggest that her success in conducting research in Sierra Leone was tied to Simeon's positive regard of her. Was she suggesting that anthropologists conduct their fieldwork to meet expectations that their "informants," or "natives," have of them? I know for sure that in my own research I was driven by my own interest rather than by the interests of those I focused on in Mombasa, Kenya. Moreover, many of the accounts I have read of anthropologists' first experiences in the field reveal that the locals are not always very welcoming or eager to be studied. Our fieldwork is often and primarily a product of both our disciplinary trends and the whims of funding agencies that support it and the local people we study or work with come in when we have already chosen our topic and our field site. I would argue that it is only after the "natives" started responding authoritatively to our ethnographies, and also when our colleagues started to challenge our ethnographic work, that we became more "sympathetic" of our "informants" and the "native" perceptions of our work. I wondered if Simeon had initially shown interest in D'Alisera's work and invited her to Sierra Leone before she decided to look for a possible field site.

What do we make of D'Alisera's dilemma in not being able to study in Simeon's country and her subsequent focus on Simeon and other Sierra Leonean immigrants to Washington, D.C.? Is it a case of the transient "natives" who, no matter where they are located, still constitute objects of anthropological inquiry? Is it a case of once a "native" always a "native"? It seems as if even when one's geographic location changes, one's alterity endures. This reality complicates our understanding of location or field site and its specific importance in constructing the meaning and identity of otherness.[47] If one can study an African in Washington and also in Sierra Leone, what does this fact do to our understanding of ethnography and the anthropological enterprise? Is anthropology's focus on alterity its own undoing?

As I have shown above, many American anthropologists are uneasy when confronted with issues within their own culture that shape their identities and impact on their everyday interactions, especially race. Further, the increasingly changing social terrain that has historically constituted anthropologists' field site has forced many to rethink both their research and writing enterprises, which have often been predicated on cultural differences. Without readily available "natives" to study—and with a diminishing resource base for ethnographic fieldwork as other disciplines use what we have traditionally considered anthropological research tools—anthropologists have had to be very creative to remain relevant and current. One such strategy has been to engage in what I call "recycling of field notes," where anthropologists continue writing about a culture they had studied many years in the past. In a sense unable to return to their initial field sites abroad and in the absence of "transient natives" within their own societies, many Western anthropologists resort to recycling old field notes as they constantly publish "new" books, essays, and journal papers.

An Ethnographic Moment or Recycling Field Notes?

One of my initial attractions to the discipline of anthropology was its ability to take account of the reality of a living people and present it with some immediacy so that others can know about the actual, everyday lives of that group of people. I remember choosing to drop history in high school because I found it too focused on the past when I was most interested in the present. In retrospect, I now see that an understanding of history is critical to anthropological analysis. Yet the phenomenon of representing a living people—what many anthropologists often refer to as the "ethnographic present"—has had its share of critiques, especially given the fluidity and changing nature of the people and cultures we study. When we write that "this group of people is . . ." (even when we studied them many years before), we tend to fix them into a time frame that denies them historicity. As Charlotte Davies states, "Whereas the ethnographer moves on temporally, spatially and developmentally, the people he or she studied are presented as if the ethnographers' descriptions provides all that it is important, or possible, to know about their past and future."[48]

This "fixing" of cultures tends to also be followed closely by many texts produced from one field study, making these cultures either irrelevant to the analysis or timeless. In 1997, for instance, Pat Caplan published a book on informants writing ethnography. The work, *African Voices, African Lives,* is primarily centered around the story of Mohammed, one of her key informants, and the diary entries he made in 1967 when Caplan first went to Mafia Island in the coast of East Africa to conduct her ethnographic research. Her using data that she recorded in 1967 to write a book in 1997 left me wondering about the lives of the people she studied. Was this a historical account or a representation of an ethnographic present? Does it mean that the people in Mafia Island never changed? I concluded that Caplan was using her thirty-year-old data to support one of the theoretical trends that was in vogue around that time. Especially since anthropology was accused of being imperialistic in its representation of "natives," many scholars had been talking about writing ethnographies and using multiple voices and narratives.

By titling the book *African Voices, African Lives,* even though the data was primarily about a single African from a small island, Caplan was making it clear that she was giving voice to Africans—doubtless, a direct response to the discipline's reaction against anthropologists' creating grand narratives.[49] T. O. Beidelman's book *The Cool Knife: Imagery of Gender, Sexuality, and Moral Education in Kaguru Initiation Ritual*—which was also published in 1997 but was based on research conducted in the 1950s in Tanzania—is another example. When I read *The Cool Knife,* I could not help but wonder why, based on data collected in 1950, Beidelman was writing about Kaguru gender, sexuality, and moral education in the 1990s. Was this part of historical anthropology, or had Kaguru sociocultural practices remained the same for forty years? I concluded that Beidelman was primarily using the Kaguru to make specific theoretical statements to his anthropology colleagues in academia. The text had little, if any, goal of accurately representing the lives of the Kaguru.

Such use of "old" field notes to make contemporary arguments is what constitutes for me academic recycling—not in the sense of trying to conserve resources by reusing them but, rather, using the same resource over and over for purposes of remaining relevant in one's discipline. Indeed, it is more than recycling. It is a game of words played by those who can. It is about narratives and theories. It is a conversation that anthropologists have with themselves, and the Kaguru, for example, serve only as a medium through which the conversation can occur. The question that remains unanswered in this process is whether or not we need to do ethnography at all, and if so, is it just to contribute to theoretical discourse? Should we just have a reservoir of data collected in the field and interpret in order to fit whatever theories come up in our academic meetings and journals? Having such a reservoir might even bring us closer to other disciplines, such as history, that some scholars have said are closely related to anthropology.[50] The direct connections that history has with anthropology often come alive when we consider the process and product of ethnography as well as when we see ethnographic texts and historical texts in their own right.

In some cases, the historicity of ethnography becomes elusive when anthropologists continue this process of using "recycled" field notes to make contemporary analyses of the discipline—as the renowned anthropologist Johannes Fabian has done. I met Johannes Fabian for the first time in Arusha, Tanzania, at the 2002 conference of the Association of Social Anthropologists in UK and the Commonwealth. I was excited finally to meet such a distinguished anthropologist, who had written a great deal about anthropology and Africa using Zaire (now the Democratic Republic of the Congo) as his ethnographic reference. I was astonished, however, on learning that this visit to Tanzania was the first time he had been back to Africa after leaving Zaire in 1986. Despite this long fieldwork furlough, Fabian had continued to write about popular culture and performance in Zaire in ways that suggested a close understanding of Zaire's contemporary social realities and sensibilities, which are best gathered through fieldwork. One wonders what role real studies of real people on the ground play in shaping our ethnographies, especially when the focus is on such fluid and changing materials as popular culture. Interestingly, Fabian's most famous book (and, in a new edition, his most recently published) is aptly titled *Time and the Other: How Anthropology Makes Its Object.* Was Fabian writing about his own practice of constructing the African Other? Was this the reason critics such as Archie Mafeje were convinced that Africanist anthropology is dead?

Toward the end of my time in graduate school in America, a colleague from the sociology department told me about a debate that had ensued between Archie Mafeje and Sally Falk Moore.[51] The debate was mediated through

CODESRIA's *African Sociological Review*, a journal that continues to shape much of sociological and anthropological thinking in Africa today. Mafeje, even though trained as an anthropologist, had long identified himself as a sociologist because of his disagreements with the discipline of anthropology, both its praxis and epistemological terrains. He states, for instance, that the problem facing anthropology "is ontological . . . in that it derives not simply from colonialism or imperialism . . . but from historically-determined white racism."[52] When I read Mafeje's critique of Sally Falk Moore's book on anthropology and Africa and read his other articles on the "death" of anthropology in and of Africa, I was both excited and discouraged—excited because I saw Mafeje's critique as an important wake-up call for African and Africanist anthropologists, urging them to pay more attention to the value of using anthropological tools to make sense of all cultures, especially Western ones. But I was also discouraged because I felt indicted by Mafeje's conclusions about the death of a discipline that I had found so intriguing and useful in understanding contemporary African socioeconomic and political challenges. I concluded that I would take Mafeje's challenge and use anthropology to make sense not only of the different African locations in which I found myself but also of the culture of academic anthropology in America, where I had spent a substantial number of years. In a way, this chapter has grappled with some of the challenges posed by Mafeje, without refuting the efficacy of anthropology as a viable discipline among others such as history and sociology that Mafeje favors in his critique of anthropology.

4

Remembering Home, Contrasting Experiences

Different Worldviews

As I argue in the previous chapter, even though Western anthropology has been dominated by the study of the Other, the discipline has and can be used to study one's self and one's culture. In this chapter, I give an example of the value of using anthropology not only to study others but also to reflect upon one's own culture. Two years into my graduate training in anthropology, I picked up a set of analytical tools that I used in critiquing not only the work of other anthropologists but my own culture as well. The more I read ethnographies and anthropological analyses of cultural phenomena elsewhere, the more I became aware of my own cultural contexts and practices. I started making sense of my own experiences and often made more specific interpretations of certain cultural experiences that I had earlier taken for granted. When I spent time with new African graduate students at the university, for instance, I found myself able to relate and understand their frustrations and excitements at a large public American university. I was able to take a more holistic approach to understanding even local experiences and could see that our shared colonial history as Africans had made us more alike than different. I started looking more for subtle cultural similarities than the assumed differences some ethnographies may project about Africa and Africans. Our middle-class values were invariably shaped by French and British cultural sensibilities, and our regard for education and social mobility was surprisingly similar. Coming to America provided for us a big opportunity to see different cultural orientations and worldviews at play and even to express those shared cultural experiences. Anthropology illuminated for me how one's cultural background shapes one's encounter with and interpretation of another culture.

Generally speaking, one of the main issues that confront many travelers or visitors to a new location is culture shock, and many Africans who come to America are no exception—especially as they try to adjust to a new sense of self. Many Africans, and particularly those who come to America for study, come already socialized into a culture that tends to socially elevate and respect those with a Western education. It is indeed the search for a better Western education that brings them to America in the first place, and for many Africans, their arrival in America is a follow-up experience that began in another education system. In many African countries, Western-educated members of society tend to define the shape that modernity takes in their local communities.

A Western education has for a long time been the best avenue through which many Africans access the advantages of modernity, often expressed through the kinds of jobs that are considered fitting for people of different education levels.[1] Tilling the land, especially by using one's hands, is reserved for those who never went to school. House help or bar tending is considered the domain of those with little or no education, and security guards are those who have no education and who still have a strong tie to their traditional cultures.[2] Because African formal education is mostly structured within an elitist system that takes on a pyramid shape (the largest number of participants at the bottom and the lowest number at the top), those with a higher education tend to have specific values that dissuade them from engaging in what would be considered "manual labor." Such labor is reserved for those who could not advance in the education system beyond elementary level.

This disparity and the clearly marked boundaries between those with a higher education and those without tend to be reconfigured when Africans move to America. Many Africans are amazed to see people who did not go beyond high school, and who do not work in a white-collar job, driving better cars than Africans with higher education. Others are shocked to learn that they have to do all their household chores for themselves including cooking, cleaning, washing clothes, and even pumping gas into their vehicles at gas stations. Those who were used to having house help back in their homes in Africa are shocked to realize that daycare is very expensive and that they, as a result, may be forced to do the babysitting and cooking for their own children. Others, because of their visa status and economic needs, find themselves working the jobs they would have despised if they were offered them in their home countries—security guards, grounds keepers, dish crew in a university dining room, house and office cleaners, nurses aides in retirement homes, or taxi drivers. Because such positions also tend to pay less than what "professional" jobs would pay, these Africans find that they have to work many hours in order to earn enough money to make ends meet. For many Africans, however, these jobs are temporary positions taken up to assist them in completing their studies, after which they hope to return to their home countries and seek better-paying jobs.

Despite these economic struggles, or what Katherine Newman calls "downward mobility,"[3] there is often an unspoken expectation and perception that having entered America is a sure sign of personal success and that no matter how hard the African may have struggled to make ends meet, when this person goes back home, he or she often projects an air of arrogance, seeking to place him- or herself above those who had been left behind at home. Even if transmigrant Africans spend most of their lives in America cleaning toilets or working at nursing homes, they never divulge such information to relatives or friends back home. Many tend to display an image of economic success and cultural sophistication. Moreover, some who never return to their homes may end up assuming an attitude toward Africa that is often displayed by non-Africans. They may start to criticize their countries, their governments, and their cultures—as was the case of some Kenyans on a Listserv list to which I subscribed while I was in graduate school: they said they would return to Kenya only if the roads were paved and there was an uninterrupted supply of electricity. Many of those projecting such a view grew up in rural communities where they had no access to paved roads or even electricity, but because they had made it to America, their values and experiences had changed and they were despising their own country, even though they had done nothing to help move it to the level of development that seemed acceptable to them.

Such a view of one's home may be the result of one having been assimilated into another culture and having thus absorbed its worldview. Maybe when Africans live in America for a long time, they inevitably see the world through Americanized eyes, or they simply inhabit cultural practices often associated with transmigrants. As Elizabeth McAlister has argued when discussing Rara, a street festival in Haiti, "transmigrants live, operate, and 'develop subjectivities and identities embedded in networks of relationships that connect them simultaneously to two or more nation-states.'"[4] Sometimes viewing life outside of one's cultural lens, as anthropology has allowed me to do, is important in changing one's initial perceptions and assumptions about others. When I was younger, for instance, I used to think that Western tourists were the richest people in the world.[5] They could afford to hire vehicles to take them to national parks, stay in the "tourist hotels," and purchase crafts (that many of my peers in Kenya considered a waste of money) costing almost five times what we thought they were worth.

When I got a chance to live and interact with Americans who were planning to— and eventually did—visit Kenya as tourists, I was surprised to learn that for a number of them, it had taken several years to save enough money for the two weeks they spent there on a safari. But when they arrived in Kenya, they were considered millionaires because they were able to spend the equivalent of a Kenyan professor's annual income in a day. This view of Americans as rich was not limited to Americans: when I had a chance to take my family on a safari in the summer of 2007, a number of my friends in Kenya assumed that I had become rich and that I was "on holiday." Given this reality, it is no wonder most Kenyans want to go to America, thinking that money grows on the proverbial trees. Many may not know the complexities involved in raising enough money to take four people from America to Kenya, even for a short period of time. When some of these Kenyans, who see America as "the land of milk and honey," get a chance to visit America for a few weeks or even months, something else happens. They feel compelled to return with a "piece" of America and, consequently, end up buying "stuff" to take back home. Buying and bringing stuff home is an important marker of "being there"—one that even provides them with some sense of elevated social status. This notion of "being there" is nothing new to anthropologists, who have for years defined their own sense of legitimacy in the discipline by invoking specific examples of having been to the unique and exotic places they write about.

On Being There

It is common for anthropologists to display in their ethnographies some proof of their having been to their fieldwork locations. The narrative of place can be enhanced by a cultural artifact that is worn or displayed at annual meetings, a photo of one in the field that is displayed in an office or accompanying a written text. Being there, however, is not a phenomenon reserved for anthropologists. During my time in graduate school in America, the same collaboration between my institution in America and Egerton University that had facilitated my entry into the anthropology doctoral program enabled two other Kenyans to make short-term academic trips to my university in

America. When some of the visiting scholars were returning home, for instance, they had to depart from a small airport close to campus and were faced with a problem because they had packed too much luggage. One of the scholars had three very large suitcases full of second-hand items from the local Salvation Army thrift store—thermos flasks, mirrors, bed sheets, clothes, shoes, jackets, lots of small appliances. Even though he could have gone to Gikomba, an open-air market in Nairobi, and gotten the same clothes, there was symbolic value for him in bringing home something from America.[6]

Most used clothes in Kenya come from America, but many Kenyans are socialized to go home from a journey with gifts for family and friends, and this scholar was just following that cultural expectation.[7] Before we took him to the airport, we had to take away four bags of used clothes from his overweight luggage, and he still was overweight by twenty pounds when we checked-in his luggage at the airport. To reduce the weight and avoid being charged for extra weight, we advised him to remove more clothes from his suitcases. What was quite intriguing about the whole ordeal, however, was his preference for the used clothes over his academic books. He, like other previous visiting scholars, had received a $200 book allowance from the host program so that he could purchase books to take home with him. For people coming in as exchange scholars and as faculty from institutions with a shortage of books, a book allowance was a very appropriate award. However, our colleague chose to remove his books from his luggage and asked that the books be shipped to him in Kenya instead of getting rid of the used clothes and other items. Imagine a scholar coming to America on an academic exchange and the only things he thought were important for him to take home with him were used clothes—and not a single book.

At a time when there were many incidents of shipped items disappearing from the postal service before they could reach their intended addressees in Kenya, an African scholar returning home from the United States preferred to fly home with used clothes and household items rather than books. How do we explain this scenario? Could it be a reflection of Kenya's material deprivation and/or an absence of a culture of literacy? Could it be some form of "mimicry and membership" to a Western cultural ideal that is explored by James Ferguson?[8] Without a doubt, there lies in this case an element of both, and my separation of these issues is primarily for purposes of analysis: there are close ties between material deprivation and a culture of literacy. That fact notwithstanding, however, I have not heard of a Kenyan, irrespective of socioeconomic status, who goes abroad and brings back a book for a relative or friend to read. Andrew Mwenda, a Ugandan journalist, provides us an example that may explain the actions of the Kenyan academic who chose used clothes over books. Mwenda shows how our worldviews and actions are shaped by our material conditions. When he was in jail (for criticizing president Museveni's leadership), a number of his friends came to visit and console him. One particular day when his Ugandan friends together with a European friend came to visit, they brought him different items that, in his view, provided an important window into cultural differences between the two sets of friends. Mwenda says:

> Blake [Lambert] had brought me a book by Norwegian journalist Asne Seier-stad titled The Bookseller of Kabul [sic]—a typical Mzungu attitude. Ugan-dans brought me food, warm clothing and beddings—things that provide material comfort, certainly a very kind and generous thing. Blake brought something that would improve my knowledge and occupy my mind. It tells a lot about how differences in the levels of development bring differences in perception of people's challenges. As fresh graduates from a peasant society, which lives on the margin of subsistence, we Africans tend to privilege mate-rial comfort over intellectual pursuits. People from industrial societies tend to privilege mental health over physical health because physical well-being is taken for granted.[9]

Mwenda's example shows how we project our own immediate experiences to circumstances we face in our daily living. Can we use the same analysis to talk about academia? Do we also project our immediate experiences into our academic and scholarly endeavors? How do we decide on the topics to focus on and the theories to pursue? I am convinced that our personal interests, experiences, and cultural contexts often shape a number of our academic pursuits. Whatever factors shape our academic inquiry, academic training factors in there as well. Two years into my academic sojourn in America and into anthropology, I had already received some anthropological training that enabled me to start applying ethnographic skills to my surroundings, even outside any well-organized research projects. My first real opportunity to do anthropological analysis came when I returned to Kenya.

On May 23, 1994, I boarded a flight from O'Hare International Airport in Chicago headed for Kenya to conduct my pre-dissertation research and see my family. I did not have overweight suitcases; neither did I carry many used clothes. I bought a few gifts for my family members. None of those gifts were books, even though I knew my family would have greatly benefited from some of the works I had read in graduate school. Indeed, it would have been quite odd for me to arrive home and hand out books as gifts to family members. I purchased a well-priced ticket from Sabena Airlines—a ticket that, I later realized, came with certain disadvantages because of its underlying economic symbolism. Being unable to afford a more expensive ticket meant that I had to contend with more flight connections and long layovers. I had, for instance, a fifteen-hour layover in Brussels and, because I did not carry a European or American passport or a visa to enter the country, I had to stay in the airport the entire time. Unlike Europeans and Americans, Africans need to have visas to enter European cities, even when in transit. Talk about contending with my Africanness and the travel limitations that come with it! I went to every store and room in the airport, slept, walked, read, and still there were many more hours of waiting. I had arrived in Brussels at 7:00 A.M., and our flight was scheduled to leave for Nairobi at 10:00 P.M. I resolved that if I chose the same airline in the future, I would have to get a visa so that I could go out into the city. I even found out that a friend from Kenya, whom I had met in America, lived in Brussels. Maybe I could apply for a visa on my way back through Brussels and visit with her. For the time being, all these plans were just that—plans.

Since I had just come from O'Hare Airport in Chicago, the airport at Brussels seemed like a joke to me, especially given its tiny bathrooms, hard chairs, and small passenger lounges. There was good food on the plane, however, so not everything about the airline was negative. We were served fish and salad, chicken, rice, broccoli, mushrooms, a dinner roll, and a bottle of wine, but I chose to eat light and avoid the wine. I was also curious to see how this European airline compared to Kenya Airways. Growing up in Kenya immediately after colonial rule, we were accustomed to thinking that European things were better than our own. I was pleasantly surprised, however, that the plane was not as comfortable as the Kenya Airways airbus I had taken two years earlier when I was traveling to America for the first time. The Kenyan Airways flight was also much smoother.

Tired of sitting in small plastic chairs in the airport lounge, I decided to walk around the airport looking for a place to rest. Comfortable lounges were strictly for first- and business-class passengers. For the rest of us, the economy-class folks, I guess we had to make do with hard plastic chairs. I even tried to sweet talk attendants at the Sabena Airlines service desk to get access to the lounges, but all I could get were two passes for food, a sandwich, and a medium drink at one airport cafeteria. Looking around the airport, I saw many other Africans at the various waiting lounges. When I asked some of the check-in attendants about this large number of Africans, I was told they were Sudanese refugees going to America for reprise as their country was in civil war. At about 5:00 P.M., I saw light at the end of the tunnel, realizing I had only five more hours to wait for my flight to Nairobi. I went to the Relax Café, where I purchased a Coke and two sandwiches with the passes I had received from Sabena Airlines.

Spending sixteen hours at an airport brought out my ethnographic skills—especially observation, which started to take the best of me. I noticed while looking outside the airport that someone brought the plane walkway to the exit door so that passengers could walk in the cover of a canopy; the fuel attendants drove their trucks very close to the plane and refueled; the toilet cleaners used their machines to suck out the refuse left by the previous passengers; and kitchen attendants restocked the kitchen in readiness for the next set of passengers. The baggage trucks came towing many carriers containing passenger's suitcases and boxes; the shuttle bus drove people to their various planes from the boarding lobby; and the fire safety personnel waited patiently on the side of the runway as planes landed and took off. I had never been as aware of activities at an airport as I was on that trip. When seen from that perspective, the airport was a hub of activity and a good site for anthropological research and analysis. Maybe being away from Kenya for two years was good ethnographic preparation that would make me more aware of the cultural realities and practices in my own country that I had taken for granted. If I were to have developed something of this awareness, then I would know I was on my way to becoming an anthropologist. I was quite excited at the prospect of conducting research at home in Kenya, even though my specific field site was not in my natal home. Supported by a grant from my department, this trip to Kenya was my preliminary field research—work that would officially introduce me to "real" ethnographic research. It was for me a case of going home and at the same time going into the field.[10]

Familiar Yet Strange

Familiar yet strange is how I would define my arrival and my stay at home in Kenya in May 1994. I arrived in Nairobi in the morning of Sunday, May 25, and went straight to the city center, where I linked up with my brother and some friends whom I had not seen in two years. Even though I was exhausted from the long trip, I wanted to stay awake all day so that I could sleep through the night. Other than the familiar diesel fumes that characterize much of Nairobi and other urban centers in Kenya, many things looked different through my new cultural lenses. I could tell that a lot had changed since I left in 1992. Life had become very difficult for many Kenyans because the cost of living had gone up tremendously. When I had left Kenya, for instance, a 2-kg packet of maize (corn) flour cost KSh 15.00, but in 1994 it cost KSh 50.00. And a 300-milliliter bottle of soda cost KSh 5.00 in 1992, compared to KSh 13.00 in 1994. A 2-kg packet of maize flour can feed a family of six for a day and a half. The minimum wage for an urban casual laborer was about KSh 100.00 per day at the time, but many people received less since there was not a strict adherence to labor laws in the country. If a family of six wished to include greens, beans or meat, onions and cooking oil, to make a full meal, they would spend almost a day's wages. This economic reality brought with it tremendous expansion of the gap between the rich and the poor—salaries for public/civil servants had stagnated, more people were unemployed, and crime rates had skyrocketed to a point where Nairobi, the capital city, was referred to as "Nairobbery." These problems added to the lure of leaving Kenya for "greener" pastures abroad and many people that I met told me I was lucky to be in America.

Later in the evening of May 25, I had dinner with my family, and some of them advised me not to be in a hurry to return to Kenya but instead to stay in America longer and "make money." The fact that I was actually a graduate student getting a PhD was not the main focus here: the message was that I was in America, and what mattered most was that I use the opportunity to make money. One relative who had been in America talked about seeing job offers everywhere including at gas stations, with some paying up to $16.00 an hour. This information caused a stir in the room as other family members were quickly calculating how much money they could earn in a month with that kind of hourly wage (about $2,500). Although I had doubts about gas station jobs that would pay that kind of money for starters (the average minimum wage at the time was $6.00), I knew that my family members' calculations did not consider other important factors such as paying for medical insurance, taxes, a car loan and insurance, utilities (gas or electricity, telephone, and water), and rent or a mortgage, which would technically leave them with less than $500.00 a month for daily expenses such as food, out-of-pocket medical expenses, vehicle fuel, and so forth. Yet this is exactly what perpetuates the image of America as a land of milk and honey.

Another relative thought that he would be OK moving to America to sweep the streets because it would allow him to make "real money." All this was said with the assumption that one could get a job easily without legal papers and that one could compare the cost of living in America with that of Kenya, where people have, for instance, live-in nannies for child care who are paid on average the equivalent of $30.00 per month. This same amount of money paid to a nanny for a month in Kenya would be only enough for a half a day of child care in the big cities in America. I wanted to tell my family members about numerous Kenyan students who had thought they would make it in America, only to realize that they constantly needed the financial support of their parents or relatives in Kenya to make it through their first few years of college. Interestingly, however, when these same struggling students go to Kenya to visit (and only a few do), they do not reveal to their fellow Kenyans that they spent their time in America working the dirtiest and most demeaning jobs that many Americans would rather not take up. Instead, many flash their credit cards around and speak with an American accent that they believe denotes progress. When they return to America, they slave away, paying their credit card debts for expenses they incurred in Kenya. Given such performances by these returning Kenyans, it is no wonder many Kenyans think America is the place where there is plenty of everything for everybody. Who would believe me when I tell my friends and family members that it is hard living in America? The best strategy may be to let them find out for themselves.

The following day, I left Nairobi for Egerton University to have my research permit signed by a representative of the institution before proceeding to my research site. I was happy to see many of my colleagues whom I had not seen in a while. We had opportunities to catch up on what was going on in our worlds, and many of them wanted to know how easy it was to study in America and whether I was planning on returning to Kenya. For me, this trip provided an important contrast between my institution in America and Egerton University. I was amazed at the meager resources available in an Egerton University classroom compared to the abundance I had left in America, where there were even television sets and projectors in numerous classrooms for use by instructors in order to enhance student learning. At Egerton, there was one large hall with audiovisual equipment, and many instructors never had a chance to use it. Instead, they lectured and used the chalkboard as students tried diligently to record every word that the instructor said. Textbooks that publishers in America would freely send to instructors to consider adopting for their courses were nonexistent in many departments at Egerton. The library also carried few, and often outdated, books that could not serve the many academic and research needs of the university community. This disparity in resources made me aware of the reality of the phrases "developed" and "underdeveloped" countries. And yet when many Kenyan students go abroad to study in America or Europe, they usually excel in their studies.

On my way back from Egerton, I took a matatu (public-transport minivan) from Egerton University's campus to Nakuru Town. This was the common conveyance for the majority of my colleagues who lived in Nakuru because only a handful had personal vehicles. In the matatu I immediately became aware of an American presence mediated through popular culture—stickers of Rambo and Hulk Hogan seemed to blend well with the music of Bob Marley that was being piped through the stereo system. I was also much more aware of the bumpy ride and the recklessness of the driver, who like other matatu drivers in Kenya wanted to maximize on the number of the trips he could make in a day. I had traveled this route on matatu many times before but was now more alert to every pothole and bump that we hit. Outside on the side roads, I could see lots of people walking or riding their bicycles with loads of farm produce on their backs or tied to the carrier of the bicycles. I could tell that many were struggling to make ends meet and that the produce they were carrying was probably being taken to the market to generate some cash they could use to purchase sugar, flour, milk, or other essential commodities to feed the family. As usual, the matatu would frequently stop in the middle of the road to pick up and drop off passengers, in total disregard of traffic laws.[11] One of these times, the driver stopped just as we were approaching an intersection that would take us to Nakuru. When I saw a police Land Rover driving in the opposite direction approaching our stopped vehicle, I thought that the driver would be in trouble for stopping there, but alas, a KSh 100.00 note did the magic as the driver was sent off with not a single ticket—only a finger of rebuke pointed at him by the police officer, who shamelessly pocketed the money. Corruption had become such a part of Kenyan society that it was almost turning into a cultural practice.[12] Seeing how easily and openly the police officer took the bribe, I realized that not much had changed during my two-year absence from Kenya. Fifteen years later, the Kenya police department continues to be regarded as the most corrupt public-service department in the country.

From Nakuru, I returned to Nairobi, where I visited with some more friends who still lived in Nairobi West, a middle-class suburb where I had lived in the late 1980s and early '90s before moving to Nakuru to teach at Egerton University. On this visit, I started with my friend Bob's house, gambling on my chances of finding him home because it was not yet five o'clock, when most people start returning home from work. Luckily I was able to find his two older daughters in the house. I was welcomed in, and we were soon in a spirited conversation about my experiences in America. They were interested in how "the States" were and what was the "in thing." Were Snoop Doggy Dogg and Dr. Dre the main things on the music scene? What about

Oprah, Arsenio Hall, and Donahue? Is there racism in America? They had more questions than I could answer, and I was quite impressed with their awareness of American popular culture. I am sure their experience growing up with television and access to international media and news gave them a very different flavor of America than what I had experienced when I was growing up in the late 1970s and early '80s in rural Kenya. I had not had access to much international news and information other than our trusted BBC world news on radio, which the more informed people in the village listened to. No controversial news found its way into the government regulated Kenyan radio at the time, and the BBC offered us a perspective on Kenya that we could only talk about in whispers. The country was under President Moi's dictatorial leadership after having inherited Jomo Kenyatta's one-party political leadership, which allowed no political dissent whatsoever. The government-regulated radio station was more of a government propaganda machine than a forum for disseminating news and information to the citizenry. I was, therefore, intrigued by the heightened sense of awareness of international culture that Bob's daughters revealed, and I realized how young people in the same country could have very disparate worldviews and experiences, depending on when and exactly where they grow up.

After some casual conversation, shared snacks, and light beverages, I asked to be allowed to leave and continue with my planned visits to see other friends living in the same neighborhood. It was now past six o'clock, and I knew that many of my friends would probably be at home. My next visit was to my former housemate, who lived in the same house we had shared four years earlier. He was excited to see me, but he—unlike Bob's daughters—was interested in knowing if there were better television channels than CNN, which he felt gave very detailed news and accounts of world events. I told him that even in the small city where I lived in the United states, we had access to thirty-four television channels, and not many of the people I knew actually watched CNN. Some of my socially conscious graduate school friends watched PBS, ABC, NBC, and other channels that broadcast national and international news, while the other students watched entertainment channels (especially sports) and hardly paid much attention to news items. We chatted a little more, had dinner, and got caught up on matters of mutual interest until it was time for me to leave. My host advised me to take a cab to South B, another residential area close to Nairobi West, where I was to spend the night at my brother's apartment. Luckily, the bus stop where I could get a matatu was at the end of the street and only about fifty yards from my friend's house. Two minutes after reaching the bus stop, I got a matatu going to my brother's neighborhood. But, given the hour of the day (9:00 A.M.), I had to pay KSh 10.00 instead of the usual KSh 7.00. Despite the price hike, it was a lot cheaper than taking a taxi for KSh 150.00 for the same trip. Finally I had a chance to sleep in a real bed. I slept throughout the night and woke up at 5:00 A.M., ready for another day at home.

I could tell that my two years of living in America, and especially the courses I had taken in anthropology, had changed my worldview and social sensibilities. I was much more aware of social class, gender issues, and international determinants of local political realities. I could not help notice, for instance, chauvinistic messages on car stickers and T-shirts as I walked around Nairobi the next day. I saw this one man wearing a T-shirt with the statement "15 Reasons Why a Beer Is Better Than a Woman"; it listed some of those reasons as "You do not have to clean a beer to enjoy it" and "A beer will not give you AIDS." I could not believe that someone would actually design a shirt that carried such a demeaning message. To think that a woman was an object to be compared to a beer was to me, to say the least, disgusting. But it was not unusual. In my MA thesis, I analyzed a song titled "Nyambura" (recorded by a Kenyan popular music group named Them Mushrooms), whose lyrics equated a man's love for a woman with his love for grilled meat. The T-shirt I saw that man wearing on the street was saying more than the printed words depicted, especially in the underlying assumption that women were the carriers of the HIV/AIDS virus, even though research has continued to show the high levels of male-to-female infections. Indeed, current research reveals that men are infecting their wives and other sexual partners at alarming rates due to extra-marital affairs.[13] I also saw some car stickers with such messages as "Behind every successful man is a woman telling him he will not succeed" and "A girl is a maize cob to be enjoyed by any man with teeth." I was now more aware of the ways in which gender norms and expectations were mobilized in public, with these stickers and captions on T-shirts capturing a certain perception prevailing in some quarters of the population. In a sense, I saw them as symbolic texts packed with cultural meanings that were useful windows into a culture that I know was not receiving much scholarly scrutiny and challenge.

A week later I went to Meru, my home area, and spent time with family and friends.[14] I remember visiting my former elementary school and being treated like a celebrity. The head teacher introduced me to the entire school and asked the students to study hard so they could go to America like me. I also noticed how discipline was maintained in the school, reminding me of my elementary school days in the '70s—although this time around, my new anthropological training enabled me to notice the phenomenon even more. When the teacher entered the classroom, for instance, all the students stood up and responded to his greetings and did not sit down until he asked them to do so. I remembered that we used to stand up whenever a teacher passed by, even if we were just sitting around with friends during recess. Teachers were highly regarded in school, especially when I was a student, and this fact may explain my shock when in America I saw college professors having casual interactions with students as if they were in the same age group.

As it is the common practice when one visits someone in Meru, we had tea with the teachers at my elementary school during my visit, and the meeting eventually turned into a question-and-answer session. The teachers asked me if there were car thieves in America, if people walked without shoes there, and if Americans were as rich as the tourists who come to Kenya. I tried to answer their questions to the best of my ability, quite often reminding them that what they had was a very limited view of America. I was determined to give them a more nuanced picture of America, even though such a picture was limited to my own observations and experiences. Ten years later, I was able to bring a few American undergraduate students to Meru, where the local community and the students were able to interact one-on-one through homestays and community projects at the same elementary school I attended. Many friendships were formed and many stereotypes were challenged, but all in all, it was the ability of the community members to feel confident that they could successfully host American students that was most satisfying to me. Many of the hosts were quite impressed that American students could eat local foods and live in the local community. My hope is that such opportunities continue to demystify perceptions of each other held on both sides. Through this interaction, I was able to bring into the community some resources that supported the community members' efforts to renovate the elementary school buildings. This support provided all the more reason for the students at the school to be encouraged to study hard to be like me.

Later that day, I went back to my home to find my dad visiting with about fifty boys and girls from our local church. These young people were members of the Boys and Girls Brigade (our church's equivalent of Girl Guides and Boy Scouts) and were paying my dad a courtesy call following the death of my stepmother. My dad was the chair of the board of our local church, and the church community had been extremely generous with their time and finances during that ordeal. They were able to raise funds to assist in paying the large hospital bill that my stepmother had left behind, and many community members also visited with my dad to console him. Being away in

America meant that I was not able to attend the funeral, and this visit was my belated participation. Dad told me that each day for two weeks during the time when funeral arrangements were taking place, there were women from our church who would come over to our home, bring food, cook, and feed all the visitors coming to console him. One of my paternal aunts also came to spend time in our home and helped with everyday chores and was still there when I visited. This was one cultural practice I think I would miss if Kenyans were to adopt the rugged individualism that I had seen in America, where everyone seemed so focused on self. Our spirit of helping each other is captured in our national slogan, *Harambee*—or "Pull Together." Help is an important form of survival for our people. My dad was a people's person, and the outpouring of gifts and help was a reflection of that social relationship. The Harambee philosophy basically means that the community puts its material weight behind an individual, who then is expected to go and acquire knowledge and other resources and bring them back to the community. Consequently, instead of an individual trying to succeed on his or her own, the community comes in to assist, but with the expectation that such an individual will return to the community and render assistance as needed. Many local schools and health facilities across the country were built through this Harambee philosophy.[15] Following this philosophy, I called my trips to Meru with my American students "Harambee" because they were based on the same notion of raising funds from friends and relatives in order to make a difference in a community.

After a few days of visiting with family and friends in Meru, I returned to Nairobi to prepare for my fieldtrip to Mombasa to carry out preliminary work on popular music among the Muslim Swahili along the East African coast. Part of the preparations included conducting some archival research at the National Archives in Nairobi. My familiarity with Nairobi as well as my earlier research in Mombasa made this trip a lot smoother than it would be for a foreigner coming to Kenya for the first time. I took a flashy matatu from my brother's apartment in South B to the city center, where the Kenya National Archives is located. It was rush hour, and I had to stand in an already jam-packed matatu. Besides the twenty-five passengers already seated, there were two others standing adjacent to each other on each row of seats. By a conservative estimate, there were about twelve other passengers in the matatu.[16] Including myself, I would estimate that we were at least thirty-seven passengers in a public vehicle licensed to carry twenty-five. This was the established culture of Kenyan's urban transportation. The drivers and touts made up their own rules, and when they got into trouble, they bribed their way out—as our matatu driver on our trip from Egerton did when accosted by a traffic police officer for stopping in the middle of the road to pick up passengers. The matatu I rode into Nairobi's city center was dubbed "Funky Pub" and was playing its music very loud. If one needed to know why the music was that loud, there was a sticker on the roof stating "I like my music loud." It also had posters of American popular culture icons such as the music group Naughty by Nature and the television series *The Fresh Prince of Bel Air*, clearly denoting some aspect of what many anthropologists have termed "the imagination" that tends to help in the ways people regard themselves and their world.[17] Being crammed inside that matatu with its loud music did not, however, provide much room for imagination, and I was relieved when we got into the city and I alighted.

I spent a few days in Nairobi before boarding a bus that took me to Mombasa to start my fieldwork on popular music. I had already carried out some research on the same topic prior to leaving for America for graduate studies in anthropology and was quite at home in the field. This time, however, I paid more attention to cultural issues and tried to apply my anthropological training to my field research. I had specifically chosen to pursue anthropology in graduate school because I had felt stifled in my earlier work in the field of literary studies focusing on popular music. I was interested in a more holistic approach to the study of poetry and popular music. It was an important transition from my earlier work for me to come back to my field site in Mombasa equipped with some anthropological tools. It was also a fulfillment of my dream to conduct research that involved the analysis of such elements as people's views of the music, the issue of certain songs being more popular than others, the specific social contexts that motivated composition of specific songs, and the various interpretations of the meanings carried in the lyrics themselves. I also found that my anthropological training was being applied in other areas of life besides my research.

I was slowly becoming aware of how much my thinking and sensibility had changed. I had gradually changed from studying anthropology to becoming an anthropologist. The many times I had been able to sit and talk with friends and family on this trip home made me realize that my being away had also enabled me to step outside my own culture and observe it from some "outside" position. I was oscillating between the emic (insider) and etic (outsider) perspectives emphasized in field research. This new set of sociocultural lenses was further made visible when I attended a departmental seminar presentation in the Linguistics and African Languages Department at the University of Nairobi. Listening to some of the statements about language and culture that were made by the presenter, I started to formulate many questions in my mind. I wanted to know the context that produced certain assumptions that were put forth by the presenter and the experiences and perspectives of the people being spoken about. How many people used the language the way that the speaker talked about? In what socioeconomic and political context did that language use occur? Was the use of that specific language unique to that population, or were there other communities with similar practices? My anthropological training was starting to bear fruit, but as I show in the next section, anthropology continues to be a very marginal discipline in Africa generally and in Kenya in particular.

Anthropology's Marginality in Africa

Despite my enthusiasm at how important my anthropological training was to understanding and contributing to scholarly discussions in sessions by my academic peers in Kenya, there is a paucity of African anthropologists and a near-absence of anthropology departments in African institutions since anthropology is often combined with sociology and anthropologists almost exclusively work as sociologists. At the time I was in Kenya, there were two departments of anthropology: one at the University of Nairobi (actually an Institute of African Studies, in which anthropology was one of the disciplines) and one at Moi University (where anthropology is lodged in the School of Arts and Social Sciences, in which—as at the University of Nairobi—students can earn a doctoral degree). To date, this paucity of anthropology departments has not changed much; consequently, it is not unusual for many of our colleagues in other disciplines to "ignore" anthropological methods and literature on culture. Indeed, this was one of my motivations for agreeing to collaborate in a book project on the history and practice of anthropology in Africa. I was curious to know why—as a discipline that is critical in understanding and presenting Africa's myriad social, economic, and political challenges— anthropology has had such a marginal presence in the African academy. After completing my collaborative book project,[18] I have had a fair assessment of why anthropology remains a marginal discipline in Africa today. First, it is because the discipline is not being sustained or expanded through the establishment of university departments or the training of anthropologists. A casual observation of new and numerous private universities in Africa shows that none of them have anthropology programs or departments. Instead, many of them focus on business administration and com-

REMEMBERING HOME · 95

puter science programs.[19] Second, and related to the first, is the absorption of anthropologists in other disciplines or departments, especially sociology, religion, and history. In other cases, anthropologists' roles are subsumed by other disciplines. As Christine Obbo notes in the case of anthropologists in Uganda who fled the country during Idi Amin's cruel regime, "when political stability returned, heads of social work and psychology refused to invite anthropologists back because they claimed to be teaching the courses that would normally be listed under anthropology."[20] Third, because anthropology as a discipline does not have much of a presence in Africa, many undergraduate students are unaware of what it entails and how it can be mobilized to yield tangible employment results upon their graduation. This uncertainty over the value of anthropology is all the more pronounced in systems of education that see a degree or diploma as a means of getting a job.

Overall, even in areas where anthropology has some presence, anthropologists have been seen to belong in the "soft" disciplines that deal with culture and people's feelings. As a result, they are deemed unable to make any recommendations or take any steps to change any social conditions of the people they study. Medical anthropologist Mary Amuyunzu-Nyamongo's example of what some of her non-anthropologist colleagues in reproductive health in Kenya say about anthropologists is quite instructive in this regard. One faculty member has asserted that "Anthropologists are like journalists: they are non-judgmental and do not make recommendations. They are people who like to investigate but fail to give educated, scientific conclusions and recommendations. You cannot engage with people's lives and not help make decisions. I see anthropologists as 'go-betweens' among scientists."[21]

On the one hand, anthropologists are regarded as passive and indecisive, unable to make concrete "scientific conclusions and recommendations" from their research data. On the other hand, there is the projection that anthropologists, by virtue of their being indecisive, are not scientific in their work; they are there to pave the way for real "scientific" work to be carried out. This is not an isolated perception of anthropology, at least in Kenya. Washington Onyango-Ouma, another medical anthropologist, shares his experiences working with colleagues in a project among the Luo in Western Kenya, where anthropology's role was again seen as peripheral. When he was involved in a multidisciplinary biomedical project with colleagues in biomedicine and psychology, Onyango-Ouma soon realized that his colleagues assumed that they were doing "real science," while he as an anthropologist did "soft science."[22] Hence—despite there being a clear indication in the project outline that the anthropologists' role was ongoing until the project was completed—Onyango-Ouma's colleagues saw his role as that of conducting "mobilisation activities to explain to the community the aim and purpose of the project. ... [and carrying out] exploratory studies on community needs and priorities for purposes of designing detailed studies and interventions."[23] He was there to clear the bushes for the "real" research to take place.

Deep into the project, however, Onyango-Ouma's colleagues in the project were faced with a crisis that forced them to seek his anthropological skills. The aim of the project was to intervene in the community's malaria problems—especially among pregnant women, as the researchers sought to understand the degree to which pregnant mothers could pass malaria to their unborn children. A number of pregnant women were recruited for the project. During the research, many women who had consented to the project refused to follow through with the researcher's request to deliver their placentas to the local health center to be tested for malaria. Upon making home visits and talking to the women and their families, Onyango-Ouma was able to establish that there was a rumor going around in the community that the researchers intended to sell the placentas. Further, some women from the community found that the placentas had been thrown away after the blood tests were carried out. If the researchers had done a basic cultural study around beliefs and practices of the target community, they would have realized that "the placenta (biero) is considered a very precious relic of a human being and as such should be buried in the family land."[24] Burying one's placenta in a specific piece of land allows the individual to lay claims to that land. The researchers (all unaware of the underlying cultural systems) were puzzled as to why people would want to take home "trash." As a medical anthropologist, Onyango-Ouma was able to see the link between science and culture in ways that were crucial to the success of the malaria intervention project.

Ugandan anthropologist Christine Obbo presents a different scenario and attitude regarding anthropology in Uganda and in other African countries. She says that educated Africans see "themselves as the proper representatives of Africa to the outside world and their voices as the authentic conduits of social and cultural truth."[25] Following such convictions, these Africans discourage any research (anthropological) contact or involvement with people in the village, who they assume are not sophisticated enough to comprehend their lives and experiences. While this attitude reveals the way that educated Africans regard their uneducated counterparts, it also reflects the overall nature of formal education in Africa. As a colonial project, formal education in Africa was a deliberate attempt to alienate Africans from their traditional way of life and insert them into a colonial (Western) modernity.[26] The content, structure, and application of formal education had no relation or relevance to many African cultural and social realities. As a result, many Africans now regard their own cultures as incompatible and, at times, a hindrance to formal education. For a Western or Western-trained anthropologist to include the voices and views of village people in an academic project is to blur those perceived boundaries between formal (Western) education and African traditional (rural) life.

There is for me a tension between, on the one hand, the practicality of anthropological knowledge in responding to Africa's sociocultural realities and, on the other, the reality of the marginal nature of anthropology as a discipline in Africa. However, as I argue in chapter 6, it takes a concerted effort—especially a more defined collaboration between anthropologists in the North and those in the South—to make our discipline successful, not only in these contexts where it is marginal but also in the North, where it is also facing its own sets of challenges. I believe anthropology is critical to our understanding of cultures anywhere in the world, including their intricately changing realities and to our ability to carry out comparative studies that allow us to become more reflective of our individual and institutional practices—as I show in the next section, with observations of my department upon my return to the United States.

Back in America

When I returned to America from Kenya that summer, I had a chance to see America differently, even though I had spent just three months in Kenya. I was able to notice a few things in America to which I had previously grown accustomed. I, for instance, became increasingly aware of the high level of waste in America. In the summer when I went home, I could tell how scarce paper was at Egerton University, but coming back to an American university, I realized that people there did not usually communicate face-to-face but instead wrote notes to each other and, in the process, used a lot of paper.[27] The amount of paper used in one day to create the flyers posted around the university announcing various activities to students and faculty would have been enough to meet the needs of Egerton University for an entire month or more. In the kitchen, the story was the same. When I worked in the college cafeteria, I was able to see how much food was wasted—making me think of all the people starving in various parts of the world, especially in India and Africa. I saw cakes, bread, soup, and even orange juice being dumped into the drainage at the end of the day. These were not leftovers but rather items meant for that day's ration that had not been used. Instead of sharing this food—with, for instance, the homeless people in town—the kitchen staff just dumped it all. Upon inquiry, I was told by kitchen staff that there were some health laws that restricted the giving out of food to other people, but I was sure that if someone wanted to give out the food, they could find a way of doing so in a legitimate and safe way.

I had also observed the wastage of water and electricity. especially in the cafeteria. There was, for instance, a water faucet that was turned on when the kitchen opened at 6:30 A.M. and left on until it closed at 10:00 P.M.— even though most of the time, there was no need for the water. There were homeless people within the vicinity of the campus, but I was not aware of any effort made by the kitchen staff to feed them. I was convinced that if the kitchen teamed up with the Salvation Army homeless shelter in town, for instance, they would be able to make available a lot of food and drinks for the homeless. Or maybe they did, and I simply was not aware of it. Whatever the case may have been, I just knew that there was too much waste in America.[28] Maybe the kitchen staff should have limited the amount of food students could put in their plates. That way they could limit the amount of waste. When I went to college in Kenya, we were served food by kitchen staff, and we got only one or two pieces of chicken or beef, for instance. As much as this idea of serving students the portion of food they could finish seemed attractive in those circumstances, I was aware that it would not fly in a culture of endless choice and abundance like the American university campus—and one where, as I have argued in chapter 3, students behave like the customers of a corporation.

Being back on campus had also opened up other opportunities for me to engage in more participant observation, and this time around, my target was, again, anthropologists. I attended a departmental meeting where we discussed new searches for faculty hires, courses, and new equipment. The meeting turned out to be a heated debate between graduate students and faculty. Students complained that certain basic course tools—such as geographic information systems (GISs)—were not available to them in the department and that they were being forced to go outside of the department and get those tools. The faculty, however, felt that the department was self-sufficient in terms of research and scholarly equipment, given its goals, mission, and capacity. I learned later from some of the students that archaeology students had met several times with the department chair and made these concerns known. This may have been why the department chair brought the issue to a faculty-student meeting, although the students that I heard from said the chair did not side with them. I thought that the chair needed the input of the faculty before making a final decision on the matter, and now at the meeting, it seemed as though the faculty had a very different take on the issue than the students. I wondered how greatly the department's overall annual budget factored into this request and the subsequent refusal by faculty to grant it.

Students next asked why they were not being offered more courses that provided them with hands-on experience, especially ones that offered direct links to the local community. They were particularly looking for courses that would prepare them for applied anthropology beyond the medical anthropology track that was available through the medical school. I was very much interested in this issue as well because I had been reminded, while in Kenya, that my training needed to make a difference in the lives of people who daily struggled to make a living. The majority of the faculty, however, did not seem attracted to this idea. Indeed, they all nodded in agreement when one of their colleagues mentioned that the demand for such courses was problematic because they would involve the matter of working with human subjects. I realized that this faculty member was talking about student projects within the college community, and yet all of us had to sign a form on the ethical treatment of research collaborators before going to conduct research in the field. I did not see why this same expectation could not be used for an applied anthropology program. The faculty was simply not willing to make any such changes in the department. Even though at times graduate students were regarded as colleagues in the department, they did not wield any real political power in the department. What I had earlier observed as an egalitarian relationship between students and faculty in the department was a surface manifestation of a relationship with deeper structures that were easily missed when the situation was casually observed.

I had another opportunity for participant observation when I was selected to join the department's graduate student admissions committee, who read the files of students applying to the department. In one of the committee meetings in which I participated, it was clear again that the professors had a lot of power in deciding who would be admitted to the graduate program and who would be rejected. I was amazed, for instance, to hear one of the committee members announce, "the two professors working in the area the student wants to go into said they did not wish to work with that student." And that was it; she was dropped from the list of prospective graduate students. It did not matter how good the candidate looked on paper. Another candidate was rejected for saying she was an Africanist and using the term "as if she was the first one to coin it," as one professor put it. GRE scores and GPAs were also useful information. The question of who would serve as the student's advisor was another issue, as was the fact of what the student had said about what they believed anthropology would do for them. But of all the statements made at the meeting, the one that surprised me most was made by a professor whom I had all along considered to be quite personable. She said that the admissions committee should be comprised only of faculty and that there was no need to include graduate students. Quite to the surprise of my fellow students on the committee, she kept repeating her views throughout the meeting. She made the same comment in a search committee meeting for a candidate for a North American archaeologist position. But the department chair had already indicated that there was a need to have graduate students on the admissions committee, especially because the issues raised were issues that affected the entire department. The whole process allowed me a glimpse, albeit a limited one, into the American university system of admitting graduate students into a program and probably gave me a sense of what may have occurred in my own case some years earlier. My training in anthropology had provided me with tools that allowed me to perform deeper analyses of what I was observing in my institution. In addition, those tools not only allowed me to understand more parts of the American culture but also provided me with some critical distance from which to observe my own culture in Africa. For me, being able to use my graduate training to objectively look at my culture was an example of anthropology as cultural critique.

5

Mega-Anthropology
The AAA Annual Meetings

For anthropology truly to become a cultural critique, anthropologists must apply the information they gather from studying other cultures toward understanding themselves and anthropological culture itself. In such anthropological studies of anthropology, I envision a systematic analysis of how anthropologists function in their everyday lives—especially when they assemble together for professional meetings such as the American Anthropological Association (AAA) annual conferences. Such a study and analysis are, in my view, very similar to those carried out in anthropology's traditional locations in far away and exotic places and not what Holmes and Marcus call *para-ethnography*.

In para-ethnography Holmes and Marcus see a distinction with classic ethnography whereby para-ethnography tends to focus on high-status professionals who are assumed to have a sophisticated understanding of culture and social change that is at times better than that of anthropologists.[1] Additionally, Holmes and Marcus suggest that the people traditionally studied by anthropologists are unlikely to have a sophisticated understanding of the workings of their own culture. Yet such a suggestion is both arrogant and problematic and does not seem to fit my idea of how anthropology can be a cultural critique. If anything, a careful analysis of anthropology and anthropologists as a specific cultural phenomenon may yield intriguing insights that would make us even more reflexive.

To assume that "simple" societies do not have a sophisticated understanding of how their cultures work is to elevate unnecessarily the anthropologist's ability to "figure out" how such a culture functions. Further, it is an attempt

YIKES

to elevate ethnographic work to almost a new positivist level. An analysis of anthropologists' practices through the prism of the AAA may shed light on this assumed sophistication of "advanced" societies. I believe it is at the AAA meetings that the anthropological ritual of what we do as anthropologists is best performed. Such a performance can yield various meanings from a symbolic-analytic approach—especially because the AAA is the largest, most powerful, and resource-full anthropological association in the world. The enormous size of the AAA may be a reflection of American economic and military power, which in turn translates into many other facets of the Association's life. At the 2005 annual AAA meeting, for instance, there were "5,125 attendees, 506 scheduled sessions, 29 poster sessions, 3,024 papers, 240 special events, 53 employers interviewing in the job placement center and 82 exhibitors."[2] In the absence of any systematic studies (that I am aware of) that focus on the AAA as a cultural phenomenon, I wonder what impact this large number of meeting attendees has on the overall culture of the discipline. With up to 11,000 members, as of 2005, the AAA constitutes a large community. Why don't we conduct studies of this enormous community and see how it operates?

Studying the AAA and American anthropology in general promises to reverse the asymmetrical relationships existing between anthropologists in the West and North of this country and those in the East and South, which have led, as Restrepo and Escobar have stated, to a situation "in which some anthropologies have more paradigmatic weight—and hence more power and implied authority—than others."[3] Consequently, even as the AAA is to be lauded for engaging other anthropologists through its membership in the World Council of Anthropology Associations (WCAA), "there will not be world anthropology without abundant anthropological studies of the most powerful nation of the world."[4] As long as the bulk of anthropological scholarship comes from Europe and North America and focuses on studying other cultures other than their own, the power differentials attendant in anthropology today will endure.

I am convinced that the same techniques and approaches we, as anthropologists, use in studying any culture or communities are equally applicable to an understanding of the AAA, which is a cultural phenomenon in itself. While my understanding of the AAA is based on my own experiences as a member of the association since 2001, from the information available on the AAA official Web site (http://www.aaanet.org) and from having attended a number of its annual meetings, I am able to make some comparisons with other anthropological associations. I know a little about other associations as a result of my experiences attending their annual meetings as well. I am familiar, for instance, with the Association of Social Anthropology in the UK and the Commonwealth (ASA) and the Pan-African Anthropological Association (PAAA). These three organizations' membership (PAAA, ASA, and AAA), the size of their conferences, and other related activities such as publications say a lot about the practice of anthropology in their representative locations. The ASA has remained relatively small because its membership, as I show later in this chapter, is restricted, while the PAAA has struggled to maintain regular membership, given the challenging working conditions facing many African anthropologists.[5]

One can learn a lot about the AAA by contrasting it with the ASA and PAAA. In all the years that I was in graduate school and even after becoming an anthropologist, I had not done what every American or American-trained anthropologist has to do: attend an annual meeting of the AAA. There are two main reasons for my absence: first, the simple fact that I could not afford to attend the meetings, and second, I did not feel confident enough to make a presentation at the meetings. Having come into anthropology after my master's degree in Swahili studies, I felt that I needed to be well-grounded in anthropology before I could make a professional presentation at the annual meetings. Not attending the AAA meetings does not mean that I did not attend other professional meetings while in graduate school, however. I attended two conferences in 1993, where I presented parts of my earlier research in Mombasa on taarab music and gender. I felt much more comfortable presenting on this research than I did of my later anthropological work until I became confident of my ability to make a convincing presentation. After those two presentations, I waited seven years before I attended another professional meeting and presented a paper. Prior to that, I had attended other meetings just as an observer, without presenting a paper. In 1996, I attended my first PAAA meeting in South Africa. It happened that I was already in southern Africa at the time of the conference, on a fellowship sponsored by the Ford Foundation for young African scholars to be affiliated with leading research institutions in Africa. It was easier and affordable for me to go to the meeting from that close location: I was able to take a bus from Harare, Zimbabwe, where I was a fellow at the Southern African Political and Economic Studies institute, to Cape Town, South Africa, for that conference. I came into AAA annual meetings much later, attending my first meeting in 2002 in New Orleans.

AAA Annual Meetings in New Orleans, Louisiana

In 2002, four years after graduating with a PhD in anthropology, I had the chance to attend my first AAA annual meeting. At the time, I was a visiting professor at St. Lawrence University, which made it easy and cheap for me to attend the AAA meetings in New Orleans. Upon completion of my training in anthropology in 1998, I had immediately returned to Kenya, where I worked for five years—with a short break between July 2002 and January 2003 when I was at St. Lawrence University. Prior to my being at St. Lawrence University's New York campus, I had been unable to attend any AAA annual meeting, not only because the trip was expensive but also because the conference was scheduled at a time when I could not get away from my work in Kenya. When I got the opportunity to attend the 2002 AAA annual meeting, I jumped at it.

I received funding from the office of international and intercultural studies and the office of the associate dean of faculty affairs at St. Lawrence University, which was enough to cover expenses for the conference. The university had also arranged for me to have a rental car to get to the closest airport to fly to New Orleans for the conference. I drove the rental car from Canton to Syracuse, left my wife and our two daughters at the home of my former student's family, and proceeded to New Orleans. I flew from Syracuse to New Orleans via Pittsburg and Cincinnati. Arriving at the airport in New Orleans, I realized I was among many of my own. It was easy to spot anthropologists. They were dressed casually, many were reading papers, and majority wore some exotic piece of jewelry or clothing that symbolized their field site—either a bracelet from Mexico or some other South or Central American culture, a necklace from a community in Africa, a tie-dyed shirt, or a multicolored scarf. I had noticed this "field-site display" on the office doors of many anthropologists in my graduate school department, where many placed pictures of people or places that they studied. The majority of the anthropologists I saw at the airport in New Orleans wore blue jeans and casual shoes and were very chatty. Upon quick reflection, I remembered seeing a few of the same anthropologists on my flight from Cincinnati to New Orleans.

The New Orleans airport was much more laid-back and touristy compared to other airports that I had been to in America. Before leaving the airport, I purchased a return shuttle ticket to ensure that I got to and from the airport without a hassle. The line for people wishing to buy the shuttle tickets was long and slow, reminding me very much of Kenya. It took me about fifteen minutes to get to the ticket counter, but luckily the airport shuttle was available every five minutes. Coincidentally, majority of the people I saw in New Orleans were Black, and the city was service-oriented. Was this the reality of only the parts I had seen, or was New Orleans's economy based on tourism? Given the architecture, the French Quarter, and Mardi Gras, the city had a reputation as a favorite destination for tourists. Unfortunately, the city went into a decline following the devastating effects of Hurricane Katrina in August 2005. At the time I visited, however, the city was alive and booming with business.

The ride from the airport to my hotel in downtown New Orleans was eighteen miles, and even though it was supposed to take about twenty minutes or so, it turned into a one-hour trip because the airport shuttle had to drop off ten other passengers. I did not mind the long ride. I really did not have any set plans once I got to my hotel. New Orleans was nice and warm, and since I was the last person to be dropped off, I had a chance to chat a little more with the driver. He complained to me about many of the other passengers he had dropped off—all of who happened to be White, except for one Asian woman. From their conversations, I knew for sure that the majority of the passengers were anthropologists. They kept making references to the meetings or anthropological work they were conducting. Some were also talking about job openings in their departments and the anticipation of meeting the candidates they were scheduled to interview at the meeting. The driver complained about "White folk," who he knew were staying in three-hundred-dollar per night hotels, had come to New Orleans, which is a tourist town, and they would not tip him. He also complained specifically about an Asian woman who gave him a "freaking dollar in four quarters." He said that these guests were receiving the luxury of a clean shuttle with someone to open the door for them— compared to "the filthy and stinking taxis"—and yet would not tip. I wondered why he was giving me all this information. Did he want someone to vent to about his frustrations with other passengers? As a passenger myself, I wondered if it was our shared skin color that made him engage in these declarations. The conversation sent a message to me. I looked at the two one-dollar bills I was holding in readiness to tip him, added an extra dollar, and gave it to him when we got to my hotel, hoping that it was not as "insulting" as the other passengers' tip had been. He smiled and said, "Thank you." When I alighted, he told me to enjoy my stay—adding that if I wanted to have some real local food, I should go to a place called Mulate's, which he said was located at the corner of Convention Center Boulevard and River Walk. I was relieved. It seemed as though he thought I did not fit the category of the other "stingy" passengers, but if I did, he did not show any such opinion at all. I had just read about Mulate's in the New Orleans visitor handbook the driver had given to each of us in the shuttle bus when we got ready to leave the airport.

When I had checked into my hotel and had time to freshen up, I decided to follow the driver's suggestion and go to Mulate's for dinner. I arrived at 7:50 P.M. to find the place packed with all kinds of people. Some wore large sombrero hats; others wore the "dung kicking" boots associated with the American South, especially Texas and cowboy culture. Others wore brightly colored shirts, shorts, and sandals. In such a heavy crowd, most people were not talking but shouting—probably because a number of them had also had one too many beers and were getting a little excited. There was a live band playing country, zydeco, and some Cajun music, and a number of people were making attempts at step and line dancing. There was a couple—I estimated them to be in their late seventies or early eighties—who were truly having fun, singing along with the musicians in a style that suggested the songs the band was playing were their favorites. When my turn to be served came, I ordered a grilled chicken breast that came with corn and roast potato. I did not have to wait long for the food to be served, and it was really tasty, with just the right kind of spices. How could food served so fast taste so good?

The ambience in Mulate's reminded me of Kenya and especially the party spirit in Nairobi during weekends. A few tables across from me, I could recognize a few faces that I had seen earlier at the AAA meeting registration desk. But with so many tourists coming to New Orleans weekly, it was hard to distinguish between the anthropologists and the tourists. In other meeting venues that I attended after New Orleans, such as those held at Washington, D.C., I was able to recognize anthropologists by the lines they formed outside of ethnic food restaurants and the choice of "ethnic" or "exotic" attire or jewelry they wore. In 2002, however, I was not quite able to sort out the anthropologists from local residents and tourists. I spent about two hours at Mulate's and then walked back to my hotel to get ready for a busy day at the conference.

Arriving at the AAA meeting venue the next day, I found it abuzz with activity as thousands of anthropologists made their way to sessions and sought out their friends. Job candidates combed the posted job opportunities in the placement center to find last-minute employers interested in interviewing them on the spot. There were more people outside than inside the meeting rooms where the papers were being presented. With that kind of crowd, things worked very differently compared to the smaller but more intimate annual PAAA meetings I had attended in Africa. There was a huge registration area with about five booths handled by personnel specifically assigned to work there for most part of the day. Participants were so numerous that there were separate booths for registered and unregistered participants. Unlike the usual practice I had observed at the PAAA meetings, participants at the AAA conference were supplied only with a book of abstracts and a program (if they paid for them) and a name tag.

There were none of the writing pads, pens, and conference bags that I was used to seeing at professional meetings of the PAAA or other disciplines in Africa. I must say, however, that culture of conference bags has penetrated the African Studies Association in America: I did receive such a bag when I registered at the 2008 annual conference in Chicago (which also marked the association's fifty-first anniversary of the association's meetings). Surprisingly, I also received a tote bag at the 2009 AAA annual meeting in Philadelphia, sponsored by Wiley-Blackwell, even though—as is common practice in other AAA meetings—all participants came to the AAA at their own cost. In Africa, in contrast, one's PAAA conference participation is almost always paid for by a "sponsor," sometimes with a moderate per diem allowance to accompany it. I guess these differences between PAAA and AAA meetings represent the socioeconomic differences in knowledge production and dissemination that exist in these two disparate locations. With a hundred years of existence, compared to only twelve for the PAAA, the AAA has truly built a strong membership base. The negative change in the American economy toward the end of the 2000s, however, may explain the presence of the unprecedented tote bags at the AAA meeting. But the differences between these two associations remain due to other factors besides economics, including the culture of literacy in Africa (which I discuss in chapter 4), where there is very low regard for academic conferences that do not provide monetary incentives for participants. Some of my colleagues in institutions of higher learning in Kenya, for instance, would rather spend some of their disposable income on social gatherings and entertainment than buy a book or pay to attend a professional conference. I remember trying to get a few colleagues from Tanzania to attend a PAAA meeting that I had organized in Nairobi in 2002, but they refused because I was unable to provide them air tickets to fly to the meeting. Luckily, colleagues from Uganda agreed to take a bus from Kampala to Nairobi and did attend the conference.

The historical complexities surrounding professional meetings and other academic activities where most African participants were sponsored by private or public institutions created an interesting culture of conferencing in East Africa. It is highly unlikely that one can find a professional meeting in

Africa where local participants do not expect to be paid in order to participate. Similar observations about African scholars in Africa always expecting a per diem allowance before they will attend professional meetings were
expressed by Africanist anthropologist Maxwell Owusu in August 2008 in
Accra at a special meeting to commemorate Ghana's fifty years of indepen-
dence.[6] Comparing this practice to the AAA meeting left me wondering if
many of my African colleagues will change and start sacrificing their own
resources to attend and participate in professional meetings. Will they begin
to see meetings as opportunities to network with other scholars and professionals, or will they continue to regard such meetings as avenues to make
some money?

The registration desk at the AAA symbolizes the enormity of the meetings, with about eight registration booths for preregistered and paid-up participants. Here, one can find one's registration material (name tag, book of
abstracts, and conference program) by going to the booth with last names
arranged in alphabetical order. Then, there are about four booths for on-site
registration, with credit card machines all ready to process participants' pay-
ment, and another booth or two for general conference information. Despite
the fact that the meeting has been in the planning stages for more than six
months before the actual event, additional material is always given to participants, often in color-coded sheets of paper inserted in the conference book.
These inserts may include special events and additions or cancellations of
events. The meeting's program book is full of information that would require
about a day or two for one to read through. If one has no idea about what
session to attend, perusing through the program is quite a task. Most of the
times I have read through the program book, I have no clue what the session
or presentation is about.

With so many sessions to choose from (at least ten running concurrently
at each hour) at the AAA, one has to be almost political about which sessions to attend. Many anthropologists attend sessions where they know the
presenters or they know that a certain session has a close link to their own
academic and research interests. The AAA is divided up into various sections
that focus on specific analytical frames and identities such as the Association
of Black Anthropologists, the Association for Africanist Anthropology, the
Association for Feminist Anthropology, the Society for the Anthropology of
North America, and the Society for Humanistic Anthropology, just to name
a few. Session presentations that are sponsored by such an association tend
mostly to attract its own members. In May 2009, a visit to the AAA's "Featured News & Commentary" Web page (http://www.aaanet.org) revealed

a total of forty sections at the conference. Given that each section needs to have at least 250 members, each session sponsored by a section at the AAA meetings has potential for many participants. Most of the sessions I attended, however, seemed like mere performances. The language used reminded me of my days in graduate school and especially the constant struggle I observed among my fellow students to articulate the "right" kinds of words and ideas in class presentations in order to sound intelligent. Given the prevalence of such performances, I assumed that conference papers were written to make the presenters sound profound rather than to communicate ideas. Terms such as "polarities," "marginalization," "subjectivity," "hegemony," "contestation," "disciplinarity," "eroticizing," "homogenizing," "sartorial identities," "commodification," "alterity," and "subaltern" seemed to be tossed around with ease and in great numbers. Maybe I was in the wrong place because I was looking for a more grounded, down to earth, presentation that explained clearly, in simple language, what the problem was and how the speaker addressed it. In fact, as I sat in some of those sessions, I slowly realized that the people and the places that the presenters were talking about were so far away and so far apart, spatially and epistemologically, that I wondered if they were real. It almost seemed as if the presenters were talking to themselves about themselves. As I have shown in chapter 3, this "theoretical" language defines the sophistication expected of "real" anthropology.

Yet for every ethereal concept and presentation I found myself cringing at, there were many other sessions and presentations that warmed my heart. I attended, for instance, an interesting panel where the speakers talked about the process of marginalization and exclusion of certain scholars and scholarship on the basis of their race. There were, for example, discussions of how Haitian anthropologists challenged the notion of race but were never "knighted," as was Franz Boas, simply because they were Black. I also attended one of those sessions where the speakers were using data collected ten or twenty years before and yet were speaking of the locals as if representing contemporary practices. This recycling of old field notes was done with short anecdotes from the field and a few foreign words to show that the anthropologists had been in the field and knew the location well. In the end of it all, it seemed as if the audience were being treated to a well-choreographed academic show in many of the presentations. Why all those complex terms and long sentences? Why the sophistication?

Anthropologists, I argue, have found a way of remain relevant by being obscure and using complex terms and long "impressive" sentences. As Edith Turner rightly states in reference to a specific section of the discipline, "It took the Society for Humanistic Anthropology to loosen the tight hold of 'sophisticated,' complex, and pseudo-scientific writing in anthropology" in an attempt to make the discipline communicate with rather than impress the audience.[7] Yet, as she goes on to show, the same obscure and obtuse language lingers on and seems to define the better part of anthropological writing (and I may add, much of the academy), as shown in an example of a sentence in the essay "Cosmological Deixis and Amerindian Perspectivism," by Eduardo Viveiros de Castro. The de Castro sentence that Edith Turner quotes goes like this: "Such a critique, in the present case, implies a redistribution of the predicates subsumed within the two paradigmatic sets that traditionally oppose one another under the headings of 'Nature' and 'Culture': universal and particular, objective and subjective, physical and social, fact and value, the given and the instituted, necessity and spontaneity, immanence and transcendence, body and mind, animality and humanity, among many more."[8] De Castro's essay (originally published in 1998) was republished in Michael Lambek's *A Reader in the Anthropology of Religion* in 2002. In a short summary of the piece, Lambek writes that De Castro "provides a brilliant and original account of the Amerindian cosmology, situating it with respect to the literature on totemism, animism, and myth."[9]

This practice of *providing brilliant accounts* seems to permeate all sectors of academia, as Gerald Graff has shown in an example of how language can obscure something that is easily understandable to a nonacademic or nonspecialist. He gives the following sentence—from Eve Kosofsky Sedgwick's *Epistemology of the Closet*—as an example: "For meanwhile the whole realm of what modern culture refers to as 'sexuality' and *also* calls 'sex'—the array of acts, expectations, narratives, pleasures, identity—formations, and knowledges, in both women and men, that tends to cluster most densely around certain genital sensations but is not adequately defined by them—that realm is virtually impossible to situate on a map delimited by the feminist-defined sex-gender distinction."[10] As Graff argues, this sentence is an example of scholars' "sound bites" that tend to turn off any general reader because the statement does not clearly set out to communicate but to impress. In plain language that would be understood by many, this excerpt seeks to ask, "How secure is the standard division of the sexes into male and female? Is this division grounded in biology, or is it socially conditioned?"[11] The question, then, is why the author of that sentence did not write it in this clear and accessible language? The answer, as I have noted above, is that if such language were to be used, it would make the text look very simple and "non-scholarly." It is the same practice that I saw in some of my anthropology seminars and that continues into papers presented at the annual AAA meetings. This obscure writing is a "culture" that makes me feel like an outsider and a culture to which I have no desire to belong.

One of the least obtuse parts of the meetings was the job interviews. My key goal at the AAA meeting was to attend some job interviews because I was once again on the job market. I had been invited to a few job interviews for tenure-track positions in anthropology in America that I had applied for earlier in the fall. One of the interviews, with Augustana College, went very well, and I felt a good connection with the two representatives from the institution. The other interview, with the chair of a department at a prestigious liberal arts school in Pennsylvania, was the worst I had ever had. The interviewer did not look interested in my candidacy and was not enthusiastic at all even about the position the department was seeking to fill. I knew I did not want to work with such a person. Luckily, I did not impress her either, and I never heard from the school again.

I heard from Augustana College a month later and was invited for a campus interview early in January of 2003 while my family and I were on our way to Nairobi for me to resume my last semester with St. Lawrence University. The interview went very well, and I had a good feeling that I would get the job. In late February, when I was already in Kenya, the dean of Augustana College sent me an e-mail congratulating me for being appointed to join the College's Department of Sociology, Anthropology, and Social Welfare. I was particularly interested in what my experience would be like in a department where I was the only anthropologist. Having trained in a large state university with many anthropology faculty and students—and having taught in Kenya, where I was in a nontraditional classroom because much of my instruction occurred in the field, often taking students for field trips that lasted up to two weeks in different locations—I was not sure what to expect at Augustana.

I came to the College in August 2003 in time to start the academic year. Being back in America, I was sure to be present at many more meetings of the AAA, but I needed some time to settle into my new institution. The next AAA meeting I attended was in 2005, and I went to all the ones thereafter. I was particularly drawn to the 2007 annual meeting because of its stated theme: "Inclusion, Collaboration, and Engagement." I was very much interested in seeing how well the meeting itself reflected in that theme.

The 2007 AAA Annual Meeting, Washington, D.C.

After my initial AAA meeting in New Orleans and subsequent relocation to America, I was able to attend AAA meetings regularly. After a number of these meetings, I began to see some emerging patterns. I decided to focus on the 2007 meeting in Washington, D.C., as a case study, hoping the conference would bring out the patterns I had so far recognized. One question that I kept asking myself was why the AAA held meetings at such expensive hotels and only in certain cities. Could the choice of those cities be dictated by the ability of their hotels to accommodate the thousands of anthropologists who attend the meetings each year, or was it the physical attractiveness of these cities? I decided to consult the AAA Web site for answers and found that meeting locations were chosen in accordance with the AAA executive board motions, which state that the meetings may not be held "in any state with sodomy laws" and that meeting planners not only "shall 'strongly prefer' meeting facilities whose staff are represented by a union" but also "shall show preference to locales with living wage ordinances."[12] Reading these guidelines for selecting annual meeting locations made me proud to be an anthropologist and a member of AAA. I was in support of respecting all people, especially workers who need to be protected against neoliberal economic mechanisms of exploitation.

Something else became evident to me as I reflected on the meetings I had attended: many graduate students attended the meetings. I wondered why I, as a graduate student, had all along been afraid of attending the meetings. Besides student participants, there were many anthropologists who attended the meetings each year, and all seemed to anticipate with keen interest the subsequent meetings. To many anthropologists, this was an important event, an annual ritual not to be missed. I too became part of the group, and now I attend AAA meetings regularly. My participation in the AAA has especially been enhanced by my membership in its Association for Africanist Anthropology (AfAA), a section where I feel quite at home. I personally know many anthropologists in this group and look forward to our annual gatherings. Such organizations within the AAA provide alternative spaces for one, in the words of Faye Harrison, to "resist and combat the politics of purging" that the larger AAA may bring upon "outsiders within."[13] Despite these small spaces for "outsiders" within the AAA, anthropology remains predominantly White and quite overwhelming to me.

I became aware of the enormity and intimidating nature of the AAA at the 2007 annual meeting in Washington, when I came out of a session hosted by the AfAA in memory of Professor Elliott Skinner. The meeting was a small and intimate gathering of colleagues interested in Africa, and since I know a number of them, we had good conversations and exchange of ideas about the discipline and the directions our research was taking us. I counted about forty colleagues in that meeting, and for a short moment, I had gotten used to a really racially mixed group. Then I came out of that small meeting and stepped into the main lobby of the meeting hotel, near the registration desk. The noise level took me aback. Everyone was talking at the same time. But above all there was a sea of Whiteness in front of me. I almost ran back to the AfAA meeting room. For the first time at one of these professional meetings, I became very much aware of the reality of being such an outsider in anthropology. I looked around and did not spot anyone I knew in that big crowd. I was overwhelmed. I walked around the continually swelling assembly, feeling out of place, and hastily proceeded to my hotel, which was located a few yards from the conference hotel. Being in the different sessions earlier had not been intimidating for me at all, but the scene at the confer-ence hotel lobby was overpowering. I had not known or recognized any of the people there, and I had been self-conscious about standing out in that group. My hotel room seemed to offer some refuge. With so many Africans and African Americans working at the hotel, I was able to get some reprieve from the sea of Whiteness I had just left in the conference hotel. As I reflected on that brief experience, I wondered why I was intimidated by such a crowd and also why I was much more aware of the racial composition of my fellow anthropologists than I usually was. Was I unable to embrace the meeting's theme of inclusion, collaboration, and engagement?

I had seen some attempts to increase the level of inclusivity at the AAA meetings and had hoped that because we are all anthropologists, it would be our identity as members of the same profession that counted and not our racial or ethnic identities. The AAA had tried to level out our social differ-ences by supplying us with name tags that did not indicate our academic rank—an effort that had somewhat neutralized the sense of hierarchy cre-ated by rank. However the name tags ended up contributing to a peculiar practice that led many participants to ignore each other. I noticed a pattern at the meetings: having a name tag meant that fellow anthropologists did not bother to look each other in the eyes; they looked only at the name tag. If they recognized the name, they would talk to that person. If they did not recognize the name, they would put on a half-a-second smile and move on. Despite this anonymity, however, there are other ways of figuring out who were the senior and the popular anthropologists, the graduate students, the about-to graduate anthropologists, and the recently graduated anthropolo-gists. The graduate students tend to move in groups at these meetings since they tend to come there in groups—mostly because they attend universities close to the meeting venue and they share hotel rooms. They are also some of the more "professionally" dressed because many use the annual meetings as sites for "networking," laying down the necessary social networks for future academic jobs. The more established professors (tenured, well-published, and easily recognized by many) rarely go to listen to presentations, unless their friends are presenting or they are participating as discussants. Many of these anthropologists are seen in groups seated in the lounges or in the coffee shops or bars. They also tend to be surrounded by a group of younger anthropologists trying to establish their own legitimacy in a competitive field by "hanging out" with the movers and shakers in the discipline.

If one wishes to meet someone in the meeting, one can use the services already provided by the meeting organizers that allow one to leave and check for messages at a desk with numerous message boxes, located close to the hotel lobby. The message boxes remind me of the older library catalog boxes where details of a book held in the library were stored. The message service is provided by the association with a few people contracted to oversee it. Yet the busiest places in the meeting, in my estimation, are the book exhibit and the placement center. These are the "real" centers of activity. In the book exhibit hall, I tried to use the number of people visiting the different booths to gauge which presses have the most prestige. Each day, I spent about two hours counting the number of visitors at each exhibit and then came up with my own list, starting with university presses such as Chicago, Duke, California, Indiana, and Illinois. In terms of prestige, Oxford, Cambridge, and Harvard university presses hold the top positions, primarily because they carry the reputation of their respective institutions. But, interestingly, Harvard University Press does not have book exhibits at the AAA meetings (at least the ones I had attended).

These presses are then followed by textbook publishing companies such as Wiley-Blackwell, Routledge, and Pearson, which—unlike the university presses—do not pretend to give the potential customers freedom to browse undisturbed through their exhibits. The personnel representing these text-book publishers tend to operate in very straightforward commercial ways. They, for instance, have numerous "freebies" to give to prospective instructors and are quick to ask visitors to their booths if they are teaching a course and then inquire about how they can assist them in meeting "their teaching needs." There are usually four or more such commercial presses at the AAA book exhibit hall each year. Other textbook publishers ask for business cards, which they use to mail promotional material to entice professors to adopt their textbooks for their courses.

Hidden in corners that are away from the "heavy traffic" areas are the in-dependent publishers or nonacademic publishers, some amalgamation of different presses from America and abroad, and individuals or small companies selling cultural artifacts such as clothing, bags, and other ethnic paraphernalia that they assume, and rightly so, would attract members of a discipline built on studying the Other. When I got into the book exhibit hall, I took a tour to see all the booths—after which, I settled on a few presses (such as Indiana, Chicago, and Illinois) that publish books in areas I am interested in, such as African studies and popular culture. As I have mentioned, I spent about two hours daily at the book exhibit hall—browsing through the numerous books, buying some, and also interacting with friends whom I seemed to meet only in this location. Besides the book exhibits, the next "high traffic" area at these conferences is always the placement center. I was curious to see what happened in this space as well, and so I decided to do some close observation. This was the space for job hunters.

Job Hunters

At the 2007 meeting, the placement center (a nice term for job search and interviewing center) was located in a spooky place on a floor that had no carpeting. It was also near the tail end of the hotel's basement, where chairs and other furniture were stored during the larger part of the year when there wasn't as much demand for them as was during AAA meetings. The placement center is usually a hub of activity, with so many interview booths that consist of tables and some few chairs separated from each other with curtains. The first time I saw the interview center, I thought of the private ward spaces at Nairobi Hospital, in Kenya, where a patient's privacy is marked by a curtain that covers the bed and is open only when the patient is gone away or when a medical attendant enters to administer some vital treatment. At each of these interview booths, there were about two to five anthropologists or representatives from the institutions looking to hire a new colleague.

There was usually no one in between these interview booths, maybe as a sign of respect for the privacy of the interview sessions—and maybe also because no interviewee in his or her right mind would venture to walk anywhere close to one of them. Yet as I walked past the tables to get to the other session hall, where wall posters showing the research outcomes of various anthropologists were displayed, I could hear animated talking coming from the interview booths as candidates tried to convince their interviewers that they were the best person for the advertised position. I did a lot of such convincing myself in 2002, when I had three interviews at the AAA annual meetings in New Orleans. After leaving the interview center, I visited the hall where the poster sessions would be held, and then I went to message boards. This latter space had about five boards, with job postings posted on each one of them as well as interview schedules for most of the jobs advertised. Adjacent to the boards were two tables with people seated behind them, flipping through folders that contained files of curriculum vitae for prospective candidates and further information about the jobs and the institutions advertising the jobs. Many prospective employers who may not have been able to secure an interviewing booth at the meetings used this message-board service to solicit for curriculum vitae and letters of interest for positions that were advertised.

I found it easy to spot the job seekers around the job-posting boards and the interview center. They usually were professionally dressed—most of the men in sport jackets and formal or semi-casual pants and the women mostly in skirt suits or pant suits. I realized that none of the casual ethnographic attire of jeans and a T-shirt seen in the meeting sessions was represented in these spaces. The job seekers also carried bags or folders, and many of them were pacing up and down along the edges of the interview booths. They were, for the most part, constantly watching the booths that they were supposed to be in—maybe in hopes that someone would give them some kind of cue about when they should enter to start the interview process. After checking some of the interview schedules at the boards and the booths where the interviews were scheduled to take place, I was able to establish the order of interviews. I sat at a distance, watching the activities around those booths, and again I observed some recurrent activities. The candidates mostly arrived about five minutes before their scheduled time and stood about ten feet away from the particular booth. They would then keep glancing at the booth and checking their wristwatch to keep track of the elapsing time. I could imagine that these job hunters had rehearsed their interview script pretty well to try to satisfy their fellow anthropologists who were in a way trying to see if these candidates were ready to join the "club" of tenure-track faculty at such-and-such institution.

Having gone through the rituals of job hunting myself, I could relate to the anxiety of these job hunters. I had had to convince particular colleagues in the discipline that I was their candidate by following certain recurring rituals that most job hunters have to enact. Even though departments of anthropology at different institutions vary in their culture, there are some standard qualities that each candidate has to articulate to the search committee in order to be competitive. The candidate should, for instance, address these three issues: the way he or she perceives his or her "fit" within the existing faculty at the institution as well as within the department culture and mission; the particular research interests that he or she has; and the way in which those interests complement, not compete with, those of the existing faculty members. Key in this process as well is one's "collegiality," which generally means that one has to be seen as a good colleague who would advance the department and the institution in the achievement of its mission and goals. The candidate must be able to project this idea of collegiality in a way that does not threaten the already existing members of faculty while also promising to be a positive addition to the department and institution. I have found, through casual observation of many departments of anthropology that are advertising jobs for new faculty, that the professional accomplishments required for a new colleague often exceed those of existing faculty members in the department. I looked at one school where two full professors in the department had no major publication and the job advertisement for the new position indicated a desire for a colleague with a strong publication record. Were they hoping to introduce a new publications culture into the department?

To expect a new colleague to do so much more than is required of other faculty members seems to go against the principle of cultural relativism promoted in anthropology, where the value of a phenomenon is judged by the local standards and not those of the outside world. If the other colleagues continue to be seen as valuable members of the department without publishing, then the same measure should determine the kinds of colleagues the department should be seeking in new tenure-track positions. Yet these seemingly double standards are a reflection of academic culture itself, where a department may be "stuck" with a nonproductive colleague simply because he or she is tenured. Not all institutions have the same expectations for their new colleagues, however. Some private and public institutions focus on teaching and, as a result, have fewer expectations for scholarly publishing than research institutions do. Job candidates who are applying for positions at research schools are generally required to do three key things: demonstrate how they would attract graduate students to the institution, roll out their research agenda for the next five to ten years, and describe the particular courses they would be willing and able to teach. Regardless of the type of institution, in naming the courses he or she would like to teach, a job candidate might be advised to be very careful not to suggest an already existing course—at least, not without seeking the view of the professor who currently teaches that course. Sometimes, professors tend to have a sentimental attachment to courses they teach and might see a suggestion to teach "their" course as an invasion of their private property.

There is, in all this adventure of getting a teaching position, a "hidden" ritual with expected practices and meanings. Once one masters the most critical facets of the ritual, one stands a better chance of being invited to join the "club" as a faculty member. But this "club" in anthropology is now facing new challenges as the classic anthropological method of ethnography has been encroached by non-anthropologists. When ethnography is no longer the exclusive domain of anthropology, then there is a real challenge to the discipline. This fact became evident, and even more disturbing, when I heard anthropologists claim that ethnography as we know it was coming to an end.

The End of Ethnography?

After leaving the placement center, I went back to the meetings hall to find other sessions to attend. I looked at the program and chose one session that had presenters with experience working outside of academia. I was curious to know what kind of ethnographic work goes on in such an arena. What was interesting about the session was that the panel had one participant who was talking about the "end of ethnography," the topic that was the reason I had chosen the session. I listened to the presentation and heard that the "end of ethnography" had come about when anthropologists began to engage in consumer research and consumer research teams engaged ethnography as part of their unique toolkit for collecting data for their clients. The presenter said that these researchers do not go for the Clifford Geertz "thick description" type of ethnography but rather the "quick and dirty" ethnography, which does not often allow for an in-depth understanding of the consumer—or of the field that is often touted as the "real" gamut of anthropology.

Consumer research strategy seems to be built around the ethnographic ideal of building intimate relations with "informants" (in this case, consumer research clients who are considered typical prospective consumers) in order to "extract" vital information that will help the researcher understand the culture or consumer under study. The challenge comes when anthropologists realize that these "informants" are actually paid for their information and that many of them might be "serial respondents/informants" who often respond to the request for participation in consumer research because they need the money. I wondered if this kind of research was ethnographic. Can we consider individuals who are paid to take consumer surveys as informants? Are the researchers who administer and analyze those surveys ethnographers? Is this pseudo-ethnography or para-ethnography? I felt a little apprehensive about this new reality that I was being exposed to and wondered if I were being territorial about who should claim to be an ethnographer.

As the presenter expanded on the topic, I learned that these "informants" register with different research agencies and that because they have participated in more than one of these projects, they often know how to respond to the initial questions that agencies ask of potential "informants" and thus readily qualify for the "work." Through this strategy, these regular "informants" can become temporary workers for these consumer research agencies. An animated discussion followed the session as members of the audience questioned the legitimacy of referring to this kind of work as ethnography. One of the panelists said that ethnography had to respond to changes in society and our old definitions of our field are no longer operative.

The use of ethnography for marketing and consumer research has become a major tool that many consultants use to sell their expertise, and anthropologists either will have to contend with this reality and reinvent themselves or become irrelevant. Much of the practice of anthropology in Africa seems to follow a similar pattern, as many anthropologists find themselves using their professional skills in consultancies than in training the next generation of anthropologists.[14] Even in institutions with departments of anthropology, anthropologists often find themselves servicing other disciplines instead of teaching anthropology courses that lead to a major.[15] Does the end of ethnography denote the end of anthropology? When I searched the Internet for consumer research and anthropology, one of the sites found was that of Jacobs Strategies, which states the following about ethnographic research: "Our marketing expertise, in conjunction with our research backgrounds, allows us to structure ethnographic research projects that target consumer opinions and product usage. By interviewing respondents in their homes, offices, and places where they actually utilize products and services, we are better able to deliver actionable results that go beyond traditional Q&A research formats."[16]

I could not help but feel a little disturbed by this oversimplification of anthropological skills, but I knew that we could no longer have exclusive "rights" to ethnography. The idea of ethnographic research expounded by Jacobs Strategies seems to be centered on finding the "right" anthropological technique for engaging an "informant" in his or her own sociocultural context. However, this approach misses the other part of ethnographic research that requires a more nuanced understanding of the "informant" through a longer period of interaction and observation. I could not hide my disappointment in this "academic take over."

My greatest disappointment with the idea of the "end of ethnography,"
however, came when I sat and listened to a prominent anthropologist discuss the papers that were given at the panel. I had read many of this particular scholar's works in my anthropology graduate courses with much fervor
and admiration, and I was looking forward to hearing him speak. When he
mumbled some incoherent statements about ethnography, I wondered if
such incoherence had something to do with smooth talkers from the marketing industry taking over ethnography. Evidently there is a big difference
between writing well and sharing those ideas in public in a coherent way
within the short period of time allowed for paper presentations at conferences. Does one's anthropological prominence rest on the kinds of books
one writes or on the successful ethnographic project one completes? Given
that ethnography is often an individual enterprise, we can only rely on the
final product (book, paper, film, or poster) to gauge the "worth" of the anthropologist. I had read this anthropologist's books and assumed he was a
capable anthropologist—until I heard him speak. It was then that I realized
we cannot elevate a person's anthropological status based only on the books
that he or she writes.

The abysmal performance by a prominent anthropologist that I witnessed
in that session made me wonder about the literature produced by anthropologists and its efficacy as a tool to gauge one's standing as a successful
anthropologist. Because much of anthropology's peer review work entails
reviewing books and research papers, it is possible to miss the holistic view
of an anthropologist. How good are we as teachers or researchers? What
kind of colleagues are we in our academic institutions and departments, and
how does that persona reflect on our discipline? Can we gauge our abilities
or worth by the ethnographies or books we write? This final question was
partially answered when I had a chance to go to another session in which
anthropologists who had substantial experience in fieldwork that spanned
up to thirty years were reflecting on their experiences. This session was important for me because as an anthropologist who did not have as much experience professionally, I wanted to learn what others think of fieldwork and
anthropology by hearing them reflect upon the many years of their work.
Would they talk about this changing nature of ethnography or the recycling
of field notes? I was curious to hear them.

When I arrived in the meeting room, I found about twenty other participants there, mostly older anthropologists chatting in a way that signaled
already established friendships. After about ten minutes, the room filled up
with a few younger anthropologists, and the organizers started the session

with an overview of what had transpired among them as they were deciding what to propose for the panel. This was a much welcome break from the panels I had attended earlier and those at other AAA annual meetings that featured obscure language and data from nowhere. I found this session very enlightening, particularly because a number of issues about the Other were discussed— including whether we should call the local person who assists in our research a collaborator, an informant, a client, or a colleague. This changing nature of the title we assign our research interlocutors is important especially, given the debate over the end of ethnography. For anthropology, how we regard informants reflects the asymmetrical nature of the relationship that exists between the anthropologists and the local people supplying the local points of view. If we call them informants, we run the risk of coming out as just engaging them for their information (as market research ethnographers do). If we call them collaborators, then we start feeling guilty when we do not include their names in our manuscripts and share equally any proceeds from sales of our research products such as books and videos. If we call them clients, then we feel as if they are coming to the anthropologist for advice or service, and we know mostly it is usually the anthropologist who seeks knowledge from the local. And if we call them colleagues, then we must have to regard them as equals, and treat them as such, and we all know too well that to adopt this stance would be to overlook the often serious socioeconomic and political differences between anthropologists and their local sources of data. We may have to settle to calling them cultural teachers, but the jury is still out on that idea. I am glad that anthropologists are still grappling with these issues because we have to continue reflecting upon and critiquing what we do in the field.

The next issue that was discussed was the value of reflecting over a number of years of fieldwork and seeing what had changed in the community and in the anthropologist. One panelist shared a case in which an anthropologist— who had been to a particular community about twenty years earlier—had chosen to focus his work on material culture, especially women's weaving, because he had not been able to get to the bottom of that one community's thoughts. When he finally put together an international exhibit of the culture's material wealth almost twenty years later, no one in the community was weaving anymore. This was a truly remarkable example of cultural change. I wondered if people who saw the exhibit and did not know much about the community studied by the anthropologist would assume that weaving was part of their cultural practice.

Another anthropologist reflected on his time in the field and said that as he looked back, he realized that at the time he was conducting his fieldwork, he had not been quite sure what he was doing. This remark elicited some chuckles among a number of people in the audience and made me wonder if this retrospective realization of an inability to be sure about what one was doing in the field ever showed up in the ethnographies that resulted from the same fieldwork. I could not believe the number of anthropologists at this session who confessed to having that view of their field experiences when they had begun their work as anthropologists. Many of them seemed to second guess their abilities to really grasp the gist of what was going on in the communities they were studying. But whenever I had read ethnographies, I never came out of it thinking "this anthropologist does not seem sure of what he or she is writing about." I wondered about the whole notion of ethnography as fiction and wished there was more reflexivity going on, especially for specific texts written by anthropologists at those moments when they were unsure of what was going on in their respective field sites. Again, was this the end of ethnography?

There was also a moment in the sharing of fieldwork experiences during this conference session when an anthropologist mentioned that when his field site had started to change, he began having difficulties with his research topics and focus. He mentioned, for instance, that when he had started his research, many of the local people were available outside of their houses, but as they became Westernized, or modernized, and started going to work and coming back home, they spent more time in their houses. This new "homebound" habit of theirs had forced him to change his research strategies. There seemed to be a difference between an anthropologist's being able to go into someone's house and being able to hang out with them on the street corner. Once the people being studied by anthropologists started adopting lifestyles similar to those of Western anthropologists, where they spent time in their private spaces in their houses, the earlier ease with which anthropologists had access to informants in the public square of rural communities diminished. In earlier anthropological field studies, it was much easier to follow someone to the field than it was, when daily activities became more centered in urban areas, to follow someone to his or her office. The lives of the local people had become more routinized and more scheduled, and they had started to face the same problems and social challenges as the anthropologist was facing in his home community. Problems such as health care, care for aging parents, finances for a college education, and child care had become major issues for a number of the local people, just as they were for the anthropologist's community back home. While this new reality made framing of research questions easier because of the anthropologist's familiarity with them through his own culture, he said he was honestly not interested in pursuing them as part of his ethnographic research. "Why go to the other side of the world and study social challenges I was going through in my own community?" he wondered. So instead, he had settled on research topics such as the way households work and the dynamic of ethnic identity in the community he studied. Even though he had not set out initially to study these subjects, he felt they were "portable topics" that were not bound to a particular community or space. Clearly this anthropologist was living up to the discipline's stated attraction to alterity. Another anthropologist said that even though she was now much more familiar with and more fully understood the culture that she studied, she did not write about that community. In fact, despite knowing the community more and more, she wrote less and less about it. After finishing her dissertation, she felt "this is it, I know it," but she was now doubtful about that confidence in knowing "it."

I was intrigued by all these reflections on fieldwork and wondered if the ethnographies that resulted from this now-abandoned work were still useful for anthropology. When asked if they would be willing to put together a book or journal articles comprising the ideas and experiences they had just shared, the session panelists had mixed responses. A number of them felt uncomfortable writing about their own experiences in the field, while others said it was a possibility. I realized that the reflexive turn in anthropology, which had dominated the discipline when I was a graduate student, was not embraced by all anthropologists and that it is easier to write about others than to write about oneself. This mixed reaction to writing about fieldwork and experiences gave me all the more reason to continue with my intent to write about the AAA. I realized that the information I had just received in that session was very hard to find in the discipline's flagship journals such as the *American Anthropologist* or *American Ethnologist*. Indeed, such information may be available only in personal blogs or in journals that are not considered mainstream. The fact that people do not necessarily want to write about their experiences in the field in itself says a lot about what constitutes anthropological knowledge, who shapes the canon, and who becomes the leading light in the discipline based on his or her writing. I also wondered if the observations I had made regarding the AAA were specific to the association or a common phenomenon among anthropologists. I decided to compare the AAA to the ASA.

ASA Meeting in Arusha, Tanzania

Comparing the AAA meeting with that of the ASA is quite telling of the nature of anthropology in the world today. Granted, I attended only one ASA meeting, and it was held in Arusha, Tanzania. But I do have a sense of its organization, especially after reading about it and talking to friends who are ASA members. One of the striking differences between the AAA and the ASA is the sheer number of AAA members and the number of those who actually attend the meetings. As the ASA's official Web site tells us, "The Association of Social Anthropologists (ASA) was founded in 1946 by Edward E. Evans-Pritchard. . . . to assist this new school of anthropology in gaining a stronger foothold within British universities, as it had previously been taught only at the LSE and Oxford. . . . Membership was by invitation . . . [for] 'persons holding, or having held, a teaching or research appointment in Social Anthropology.'"[17]

Today, membership in the ASA continues to be by "invitation of the Association" and "restricted to people who, by virtue of their training, posts held and published works, can be recognised as professional social anthropologists."[18] Moreover, the association's "aims broadly parallel those espoused in 1946, with the additional objective of supporting and promoting the professional practice and application of anthropology outside the academy."[19] By contrast, membership in the AAA is open to "Any person having a demonstrable professional or scholarly interest in the science of anthropology": "A professional interest in the science of anthropology is defined as a serious concern in the subject in accordance with the standards generally accepted in the profession, whether or not the interest is a source of livelihood."[20]

The one distinction between these two associations as far as membership is concerned is that in the ASA, a prospective member needs two existing ASA members to act as referees, and no such requirement exists for AAA. When I joined the AAA, I did not need any referees to support my membership bid. Considering the annual membership dues required for good standing in the associations, however, it is safe to state that both associations have some restrictions as to who can join. The ASA, however, continues to have a smaller membership—a fact that may explain its ability to host its annual meetings outside of the UK, including Africa, with meetings held in Zimbabwe and Tanzania in 1997 and 2002, respectively. Realistically, it is much cheaper for anthropologists to travel to Africa from Europe (where many ASA members are located) than from America. Historically, American professional associations have tended to be very inward-looking and provide little interest or incentive for members to interact meaningfully with members of other associations or those who live in locations outside America.

At the ASA meeting I attended in 2002 in Arusha, there were ninety participants (either as presenters, panel chairs, or keynote speakers) from half as many countries. Because of its proximity to the meeting venue, Kenya had the most participants from a single nation. Due to the small number of meeting participants, there were no concurrent sessions—a situation that meant all sessions were well attended. With papers being presented by archaeologists, social/cultural anthropologists, physical anthropologists, sociologists, historians, linguists, and scholars of religion, this meeting was as interdisciplinary as I have ever seen an anthropology meeting. There were fourteen panels altogether, and only one of them was convened or chaired by scholars who were all from the same country. The limited number of conference attendees may be attributed to the location—even though, in comparing it to other conferences, one may realize that venue has little to do with the size of attendance. For example, in the 2007, at the ASA annual meeting held in April at the London Metropolitan University, there were 154 participants (as either presenters, chairs, or keynote speakers) and twenty-nine panels. ASA annual meetings as well as membership have remained small. Because of the sheer numbers of anthropologists in the AAA—an average of five hundred or more panels and more than five thousand participants at annual meetings— other anthropology association meetings do not have the same international clout as does the AAA. In the next chapter, I take a look at emerging trends among anthropologists who seek to create a systematic connection among all the different anthropological associations and traditions.

Looking back at my experience in the 2007 AAA annual meeting, I can say that there is a great need for us as anthropologists to keep our ethnographic eyes on ourselves and our professional associations in order to understand how best we can be inclusive as well as collaborative. We need to work diligently to reinvigorate the discipline and its practices so that we remain relevant in our own field, at a time when other disciplines are assuming they can readily and successfully carry out our roles. If professionals in these other disciplines do end up in the role of the anthropologist, doing work such as ethnographic research and cross-cultural analysis, and we do not respond accordingly, we will soon become irrelevant in a world where neoliberal economic models have already prevailed, even in higher education. This threat is even more present in the practice of anthropology in countries other than the United States—as well as in the relationship that the AAA has with other national and regional associations.

6

A New Paradigm for
Twenty-First-Century Anthropology?

What is the future of anthropology in a world that is becoming increasingly connected by new forms of globalization that hinge on a neoliberal economic model? What is the role of anthropology in highlighting and analyzing this global neoliberal condition, especially as it reflects not only anthropology's quintessential research subject—the Other—but American anthropology's relationship with other anthropologies? Faye Harrison offers an important starting point in *Outsider Within* (2008) for answering these questions by providing what she calls in her subtitle a "reworking of anthropology in the global age." She then goes on to provide nine critical objectives toward this reworking of anthropology. Her ninth objective of "developing a commitment for decentering Western epistemologies and promoting a genuine multicultural dialogue in the study of humanity" greatly informs the discussion I undertake in this chapter.[1] In order to exemplify how the future of anthropology is tied to reworking relationships that exist between the AAA and other world anthropologies, let me start by contextualizing my own academic identity as an Africanist anthropologist.

Coming to America in the early 1990s to study anthropology also meant my entering into a formal area of study commonly known as African studies. As an African who had lived all my life (before coming to America) in Kenya, studying and conducting research and writing about things African, I never at any one time considered myself an Africanist. What makes one an Africanist anyway? And what are the specific research tools that constitute an Africanist research approach? These and other questions would occupy me in much of my academic life in America as I entered an arena in which my previously taken-for-granted Africanness demanded to be reflexively considered. The fact that I did not consider myself an Africanist does not mean that when I entered into anthropological training in America, I ceased to be African; rather, I had a new set of eyes and new discourse through which to regard that reality. I found myself, for the first time in my academic experience, entering into a conversation about Africa—its identity and its inhabitants.

The first academic home for anthropology in Kenya was the Institute of African Studies at the University of Nairobi, which until the early 2000s was heavily regarded as the "anthropology program" home at the institution. Today the Institute reflects its anthropological identity in its name, the Institute of Anthropology, Gender, and African Studies—clearly establishing that anthropology, gender, and African studies are independent spheres of knowledge production and study. When it was started in 1966, the institute (known then as the Institute of African Studies) "was charged with the responsibility of promoting and conducting original researches in the field of African prehistory and history; musicology and dance; traditional and modern arts crafts; religion and other belief systems"—clearly placing anthropology within a multidisciplinary context.[2] At Kenyatta University, where I trained for both my bachelor's and master's degrees, there was no institute or center for African studies, and it remained so into the 2000s. But we did attend to research grounded in what I now know as African studies. Maybe all I needed was to come into anthropology to finally be legitimized into my own academic identity as an Africanist.[3] Intrigued by this new academic identity as an Africanist when I entered American higher education, I decided to spend some time looking back at the history of my "new" field of study. In this historiography of African studies, I also wanted some answers to explain why I had sensed some hostility toward anthropology among some fellow graduate students in disciplines such as sociology and political science. Coincidentally, these fellow students were all in the field of African studies.

Renowned American sociologist Immanuel Wallerstein would provide for me a much-needed historical context for a discussion about African studies. Wallerstein argues the following in relation to anthropology's interest in the Other and especially the African:

> The fact that the study of Africa was thus limited of course reflected the division of intellectual labour that had been carved out in the late nineteenth century, among whose features was the division of the world into three geographical zones: modern European and European-settler states, which were

studied by economists, historians, political scientists, and sociologists; non-Western areas with a long-standing written culture and a preferable so-called "world religion," which were studied by so-called Orientalists; and backward peoples, which were studied by anthropologists.[4]

I had just finished reading the Wallerstein paper from which I take the passage quoted above, when I had a discussion with a colleague from sociology who insisted that anthropologists had for many years dominated African studies in America and that certain White "gatekeepers" had systematically blocked African American anthropologists from entering into the "African studies kingdom." At the time of this discussion, I was just starting to get a grip on the history of the discipline and was ill-prepared to make an educated defense of anthropology against those accusations about "gatekeeping." I did wish, however (as I discuss in chapter 1) that these allegations were untrue and that my area study focus had a good history. Here I was in my initial years of graduate school, trying to embrace a discipline that had excited me when I was searching for attractive paths in doctoral studies.

Over the next few months of graduate school training as a cultural anthropologist, I embarked on reading about anthropology's history and gradually realized that my sociology colleague knew a whole lot more about the history of African studies than I had imagined. I found out that indeed there was a history of White Africanist gatekeeping that dominated the field of African studies and that some of the key players were also anthropologists. This fact disappointed me. I realized, for instance, that Merville Herskovits was one of the culprits. While often regarded as the "father of African studies" in America, Herskovits was also one of the earlier gatekeepers. There is enough research now to confirm these earlier notions, which had seemed fuzzy at the time I was beginning graduate work in anthropology. As Pearl Robinson tells us, after Herskovits graduated from Columbia University with a PhD in anthropology under Franz Boas, he went to Howard University in 1925 as a lecturer in anthropology. At Howard, Herskovits would be remembered for claiming that there were no traces of Africa in American Blacks, a position he later rescinded when he moved to Northwestern University two years later.[5] Herskovits's ambivalent position on the connections between Africans and African Americans was temporary and most likely shaped by contradictions that are common in much of the academic world. Faced by a growing anti-Semitism that engulfed much of America's academic world in the 1920s and '30s, Herskovits would, not surprisingly, find his own scholarly foothold studying a marginalized community in America: African

Americans. From this scholarly work Herskovits went on to write *The Myth of the Negro Past,* which became the most important text linking African American cultural roots to Africa. However, this connection between Africans and African Americans did not produce a unified academic area of inquiry under the African studies program developed in the United States by Herskovits. Instead, African studies as a field focused primarily on Africa and its people within the continent. His earlier straddling between the African and the African Diasporic worlds did not produce a field linking the two areas of study. Instead, African studies and Afro-American studies developed as two separate entities. Indeed, Elliott Skinner—one of the most successful and prominent African American anthropologists and one whose work sought to clearly link Africa with the African Diaspora worlds—was named Franz Boas (not Melville Herskovits) Professor at Columbia. In a way, this position may strategically and symbolically point to the chasm that developed between African American anthropology (represented by Boas, following his contributions to and support of African American anthropology, including his encouraging Zola Hurston in her own work) and Africanist anthropology (represented by Herskovits, especially through his work at Northwestern University, where he established the African Studies Center). These contradictions in areas of study were to reveal the realities of the academy and continue to do so today.

Indeed, the contested perception of the connections between the African Diaspora and continental Africa led Herskovits to define Africa and African studies differently from the definitions preferred by African American scholars of his time. He focused on Africa south of the Sahara, while Diasporic African scholars considered *Africa* to mean the continent as a whole (including North Africa) and the African Diaspora. Interestingly, Herskovits's research took him to Suriname, Dahomey, Haiti, Trinidad, and Brazil, where there are large communities of Africans and people of African descent. Yet the divide exemplified by the difference between Herskovits and Diasporic Africanists in their regard for African studies has continued to shape mainstream Africa Studies programs in America, especially those with a Title VI African Studies Center, like the university I attended.[6] Only recently have some academic departments in America been amenable to combining the study of Africa and the African Diaspora into Africana studies. A reworking of anthropology, I would argue, has to acknowledge and contend with this history of truncated engagement with Africa, the African Diaspora, and other anthropologies. As anthropologists, we have to inhabit our historical realities in order not to repeat the same mistakes today. We must engage the history of knowledge production, be it in anthropology as a discipline or in Africa, which continues to be a central source of anthropological knowledge.

Such historiography seems to be carried out by a few scholars who—many decades after Melville Herskovits founded the African Studies Center at Northwestern University—continue to critically look at his legacy. The series editors' introduction to Jerry Gershenhorn's book on Herskovits states, "That Northwestern was where Africanists were produced is widely known. Less well known is how Herskovits blocked from the means of production . . . those not indebted to him or not supporting his positions . . . during the era when area studies was heavily funded by the U.S. government and foundations."[7]

While at Northwestern University, Herskovits managed to gain an important foothold in the study of Africa, allowing him to have power over the production of knowledge across the country, including—and even among—African Americans. As Martin and West write, Herskovits "sought to deny funding for . . . W. E. B. Du Bois's *Encyclopedia Africana*" because he felt that "Dr. Du Bois was not a 'scholar'; he was a 'radical' and a 'Negrophile.'"[8] History did prove Herskovits wrong, but his sentiments are not new in academia and especially in anthropology, where its own brand of gatekeeping endures—as I mention in my earlier discussion of who gets hired where and whose texts are regarded as part of the canon.

This history formed the context in which I entered anthropology through African studies, a field that itself is embedded within larger structures of academic activity. I want to take a moment to look at how the discipline of anthropology, and the attendant area studies from which we derive our scholarship, may become relevant in an era that seems configured quite differently from that which gave birth to both anthropology and African studies. How will anthropology, a discipline very central to African studies, reinvent itself in this new century in order to address the crises and challenges facing us as professionals? For me, this is a question not only of academic interest but also of personal concern because I would like to understand how my own training as an anthropologist, my academic identity as an Africanist, and my subjective identity as an African interested in positive representation of Africa will feature in the discipline's future. Will anthropology have a paradigm shift? Will anthropology—especially the one emanating from the hegemonic centers in America, Britain, and France—be more reflexive, decentered, or cognizant and even celebratory of other anthropologies? Will anthropological knowledge and its subsequent values continue to be predominantly disseminated through the English language in the twenty-first century? What place will other large anthropology communities such as those in Japan, Colombia, and Brazil occupy in such a new paradigm? How about funding and research: will research funding continue to be dominated by institutions and foundations in the hegemonic centers with monies going to anthropologists in the prominent centers? Or will there be new funding sources interested in cross-border, interdisciplinary, and cross-generational themes rather than area-based research? Will there be new gatekeepers like Herskovits?

To answer these and many related questions, I offer two threads of analysis that focus, first, on recent developments in the field that is now referred to as "world anthropologies," where I see some ray of hope for a more global and sensitive anthropological practice and, second, on the practice of anthropology in Africa. Regarding the new field of "world anthropologies," I am especially interested in seeing if we can discern an emerging pattern that can promise to bring change in the way anthropology and anthropologists of the center perceive, relate, and interact with those of the margins or peripheries. Will "world anthropologies" be a true indicator of the discipline's shift from "business as usual" and start to be regarded as the discipline not defined by its object of otherness or alterity? Let us explore some recent developments in this field.

In the March 2008 issue of *Anthropology News,* the American Anthropology Association's newsletter, there is an item by Fran Rothstein announcing the formation of the Commission on World Anthropologies (CWA), which was charged with the following: "Developing policy recommendations for enriching US-based anthropology; Assisting in organizing sessions and meetings at the AAA Annual Meeting that bring the anthropological knowledge production of the Global South to US-based anthropologists; Proposing and facilitating joint meetings with anthropological associations from outside the US; and Facilitating the translation, presentation and publication of research from world anthropologies."[9]

This announcement and the gesture that had preceded it were not a small feat for anthropology. As I state in chapter 5, the AAA is one of the strongest anthropological associations in the world. With a membership today averaging over ten thousand—and pricy membership dues—the AAA is an economically stable association as well. For the AAA to be interested in forging relations with other anthropologies is both a welcome opportunity as well as a challenge—an opportunity if the AAA's success as an association can be spread out to other associations as a strategy of sharing best practices as well as a partnership for mutual success, and a challenge if the AAA, because of its economic strength, will end up dominating such a relationship.

The desire to have a more connected world of anthropologies and anthropologists is, however, not a new idea in anthropology. The International Union of Anthropological and Ethnological Sciences (IUAES) has been in the business of creating a forum for cross-national and international exchange and communication between anthropologists and other disciplines since 1948. While the AAA has had an ongoing relationship with the IUAES—as a member organization—for many years, the AAA has, not surprisingly, largely pursued its own domestic agenda of growing and sustaining its own practice and identity. In 1990, as Marietta Baba explained, "the American Anthropological Association (AAA) Board of Directors suggested that an international commission created for the purpose of globally connecting applied/practicing anthropologists be established within the International Union of Anthropological and Ethnological Sciences (IUAES)."[10] But besides these suggested collaborative activities, the AAA has remained very aloof and hegemonic, leaving most of the other anthropology associations to seek ways of working with the AAA but on the AAA's own terms. The question remains, therefore, as to whether this new initiative by the CWA will bear fruit in ways that other initiatives have not in the past. Besides this attempt to internationalize anthropology through IUAES, there have also been other attempts to make anthropology truly a world discipline.

Almost ten years before the formation of the CWA, there were indications of a new form of expansiveness in the discipline with a goal of critically examining how anthropology is organized and practiced throughout the world. This initial thinking led to the emergence of the World Anthropology Network (WAN), which was initiated by Arturo Escobar (University of North Carolina, Chapel Hill) and Marisol de la Cadena (University of California at Davis)—who were later joined by Gustavo Lins Ribeiro (Universidade de Brasilia) and Penny Harvey (Manchester). These diversified voices and more connections in anthropologies in the world point to a desire to transcend the national anthropology hegemons and usher in more partnerships and collaboration.

In an opinion piece that was originally published in the November 2005 issue of *Anthropology News,* WAN presents itself as "a project of intervention to legitimize the voices of other forms of anthropology, one which recognizes these forms as anthropological knowledge in their own right, independent of, yet in conversation with, hegemonic centers of knowledge around the world."[11] The conversation that led to the formation of WAN was happening as early as 2001. In 2003, Gustavo Lins Ribeiro and Arturo Escobar organized a Wenner-Gren-funded international symposium in Pordenone, Italy, March 7–13, under the title "World Anthropologies: Disciplinary Transformations with Systems of Power." The symposium would later be transformed into an edited volume with the same title, which was published in 2006 by Berg Publishers. Participants at the symposium were Arturo Escobar (United States), Gustavo Lins Ribeiro (Brazil), Michal Osterweil (United States), Nikolai Vakhtin (Russia), Eduardo Archetti (Argentina), Shinji Yamashita (Japan), Eeva Berglund (England/Finland), Verena Stolcke (Spain), Johannes Fabian (Netherlands), Esteban Krotz (Mexico), Roberto Cardoso de Oliveira (Brazil), Marisol de la Cadena (United States), Josephine Smart (Canada), Sandy Toussaint (Australia), Susana Narotzky (Spain), and Shiv Visvanathan (India). Otavia Velho (Brazil), Arlene Davila (United States), and Paul Nkwi (Cameroon) were invited but unable to attend. As the sponsor of the meeting, the Wenner-Gren Foundation was represented by Richard Fox and Laurie Obbink.

All the participants at the symposium—except Michal Osterweil, Verena Stolcke, Roberto de Oliveira, and Arlene Davila—contributed a chapter to the edited volume on world anthropologies. What is interesting about this volume, like many other volumes on world anthropologies, is that individual chapters often focus on the practice of anthropology in a specific country. While this approach is important in bringing to the larger readership the practice of anthropology in locations outside of the dominant centers, the multiplicity or practices, traditions, and values that emanate from anthropologists' own training and travel outside their home locations can easily be overlooked or underplayed. Are national anthropologies really that distinct and autonomous? Are anthropological traditions of the "margins" very different from those of the "centers," or are they, as George Stocking Jr., says, "neither so nationally varied nor so sharply divergent from that of the center"?[12] I have argued in the case of Kenyan anthropology, for instance, that Kenyan anthropologists and the programs they develop and support tend to reflect their varied training in Europe and America and do not necessarily constitute a Kenyan anthropology tradition.[13] So are these conversations about world anthropologies going to end up as full menus of what happens anthropologically in different parts of the world, or will they provide real practical expressions of collaboration and exchange, recurrent and emergent among and between anthropologists and anthropologies? Is this the shape of collaboration that will emerge in this new initiative under the CWA?

It seems prudent to opine that there are no bounded, distinct anthropological traditions or practices. What we have are traditions born out of interactions and exchanges occurring at various levels between anthropologies and anthropologists, especially following such processes as imperialism and globalization. No anthropology can claim to be unique and distinct, even though academic analyses tend to seek out distinctions for purposes of discussion. Indeed, as George Marcus argues, "There is now likely to be a much greater affinity of concern and interest in a globalizing and relativizing world between anthropologists of the center and anthropologies of the margins even though the distinction is still held in place by the prestige of relative wealth and status enjoyed by the former."[14] Marcus bases these observations on the critiques of American anthropology that emerged in the 1980s (especially those challenging positivist representation of fieldwork, those challenging classic ethnographies by injecting newer studies into the analysis, and those pushing for a more public anthropology) and demonstrates this affinity between center and margin. In a sense, anthropological traditions across the board have followed patterns similar to the ones observed in the growth or expansion of socioeconomic and political structures, both domestically and abroad. The same colonial systems that developed political and economic interdependence between colonizers and the colonized, for instance, have tended to be reflected in the academic traditions that emerge. In this sense, it is not surprising that Anglophone anthropological traditions in Africa have followed the British, and later the American, model of anthropology, while their Francophone counterparts have followed the French model.[15] Are the new initiatives by the CWA or WAN going to dismantle this anthropological tradition of hierarchy and asymmetry?

Expanded Terrains or New Anthropological Centers?

In 2004, another meeting on "World Anthropologies" was held in Recife, Brazil, under the sponsorship of Wenner-Gren and attended by presidents and chairs of anthropological associations and societies from different parts of the world. It was at this meeting that the World Council of Anthropological Associations (WCAA) was formed, following discussions among the fourteen participants representing nearly as many anthropological constituencies.[16] Among the attendants were Annie Benveniste, president of the French Association of Anthropologists; Ajit Danda, president of the Indian Anthropology Society; David Bogopa, president of the Pan African Anthropological Association; Elizabeth Brumfield, president of the AAA; Gustavo Ribeiro, president of Association of Brazilian Anthropology; Hendrik Pauw, president of Anthropology Southern Africa; James Waldram, president of Canadian Anthropology Society; Joal de Pina Cabral, president of European Association of Social Anthropologists; Junji Koizumi, chair of the Committee for International Relations of the Japanese Society of Cultural Anthropology; Luis Vargas, president of International Union of Anthropological and Ethnological Sciences; Milka Lucic, president of Latin-Americans Association of Anthropology; Richard Fardon, chair of the Association of Social Anthropology in the UK and Commonwealth; Thomas Reuter, president of Australian Anthropological Society; Victoria Malkin, Wenner-Gren Foundation for Anthropological Research, Inc.; Yuri Christov, president of Russian Association of Anthropologists and Ethnologists; and Paul Little and Aline Sapiezinskas, both from the University of Brasilia in Brazil, where the conference was held.[17] This is truly an impressive list of representatives of many anthropology associations, and it points to the possibility of building a very strong network of anthropologists across the world.

This notable flurry of activity in favor of "world anthropologies" is important, especially because of the centrality of anthropological "centers" represented by British, French, and American anthropology. Yet we must also acknowledge the fragility of these new projects, particularly because they too could become the new centers of anthropology in their respective locales. The WAN Collective, for instance, lists twenty members, none of whom represent any African institution or professional association such as the PAAA. Curious about this membership in WAN, I visited the network's Web site (http://www.ram-wan.net/html/people.htm) and learned that membership in an organization or network can point to the possibility of the formation of new centers within a decentering project. Even when there is an indication of a spreading out of networks of anthropology, certain centers may emerge, as is exemplified by table 1, which lists the initial members of WAN. The specific number of individuals from the different countries is given in parentheses.

From this data, we can see the distribution of membership in WAN based on the country where the member is primarily located. Granted, there are fourteen different countries represented—a reflection of a diverse member-

Table 1. Members of the World Anthropologies Network, by Continent and Country

Asia	Europe	South America	North America
India (4)	UK (3)	Colombia (14)	U.S. (10)
Indonesia (1)	Spain (3)	Brazil (4)	Canada (1)
	France (1)	Argentina (7)	Mexico (2)
	Belgrade (1)	Chile (1)	
	Portugal (1)	Peru (4)	
	Netherlands (1)	Ecuador (1)	
	Denmark (1)		

Source: WAN (information as of October 14, 2008), http://www.ram-wan.net/html/people.htm.

ship, but one that does not match the representation of various constituencies seen in the WCAA. A more careful look at the membership representation reveals an imbalance: Colombia and America, for instance, have the highest number of members in WAN. There are a number of possible explanations for this large figure. The total number of anthropologists practicing in those countries is high, and therefore their representation in WAN is relative to the size of the community of anthropologists based in those countries. Yet it so happens that Arturo Escobar, one of the founding members and the engine behind the World Anthropologies project, has close personal and academic ties to both Colombia and America. Escobar is originally from Colombia, where he received his training in science, but he currently teaches at the University of North Carolina, Chapel Hill, and frequently teaches a course titled World Anthropologies. Could Escobar be the reason why Colombia and America have more members than other countries?

Escobar is central in this regard, but his position and role also symbolize the shape that a world anthropology collaborative will take. It is the shape that recognizes the fragility of national associations, on the one hand, and the strength of individual connections between anthropologists, on the other. Seeking to create an anthropological network as WAN has done is indeed one of the surest ways of expanding anthropology beyond its bounded territories of associations, such as the AAA and the ASA. It is not that associations are not functional but rather that individual connections and relationships among anthropologists across racial, geographic, and class boundaries will lead to more sustainable collaborations. Anthropologists' ability to form strong one-on-one bonds with research interlocutors can be extended to our professional relationships with colleagues at home and abroad. Such connections and collaborations have to, however, be cautiously and vigilantly organized so that they do not result in new centers of power and exclusion.

In a paper on the state of anthropology in Spain presented at a presidential session at the 2007 AAA annual meeting in Washington, D.C., Hugo Valenzuela and Jose Molina argued that there were centers within peripheries and peripheries within peripheries in what they referred to as the "Matrioshka nest doll" dilemma.[18] The Matrioshka doll (from Russia) has many dolls fitted inside of each other in decreasing sizes, and one can miss the number of dolls present if one focuses only on the larger one into which the others fit. Using this metaphor of dolls, we can expand our analysis of anthropology centers and margins to refer to those in America and Britain as well as those in the metropolis in other countries. We must be careful when we try, in Ribeiro's words, "to create and consolidate a more plural anthropological community as well as to offer more diversified access to global anthropological knowledge."[19] We want to avoid creating new centers of power and cartels of exclusion. However, even if we do not quite form such strong groups, we may end up with closed networks comprising of academic kinship ties that beget a certain level of exclusion that could produce a predictable anthropological tradition. As Ulf Hannerz shows in reference to the common kinship of the European Association of Social Anthropologists (EASA), out of the first eight chairpersons of EASA, between 1989 and 2005, four were British (one of South African origin), one was Danish, one Swedish, one German (although teaching in the Netherlands) and one Portuguese—but I was the only one among them without a doctorate from the United Kingdom.[20]

Is this coincidence or evidence of ties that bind? The reality of our profession, like other professions, is that we work within established structures of power—many of which we have little or no control over, especially in terms of funding and communication networks. Such structures of power are so dominant that even where anthropologists share the same linguistic mode of communication, for instance, they do not necessarily decenter the global flow of knowledge, as Hannerz notes when he states that "the obstacles to communication are not entirely linguistic, but have to do with the organization of publishing as well. It is clear that some non-metropolitan English-language publications—Canadian, Australian, Indian—do not really reach out as widely as those of established American and British publishers."[21] Even though all these publications are in the English language, they reflect the relative power of their respective countries within specific politico-economic and cultural realities.

In our conversations and in our mandates to create networks of anthropologies, it is important for us to include a heightened sense of self-reflexivity and vigilance in order to avoid becoming victims of what we critique. As we celebrate the emerging efforts to decenter anthropology and as we forge better relations in world anthropologies, we need to be cognizant not only of the asymmetrical structures within which all anthropologies work but also of the tendency for academia to reproduce its own problematic structures. Not all national anthropologists work within an established association, and not all work outside a national mandate. Using an example of the practice of anthropology in Mexico, for instance, John Gledhill argues that "there are many countries in the South where anthropology enjoys no institutionalized existence and its practitioners find themselves obliged to teach and research about other matters."[22] My own research on the practice of anthropology in many African nations—where, for instance, anthropology remains largely a tool kit to be used by other more established disciplines—confirms this observation by Gledhill.[23] Numerous challenges abound, therefore, in our attempts to make the world anthropologies project successful.

A Ray of Hope

Things are, however, looking brighter regarding world anthropologies as more and more steps are being taken to make sure the momentum started at the turn of the century to make the project successful, remains active. In July 2008, for instance, Setha Low, then president of the AAA, attended the second meeting of the Association of Presidents and International Delegates of the WCAA in Osaka, Japan. Low agreed to serve on the WCAA organizing committee for four years "to signal AAA's commitment to recognizing and connecting diverse world anthropologies." Especially encouraging, Low remarked, was the added objective of "disseminating anthropological knowledge" because, with increased communication brought by the Internet, anthropological knowledge can travel and be utilized widely.[24] As I mention earlier in this chapter, the AAA's formation of the CWA further points to this momentum, but there is need for a sustained exploration and then concretization of this collaboration.

As a member of the CWA myself, I have been excited by the discussions we have had on how to make the AAA part of the larger body of world anthropologies through joint professional meetings, translation of research findings into multiple languages, participation in international meetings hosted by other anthropology associations, and so on. The CWA also has a column in the Anthropology News, with a specific focus on world anthropologies. What is even more exciting about the CWA is that it has the support of the past president of the AAA, Setha Low (2007–09), and the current president, Virginia Dominguez (2009–11)—both of whom are members of the commission. To be realistic, however, I must state that many of the proposals put forth by the CWA, WAN, and the WCAA will have to be undertaken with caution. Some tasks can be achieved faster and more efficiently than others. Having a shared Internet portal that builds and distributes information about world anthropological associations and their activities is, for instance, one way to achieve the goals of the world anthropologies project faster. Such an approach would, however, have to negotiate carefully a context of existing inequalities in Internet access and other related economic activities that different anthropologists bring to this table of collaboration. Not all anthropologists have access to computers or to the Internet, and although connecting them through an Internet portal may prove adequate only for a few, it would be an important step toward collaboration. Hosting joint annual meetings that require participants to travel outside their areas of normal operations (such as abroad, especially in areas where the cost of travel is still prohibitive for many) will be less practical. We must choose our tasks carefully and deliberately if we are to succeed. Having practiced as an anthropologist in Africa and as president of the PAAA, I can attest to the different strengths and challenges that anthropologists on the margins bring to the discipline. Many cannot afford to attend international conferences, have no easy access to current and relevant books and journals, and get virtually no research funds to carry out work in their specialties. True collaboration will have to be cognizant of and proactively engage with these realities. Such collaboration has also to work with existing structures established by associations such as the IUAES, which has the real potential to decenter hegemonic anthropology and create networks of world anthropologists.

Recent advances in technology have created numerous possibilities that can make some of these challenges achievable in due time. The sharing and distribution of research outcomes through open-source access to publications as well as joint research projects can be achievable with the right kind of goodwill and support across boundaries. Ultimately, for my own work, the goals of world anthropologies will become expanded when anthropologists from the margins study and write about anthropologists in the centers in reciprocal and equal terms and their work becomes central to the formation of the cannon. This book is one major step toward such a reality. To do this, however, anthropology has to be more about collaboration than cooptation, and this point brings me to my second thread of analysis, which I develop with an extended discussion of the practice of anthropology in Africa in a neoliberal era.

Anthropology and Other Disciplines

In a presidential address to the forty-ninth meeting of the African Studies Association held in San Francisco, November 16, 2006, historian Joseph Miller asked fellow Africanists to make explicit their commitment to reenvisioning the postmodern world by emphasizing Africa's cultural, political, and economic plurality and by building collaboration with African scholars and professionals in order to emphasize Africa's contribution to world cultures. Miller went on to share his hope that African studies scholars in the West would infuse their experiences and expertise of Africa in all disciplines. He gave the example of Clifford Geertz's profound contributions to the "intellectual vitality of different schools and departments as expressed by numerous scholars gathering at a conference in the University of Virginia in 2003" and, by extension, showed his colleagues that African studies can be infused in the Western academy in the same way.[25]

It is quite refreshing, at least to me as an Africanist anthropologist, that an anthropologist can have such profound influence on the Western academy (which itself has had a history of highly visible disciplinary boundaries) and that such influence can be a model to be emulated by Africanists through an appeal by a historian. It is also encouraging given that anthropology as a discipline continues to be dogged by its historical relations to Africa that often (and quite selectively) highlight its complacent relationship with colonialism and its dislocation from real political and economic challenges of specific countries in which anthropologists work. Yet anthropology's relevance and viability as a tool for understanding, recording, and even intervening in the socioeconomic and political changes occurring in Africa cannot be overemphasized. I want to argue here that while anthropology in Africa is ready to shed—and, in many ways, has already shed—the baggage of its attachment to colonialism, there still remain a number of roadblocks to the discipline's efficacy as a tool for writing and understanding Africa as well as a viable discipline in the African academy.

These roadblocks include three main issues that I will discuss at length here. The first is anthropology's research methodologies, which are predominantly relational and which, in turn, make our fieldwork interlocutors continually expect us to intervene positively in their immediate lived experiences—a role that we cannot always fulfill. The second is the assumption by many researchers that they can do ethnographic research and consequently reduce anthropology to a tool kit to be appropriated by other disciplines and not as a discipline to be embraced in its own right in the academy. And the third is the fact that anthropologists have not asserted themselves well enough to ward off various critiques of their disciplinary practices as well as to challenge those from other disciplines who do a poor job of ethnographic research and cross-cultural studies. At times anthropologists have quickly embraced critiques of their work, especially by postmodernists and, in the process, have thrown the baby out with the proverbial bath water. They have almost solely focused on the writing of ethnographies rather than the content of such ethnographies. This "narcissistic" turn in anthropology has made anthropology less "useful" for the expansion of issues pertaining to the people we study or the associations they belong to. Indeed, as Philippe Bourgois rightly states, "An ethnography that engages theory with politics in ways that are relevant to the people being studied has remained marginal to the overall discipline of anthropology."[26]

Anthropology and Its Dual Identity in Africa

Let me contextualize these three arguments with two stories that, although unrelated in terms of their sources or contexts, do tell a lot about anthropology and Africa today. When I arrived in Washington, D.C., for the 2004 American Anthropological Association conference, I took a cab from the airport and headed to my hotel. The driver of the cab I boarded was a man from Ethiopia who, I gauged, was in his mid-forties. We started a conversation about random things, and when I told him I was attending the annual anthropology meeting, he asked where I was from. I did not "speak like an American," he said. He was excited to know I was from Kenya and commented that our countries were neighbors. He then told me that he too was an anthropologist and that he was trained in Eastern Europe, where he had received a master's degree in archaeology, after having earned a bachelor's degree in anthropology in Ethiopia. Realizing he had captured my interest, he went on to tell me that he did not trust "Western anthropologists" because they "steal our continent's resources and put them in their museums and private collections." He shared an example of an incident in Ethiopia, in which a Western anthropologist had taken away artifacts from archaeological digs in Ethiopia with the intention of transporting them to his home country. His thievery was discovered at the airport, however, and he was relieved of the artifacts. I did not know how to respond to this piece of information, especially since it had become clear to me that the cab driver felt a certain level of contempt toward Western anthropologists. I wondered if, by telling me this, he was indirectly asking me to be cautious of "Western anthropologists" and, by extension, was expecting that as an African, I should actively work toward blocking such exploitation of the continent's artifacts.

The second story also refers to artifacts in East Africa but this time involves Western anthropologists intervening on behalf of local individuals and communities to return sacred objects taken from their homes and transported abroad. It is a story about two anthropologists—Linda Giles and Monica Udvardy—who have been involved in the process of pushing for the repatriation of the memorial statues commonly known as vigango, which are owned by the Mijikenda people of the East African coast. Both Monica and Linda have worked along the East African coast, using their ethnographic research to learn about local belief systems and practices.[27] Through their fieldwork, they came to know and befriend many local people, some of whom had their vigango taken away and sold to American collectors. Some of the artifacts have already been returned to their original homes, much to the joy of local Mijikenda. Monica and Linda's efforts together with those of others working with them, for instance, bore fruit in June 2007 when two vigango that belonged to the family of Kalume Mwakiru of Chalani village in Kilifi District in Kenya's coastal region were returned. When asked about the significance of the return, Kalume Mwakiru's family said that "it has suffered numerous tragedies in the last two decades including sickness, bad harvests and the death of their family patriarch. And they insist that this is because the two vigango were stolen from family graves."[28] The statues had been found at two different university museums, the Illinois State University Museum in Bloomington and the Hampton University Museum in Virginia—a fact that reveals an interesting relationship between universities, collectors, and cultural property.

These two stories of anthropologists in East Africa present us with anthropology's dual identities: it is represented and identified with those who take away (the takers) and with those who give back (the givers). In this case, the takers are exemplified by the anthropologist in Ethiopia described by the taxi driver, and the givers are exemplified by the efforts of Monica and Linda to return vigango to Kilifi. These qualities of taking and giving, I argue, are simultaneously embodied in each of us as anthropologists and vary only in degree to which they are stoked and mobilized. We often take away confidential information, images, and even artifacts from our fieldwork sites and bring them back to our institutions or homes to be used to enhance our careers and even our individual identities. We also give back to individuals and to our research communities various resources in the form of paid assistantships, limited medical assistance, collaborative and applied research to highlight local interests, and even new ways of seeing local realities.[29] In addition to acting in these dual roles, anthropologists often find themselves torn between their academic expectations and obligations and their local commitments and relationships in the field. Because of their close contact and rapport with people on the ground, anthropologists are expected to engage more closely and consistently with the local social realities. These expectations, together with anthropologist's successful research methods, have complicated rather than popularized anthropology in Africa. Let me explain.

Anthropology, Relationships, and Agency

Donna Haraway has rightly stated that all knowledge is relational.[30] But ethnographic research methods, in particular, embody relationality more perversely than do other social science research techniques because the ethnographic approach operates, as Gracia Clark has written, in a context of "intentional personal interaction."[31] Ethnographers stay with communities for long periods of time, learning their ways as they try to make sense of their research questions and social realities. In the process, anthropologists stumble over their own cultural, academic, and personal inadequacies that, when not masked or glossed over, help free ethnographies from any cosmetic presentations or cookie-cutter constructions of cultural realities. By acknowledging and even mobilizing their identities, fears, and inadequacies during fieldwork, anthropologists are able to produce credible ethnographies while also building strong relationships in the field, with colleagues, and even those with whom they usually do not interact.[32] Through these relationships, anthropologists not only share their own individuality in the field but also gain access to personal stories, fears, anxieties, experiences, perspectives, and other data from their interlocutors that allow for a comprehensive and holistic understanding of an individual, community, or even phenomenon. Such a research process and technique have, however, resulted in vehement challenges to ethnography's knowledge claims and have also led to situations where anthropologists are increasingly expected to intervene socially and politically on behalf of their research participants or interlocutors. In the colonial period, anthropologists created enmity with the elite, nationalist leaders, and even Western development advisers when the anthropologists doubted the validity of the development processes that African leaders and their foreign advisers wholeheartedly embraced.[33] Others were considered difficult folks to work with by colonial administrators.[34]

There is no doubt that anthropologists, often privileged by class and/or race, work with underprivileged and often disenfranchised communities and individuals—a situation that subsequently creates a context for expectations that the anthropologists will provide material assistance to research participants, in the same way that other nonlocal people in the community are expected to do. What is different for anthropologists, however, is the relational nature of their ethnographic methods that places them in contexts where much more is expected of them by their research participants. The fact that anthropologists get accepted into communities through being adopted into local kinship structures, and through being welcomed into the homes and lives of their interlocutors, means that anthropologists are subject to social expectations and obligations that prevail in the local social framework. As anthropologists, we pride ourselves in making real local connections, and through such connections, we are able to understand the sociocultural realities in communities with which we work. In the same way, we are quite often adopted into families, communities, and clans. Through such acceptance, we take up social and filial (fictive or otherwise) roles and obligations. Many of us can give numerous examples of inquiries and requests to assist our research participants, as well as other members in our research communities, with money or opportunities to go abroad. Some even get marriage proposals or are asked to intervene in the process of applying for travel documents to Europe and America. At times, some of our interlocutors may agree to work with us because of the benefits they believe they can access through such a relationship. We as anthropologists may also seek specific individuals in the research community because of the advantages to our research that we believe may accrue from such a relationship. This strategic approach to selecting interlocutors shows, as Gracia Clark aptly puts it, that the ethnographer and research participants both have "personal agendas" in the ethnographic project and that there are numerous social and personal negotiations that accompany anthropological work.[35] With such strong ties to acceptance and even agendas, it is no wonder that much more is expected of anthropologists than is imagined of scholars in other disciplines, where extended and intimate fieldwork is not the default research methodology.

Appropriating and Marginalizing Anthropology

Such an ethnographic method that entails expanded periods of time in the field engaging in participation, observation, interviewing, and negotiating everyday activities in a given location or community has been the quintessential defining practice of cultural anthropology. Even when sociologists engage in ethnography—as is common among those from the "Chicago School"—ethnographic methods have almost always been associated with anthropology. In Africa, where academic research has tended to demand immediate social and political application or applicability, the ethnographic method has had a very strong appeal but in a modified form that demands short-term research propelled by consultancies.[36] In this regard, anthropology and its strengths in ethnographic research are not only attractive but also greatly needed in Africa today. However, the sad part of this reality is that a number of times, our colleagues in sociology, political science, religion, and even communication studies have stepped in and taken up the role of anthropology by simply conducting ethnographic fieldwork or what they consider ethnographic research. This practice has greatly jeopardized the discipline.

It is almost as if our colleagues are asking why they should bother training in another discipline when they can take up its tools and improve their existing discipline. What is more, in a context of higher education in Africa (and elsewhere) where courses and disciplines are often gauged by their pragmatic value in enhancing economic progress (such as in getting jobs or solving social problems), anthropology as a discipline is at the risk of being ignored. Anthropology has not cultivated itself as a discipline to be associated with training graduates for work outside of academia. With very few anthropology degree-granting programs in Africa, the discipline must produce more anthropologists in order for it to survive. Such training must demonstrate a cognizance of prevailing human resource needs in Africa. The low percentage of trained anthropologists in higher education is not limited to Africa alone. It is quite telling, for instance, that in comparing the number of PhDs awarded in 2006 to students in anthropology and in sociology departments in North American and European institutions, there are more in sociology than in anthropology.[37] Yet my experience sitting in a search committee for tenure-track positions in both anthropology and sociology in a small liberal arts college in America in 2006 revealed a large number of anthropology applicants compared to the small number of applicants for the sociology position. Are we producing anthropologists who are able to find work only in academia, or are we not looking outside of academia for work? I am afraid the answer is not very flattering. There are a growing number of applied anthropology programs, but their numbers are really small compared to "pure" anthropology. And therein lies the problem: anthropology in Africa requires anthropological interventions in the applied realm, and very few anthropologists are being trained in the subdiscipline—even though the majority of anthropologists in Africa often end up in consultancies that require them to apply their anthropological skills in solving real social problems.

In East Africa, for instance, the largest number of anthropologists who are visibly active in and outside of academia are those in the subfield of applied anthropology, especially in medical anthropology, or those working in the field of reproductive health.[38] This they do through consultancies in health-related research especially in the areas of malaria and HIV/AIDS. If colleagues in other disciplines can carry out "anthropological research"—and there still exists the current paucity of applied anthropologists being trained— what will happen to the discipline? This question seems to be recognized by many anthropologists, and the anthropology program at the University of Kwazulu-Natal seems to give an interesting response. In the program that is based at the University's Howard College Campus, anthropology has three professors and five different courses that, although taught by anthropologists, are not strictly limited to anthropology. Indeed, out of the five courses, only one carries the word "anthropology" in its title: "Culture and Society in Africa," "Health and Socio-Cultural Context," "Understanding Families and Households," "Anthropology and Public Interest," and "Research plus Special Topic." As the Web page that describes the University's undergraduate anthropology program shows, this is a strategy to infuse anthropology into all other disciplinary perspectives and probably in response to the prevailing realities of the discipline on the ground:

> Five recently revised courses are offered, one first-year level course and four second and third year level courses. Instead of following the usual rule that you may major in a subject only if you have completed the three-year sequence, these courses require only that you have accumulated sufficient credits— whatever subjects—to be able to do the course at second and third level. This means that students who develop an interest in or need for our subject in the midst of their studies can still enter any of our courses.[39]

In this case, anthropology becomes a service discipline, assisting other disciplines to prepare students for the diverse and changing world and not graduating its own majors. It is also—at least judging by the language used here—presented as a discipline willing to create no hurdles in order to attract students.

A discipline that does not reproduce itself in the academy through majors is a dead discipline. Yet the scenario projected in the case of anthropology at Howard College is very instructive. On the one hand, it is showing that anthropological skills and techniques can and have been used successfully in other disciplines. In this regard, anthropology is the framework through which other disciplines can approach and understand contemporary Africa and its combination of social, economic, and political issues. On the other hand, it is a prediction of the eminent demise of anthropology as an academic discipline in Africa. I have argued elsewhere that as a recent entrant into the African academy, anthropology does not have a specific tradition, tending to reflect the traditions of the (Western) countries where African anthropologists are trained.[40] Given the high number of African anthropologists trained in Europe and North America, and the emphasis on academic (pure) anthropology in these programs where most Africans are trained, it is highly unlikely that such an anthropology would survive in Africa today. Zambian anthropologist Owen Sichone puts it bluntly when he says:

> Many African scholars dislike anthropology intensely. I have frequently heard many political scientists and economists insult each other by referring to aspects of their work as "anthropological." The tarnished reputation of the

discipline is blamed on anthropology having participated in the imperial strategy of divide and rule. But was anthropology the handmaiden of imperialism in a way that geology, cartography and land surveying were not? Christianity has continued to flourish in Africa despite its well-known contribution to European cultural imperialism. The reason for anthropology's bad name should be located in its own name.[41]

This nature of anthropology is its fascination with theory and academic jargonism that makes sense only to a selection of anthropologists. Anthropology started off as the only discipline willing to give voice to "non-modern" people living in rural areas.[42] But it will lose its usefulness in that sense if it stops recording the lives of those people (and of others) and instead translates them through obscure, irrelevant academic jargon.[43] No other enterprise has rendered anthropology useless in Africa as has the postmodern turn and its attendant literary rituals.

Reflexivity, Poetics of Ethnography, and the Demise of Anthropological Authority

I am convinced that anthropologists have been slightly cowed by the onslaught of postmodern critiques of ethnography and their ability to represent other people's social realities. As a result, there has emerged a certain level of second-guessing the anthropological enterprise itself—and, in turn, our own inability to assert the efficacy and value of the anthropological method to our colleagues in other disciplines. No doubt postmodern critiques have allowed for new and creative ways of regarding ethnography, but this is not totally new to anthropology. Although postmodernists' critiques of anthropology were highly acclaimed in the 1980s and '90s, anthropologists and other social scientists had earlier engaged issues of subjectivity (which are central to the postmodernist critique) and problems of meaning-making in cultural practices and encounters. As Melford Spiro argues, anthropologists allied with the "Culture and Personality School," such as Margaret Mead and Ruth Benedict, were already engaging with issues of subjectivity in ethnography.[44]

It was only when subjectivity became the central issue in the academy due to postmodernism that much more attention was paid to this well-established anthropological enterprise. To my knowledge, postmodernism was not enthusiastically embraced in Africa, least in African anthropology. As Tejumola Oliniyan states, "There are three major arguments against postmodernism from the perspective of its African critics: its de-centering of the subject, its privileging of culture, and its abstrusive language."[45] One of the major achievements made by postmodernist critiques of Western epistemology is the decentering of the European/Western grand narratives of history and civilization that have always placed Europe at the center and the rest of the world, especially Africa, at the margins. This decentering has finally acknowledged and maybe even embraced efforts by many African critics to fight Western political, economic, and cultural imperialism through anticolonial movements, negritude, and even alternative political arrangements such as those described in Julius Nyerere's Ujamaa: *The Basis of African Socialism* (1962) in Tanzania. Being part of this large Western hegemon of knowledge production in and of Africa, anthropology was negatively perceived alongside other Western disciplines but more so because of its perceived intimate relations with colonialism.[46]

During the euphoria of postmodernist critiques of Western academic enterprises, anthropology suffered yet another attack from African critics, especially as anthropology acknowledged and even embraced postmodern critiques of its methods. The late Archie Mafeje, for instance, argued that anthropology is a colonial project more than sociology, economics, and political science are because anthropology is "ontologically based on alterity that is racialized."[47] Indeed, much of anthropology's methodological framing has been shaped by an analysis of otherness and the study of the Other, the non-Western object. Yet alterity, especially as framed by Western scholarship and imagination toward Africa and Africans, has been the dominant Western epistemology—and not just in anthropology. If anything, as Immanuel Wallerstein has argued, anthropology's focus on the Other is a product of the larger Western academic division of labor that, in the nineteenth century, allocated the study of modern European and European-settler states to economists, historians, political scientists, and sociologists; non-Western areas with a long-standing culture to "orientalists"; and "backward" peoples to anthropologists.[48] In this way, anthropology is but a piece of a larger Western epistemological grand plan that was grounded in a Eurocentric regard and understanding of the world. Indeed, as Bernard McGrane has argued, Western perception and, specifically, its subsequent relationship to the alterity of Africa has been consistent in all disciplines and can be seen through an archaeology of Western epistemology. McGrane says, for instance, that before the eighteenth century, "it was Christianity which came between the European and non-European Other. Anthropology did not exist; there was, rather, demonology, and it was upon this horizon that the Other took on his historically specific meaning."[49]

McGrane identifies this Christian regard of the non-European Other, including Africa, within four paradigms that shape the dominant Western epistemology—theological, enlightenment, sociological, and cultural. Demonology falls under the theological paradigm, and it dominated European thinking until it was challenged and replaced by the Enlightenment, which emphasizes alterity as based on superstition and the lack of a scientific worldview. In the nineteenth century, when anthropology comes to life, the dominant paradigm is a sociological one that regards human societies within an evolutionary continuum, in which the Other—especially the African—is located at the base of the social ladder, while the European Other is at the peak. The prevalence, for instance, of Edward B. Taylor's ideas on social evolution is grounded in this sociological paradigm. Finally, within the cultural paradigm of the twentieth century, alterity was based not on a continuum but on ways of living in which Africans were different because they had a different culture. In this most recent paradigm, postmodernism found its foothold—whereby, as Emmanuel Katongole says, "there is something sinister about the postmodern celebration of difference, which at the same time renders differences ineffectual or inconsequential. In other words, the ability to recognize otherness and difference everywhere might just as well amount to an ironic shielding of oneself from listening or attending to the particular and historical claims of the 'other.'"[50] Reflecting upon the influence of postmodernism on anthropology, Thomas Eriksen asserts: "Postmodernism taught a generation of anthropologists to dissect the menu without bothering to look at the banalities of food; it concentrates on the wallpaper patterns instead of the quality of the woodwork."[51] This misplaced focus would seem to lead to African anthropology's own undoing or, at least, to the lack of a vibrant culture of African anthropology.

Anthropology in Africa has to continually focus on the "food" and "woodwork" instead of the "menu" and "wallpaper patterns" because as a discipline anthropology in Africa cannot afford to major in the minors. The African academy is in its infancy, and cannot pursue the same issues or theories that preoccupy its counterparts in the West. Furthermore, how can anthropology subscribe to postmodern notions of problematizing representations of peoples and their lives, just when Africans (who have been subjected to sustained anthropological inquiry) are gaining ground on attempts at self-representation? How can cynicism toward all claims to truth and skepticism toward all political positions be embraced by Africans struggling to keep their academic departments alive? Melford Spiro cites Marcelo M. Suarez-

Orozco as having asked "how can such an anthropology [that has an affair with subjectivity] be of use to our understanding—and dismantling—of ethnic cleansings, rape camps, and torture camps?"[52]

For anthropology to be relevant and survive in the African academy, it has to do more in solving problems or suggesting concrete solutions to social challenges and do less of a "dance" with subjectivities and poetics of its writing culture.[53] If it does not close the gap between theory and practice, anthropology will have no practical value in Africa and will be reduced to what Paul Zeleza refers to as "the superficial travelogues" of "foreign fly-by-night academic tourists."[54]

Culture has been and continues to be the mainstay of anthropology (especially sociocultural anthropology), and postmodernists' privileging of culture could be an added advantage to anthropology's role in the academy. However, instead of focusing on historicized actions and events of culture as many African scholars have, postmodernists prefer to use discourse, narratives, and symbolic relations—thereby privileging subjectivity over, in Tejumola Olaniyan's words, "the concrete sociopolitical struggles that most African scholars believe to be where the solution to the continent's unending exploitation by the West lies."[55] If and when anthropology embraces the abstrusive language of postmodernism highlighting the poetics of ethnography and self instead of Cliford Geertz's "thick descriptions" of the everyday lives of real people in real places, then it will have gone astray. It will have reflected, as Olaniyan writes, "its disconnection with the lives of the masses, for whom such language is nothing but another characteristic and incomprehensible indulgence on the part of university eggheads who do no real labor."[56]

Should all anthropology in Africa be located in applied research? Not quite. What these critiques subtly reveal are the material differences that exist between many African scholars and their Western counterparts and between the associations they represent as I have shown above. Western scholars, it may seem, can have the luxury of an academic activity centered around discourse and narrative because their basic human needs as well as their professional needs are met. In many African institutions, many scholars can barely survive due to many economic challenges that they face and that often force them to devote much of their time to paid consultancies that do not allow for theoretical and interpretive rigor enjoyed by their Western counterparts. In order for African anthropology and, by implication, World anthropologies, to grow and thrive, there must be a change in the material and economic reality of its practitioners. Further, anthropology has to grow as a discipline through academic programs and courses, with students graduating with majors in anthropology. African anthropologists also have to start placing more priority on the life of the mind (buying books, attending professional meetings, and joining professional associations) whenever they have some disposable income. Books, academic journals, and professional meetings must be on their priority lists when they are making decisions about how to spend such funds. The more established anthropologists in America and other economically stronger countries will in turn have to collaborate with these other anthropologists for the survival of the discipline. Their fates are intricately tied together.

Notes

Preface

1. For a more developed discussion of Kenyatta and anthropology, see Ntarangwi, Mills, and Babiker (2006), especially pp. 13–16, and Ntarangwi (2008).

2. At the time, I read Evans-Pritchard's *The Nuer* (Oxford University Press, 1969); Fortes's *African Political Systems* (Routledge, 1994); Marcus and Fisher's *Anthropology as Cultural Critique* (University of Chicago Press, 1986); Clifford's *The Predicament of Culture* (Harvard University Press, 1988); and Mohanty, Russo, and Torres's *Third World Women and the Politics of Feminism* (Indiana University Press, 1991).

3. Malinowski (1938:vii).

4. Rabinow (1986:241).

5. While I agree with Faye Harrison's rendition of the "Anglo-French axis" (2009:235) by which she means English and French have dominated mainstream anthropology for a time, there are many other anthropological traditions in such locations as Denmark, Germany, Holland, and Norway, where anthropologists have produced and continue to produce important anthropological literature, especially on the subject of Africa and Africans.

Chapter 1: Imagining Anthropology, Encountering America

1. See, for instance, Geertz (1973), Gottlieb and Graham (1994), Behar and Gordon (1995), Dettwyler (1994), Nathan (2005), Ortner (1997), and Yu (1997).

2. Examples include Clark (2004), D'Amico-Samuels (1991), Harrison (1991), Page (1988), Reagon (1983), B. Smith (1984), and Ulysse (2002).

3. Notable here is James Clifford, whose 1988 critique *The Predicament of Culture* is not far-fetched, given that anthropologists Richard and Sally Price, Margery Wolf, Michael Jackson, Oliver La Farge, and many others have written commendable works

of fiction that often borrow from their own ethnographic fieldwork. Kirin Narayan (1999) also has a good analysis of ethnography and fiction worth reading.

4. Exemplified by the work of Lila Abu-Lughod (1991).

5. Exemplified by such works as those by Dettwyler (1994), Gottlieb and Graham (1994), and Yu (1997).

6. Some exceptions here include Behar and Gordon (1995), Harrison (2008), Frankenberg (1993), Nathan (2005), and Ortner (2003).

7. World Anthropologies Network Collective (2006:9).

8. See Geertz (1973).

9. See Spiro (1996).

10. See Harrison (2008).

11. Ibid.

12. Nader (1969).

13. Harrison (2008:1).

14. Drake (1978, 1980, 1987), Harrison (1991, 1992, 1995).

15. I stumbled upon these anthropologists when I first read Faye Harrison's edited volume *Decolonizing Anthropology*, initially published in 1991.

16. Harrison (2008:1).

17. See Ntarangwi (2003b).

18. By the time, I had already decided to look at graduate programs in America, where my favorite professors at Kenyatta University had been trained. Furthermore, given the other options I had for graduate school training abroad (in Britain or Germany), America was economically and culturally more attractive, particularly because it included the possibility of my getting a research or teaching assistantship.

19. My case was taken up by Professor Nyaigotti-Chacha, who argued that my project was well within the purview of Swahili cultural studies.

20. Geertz (2000:ix).

21. This path to anthropology is not unusual, as I came to find out later. Roy Rappaport, for instance, had come into anthropology after many years of working in the hospitality field running a country inn in Massachusetts. He went on to teach anthropology at the University of Michigan and even became president of the AAA.

22. Bruner (1984, 1991, 2005), Geertz (1973, 1974, 1983), Gottlieb (1982, 1997, 2004), Ortner (1983, 1997, 1999), E. Turner (1985), and V. W. Turner (1967, 1974, 1980).

23. Spencer (1996).

24. Ortner (1984:129).

25. Ortner (1984:131).

26. Geertz (1973), Turner (1984).

27. See, for instance, Abu-Lughod (1991), Clifford and Marcus (1986), Mafeje (1998a), Magubane (1971, 1973), Thornton (1988), and Marcus (1998), among many others.

28. See, for instance, Said's (1978) critique of Orientalism.

29. See Turner (1974, 1980).

30. Ortner (2005:36).

31. See, for instance, Ntarangwi (2003, 2009).

32. See Clifford (1988) and Clifford and Marcus (1986) for examples.

33. A casual review of anthropology papers presented at the AAA annual meetings, as well as new anthropology books published between 2002 and 2006, confirms my view here that anthropology (at least sociocultural anthropology) remains a discipline in pursuit of the Other. Even in cases where there are studies of Western communities, these analyses tend to focus on minority populations—or on what would be considered alterities, such as different sexual orientations and alternative work arrangements such as drug dealing and prostitution.

34. See Schneider (2006).

35. See, for instance, Clifford and Marcus (1986), Goffman (1989), Harrison (1991, 1995, 2008), Jackson (1999), Mafeje (1996, 1997, 1998a, 1998b), Owusu (1978), and Van Maanen (1988).

36. For the exceptions, see, for instance, Buck (2001), DeVita and Armstrong (2002), Di Leonardo (1984), Dominguez (1986), Frankenberg (1993), Hartigan (2005), Nathan (2005), and Ortner (2003).

37. See, for instance, H. Lewis (1999) and MacClancy (2002).

38. Examples, among many others, are Asad (1975), Chilungu (1976), Mafeje (1996, 1997, 1998a), Magubane (1971, 1973), Nzimiro (1979), Owusu (1978, 1979, 1986), Said (1978), and Sichone (2001).

39. Examples are Clifford and Marcus (1986), Fabian (1983), Goddard (1972), Gupta and Ferguson (1997a, 1997b), Harrison (1991), Hymes (1972), and Rigby (1996).

40. See Mudimbe (1988, 1994).

41. See, for instance, DeVita and Armstrong (2002) and Kim (1977).

42. See Ogbu (1974, 1978, 2003).

43. See Harrison (2008).

44. See, for instance, a list of scholarly works focusing on North America available at http://sananet.org/bibliography.html. This list came as a result of a SANA graduate-student caucus at the 1997 AAA annual, meetings where a need to develop such a bibliography was raised.

45. See the introductory chapter in Grinker and Steiner's 1997 volume *Perspectives on Africa,* which contains forty-four selected essays on Africa by scholars from different disciplines and geographic locations.

46. These figures were gathered from information available on the department Web sites of four institutions: University of Chicago (http://anthropology.uchicago.edu/faculty/), Princeton University (http://www.princeton.edu/anthropology/faculty/), Washington University in St. Louis (http://artsci.wustl.edu/~anthro/anthfac2.html), and University of Michigan (http://www.lsa.umich.edu/anthro/faculty_staff/index .htm).

47. Harrison (1997:5–6).

48. See Spivak (1988).

49. Harrison (2008:25).

50. See Geertz (1985).

51. See Mazrui's "Islam and Acculturation in East Africa's Experience," a lecture given at the National Defense College of Kenya (near Nairobi), on July 27, 2004 (online at http://igcs.binghamton.edu/igcs_site/dirton20.htm).

52. See Clifford and Marcus (1986) and Fabian (1983).

53. Marcus and Fischer (1986).

54. Carroll (1987:9).

55. Medicine (2001).

56. For an anthropological account of my teaching these students in Kenya, see Ntarangwi (2006), chapter 11.

Chapter 2: Tripping on Race, Training Anthropologists

1. See Mafeje (1998b:95).

2. I am cognizant of the role played by such entities as research agencies that decide what research will be funded and why, and I understand that this role shapes trends in the profession. Yet I am also aware of the power of the discipline to reproduce itself through course offerings and textbook content.

3. Throughout this text of this book, whenever I use the term *America,* it will denote the United States unless I indicate otherwise.

4. See Frankenberg (1993).

5. Many scholars have written about White flight and the economic resegregation of residential spaces in the United States. See, for instance, Anderson (1992), Bourgois (2002b), Di Leonardo (1998), Drake (1990), and Sacks (1974).

6. I was a little disappointed when I read Allison Truitt and Stefan Senders's edited volume *Money: Ethnographic Encounters* (published in 2007 by Berg Publishers), especially because the volume does not devote any serious attention to informant-ethnographer asymmetrical relations produced by money that the anthropologists bring to the field.

7. See, for instance, Anderson (1992) and Bourgois (2002a).

8. See Abu-Lughod (1991), Clifford (1988), Geertz (1973).

9. See, for instance, Appadurai (1996), Gupta and Ferguson (1997a, 1997b), Marcus (1998), Narayan (1999), and Ortner (1997).

10. See Ogbu (1974, 1978).

11. See Sterk (2000).

12. Obbo (1990:291).

13. See Miner (1956).

14. See Ntarangwi (2003b), especially chapter 1.

15. This was the second time I learned of intentional discussion groups comprised of

African Americans meeting to focus on race. I wondered if Whites, as the dominant race, would have weekly or monthly meetings to discuss race. For many of them, the issue of race was not part of their everyday predicament, so there may have been no urgency to have such a discussion.

16. Di Leonardo (2009).

17. Frankenberg (1993:147).

18. Monzo and Rueda (2009:21).

Chapter 3: Of Monkeys, Africans, and the Pursuit of the Other

1. Harrison (2008:19).

2. Harrison (2008:22).

3. Quoted in Harrison (2000:xiv).

4. Examples here include Marcus and Fisher (1986) and Said (1978).

5. Edmond (1993).

6. The spring 2009 issue of *Transforming Anthropology* is devoted to the study of Whiteness and shows how, despite the fact that Americans have elected their first Black president, race is still an insidious cancer that continues to gnaw at the social fabric of the United States.

7. Visweswaran (1998:70). I would argue, however, that the recent Race Project, spearheaded by the AAA (http://www.aaanet.org/resources/A-Public-Education-Program.cfm), has clearly centered the discussion of race and racism within anthropology.

8. Marcus (1992:vii).

9. Frankfurt (2005:63).

10. See Lutz (1995).

11. See Harrison (2008) for a discussion of the importance of story and fiction as theoretical interpretive frames and explanations often used by black women writing about culture and power dynamics involved in cultural, racial, and gendered differences. In an earlier essay (1990), Harrison discusses the value of using stories and first-person narratives in teaching anthropology courses dealing with dynamics of social justice and community building.

12. Graff (2003: 134).

13. Du Bois (1955:1237).

14. Ibid.

15. Nachbar and Lause (1992:90).

16. D. Lewis (1973:589–90).

17. See Landman (1978). For a global overview of this phenomenon, see Baba (1998).

18. "Purpose and Vision," Society for Applied Anthropology, http://www.sfaa.net/sfaagoal.html.

19. See, for instance, hooks (1994), where she talks about her experiences as a

young Black female attending a predominantly White school and being unable to bring her Southern cultural practices to bear in a classroom shaped by White middle-class values.

20. Harrison (2008:271).

21. See, for instance, the work of John Ogbu (2003, 1978), in which he shows how minority students disengage from their academic experiences so as not to be assimilated into mainstream American culture.

22. This paucity of anthropological studies of the corporatization of academia continues despite calls for such studies by Baer (1995).

23. Faye Harrison's chapter "Academia, the Free Market, and Diversity" in her 2008 book is a much-needed voice in this research area, but the subject still remains a fertile ground for anthropological inquiry. Also, even though many anthropologists work outside academia, the AAA is dominated by anthropologists working in higher education and thus providing them ample opportunities to study their work places—their students, colleagues, and institutions.

24. See Harrison (2008:272) for an example of how a Black female professor was harassed by White students because of her insistence on teaching about the subtle workings of racism.

25. Cornwell (2005:3).

26. R. T. Smith (1984:467).

27. Ortner (2006:20).

28. Gans (1999:39).

29. See Ortner (2006).

30. Rebekah Nathan (2005) has attempted this kind of ethnography by enrolling in her university as a student and seeing the classroom and the entire college from a student's perspective.

31. Ortner (2006).

32. hooks (1994:178).

33. See Ortner (1991:169–72).

34. MacLaren (1987:75).

35. See Ramos (1992).

36. MacClancy (2002).

37. See Asad (1975), Magubane (1971, 1973), Mafeje (1996, 1997, 1998b), and Said (1978), for some examples of this discussion.

38. David McCurdy (2006:433) gives an example of an anthropologist consultant hired by a utility company to find out why suburban customers were failing to reduce their consumption of natural gas, even though their questionnaire responses indicated an attempt at conservation. To gather information, the anthropologist conducted ethnographic interviews with several families and also installed video cameras aimed at the thermostats in private homes. The interviews and video recordings came in handy in the absence of the participant observation that often defines many studies of the Other in places away from home.

39. A good example here is Sherry Ortner, who did most of her research in Nepal before switching to New Jersey to study her high school graduating class

40. Löfgren (1989:366).

41. D'Alisera (1999:6).

42. D'Alisera (1997:5–6).

43. D'Alisera (1997:55–56).

44. See Stoller (1999, 2002).

45. For instance, Stoller (1995, 1997, 2004).

46. D'Alisera (1997:57).

47. Gupta and Ferguson (1997a).

48. Davies (1999:156).

49. As an author myself, I am aware that the final title of a book is not entirely the decision of the author and could have been decided for marketing purposes in a process that Caplan had no control over.

50. George Stocking (1995) is one such scholar.

51. See Mafeje (1996) and Moore (1998).

52. Mafeje (1998b: 95).

Chapter 4: Remembering Home, Contrasting Experiences

1. One's level of education seems to determine the income he or she can earn at a job even in the United States, where those with only a high school diploma tend to earn significantly less than those with a college degree.

2. In Kenya and Tanzania, for instance, the Maasai are considered the most traditional and resistant to Westernization. Interestingly, they are also overwhelmingly represented in security jobs for both private and public premises and for homes, especially in urban areas.

3. Newman (1988:9).

4. McAlister (2002:16). In her statement here, McAlister quotes from *Nations Unbound: Transnational Projects, Postcolonial Predicaments, and Deterritorialized Nation-States,* by Linda Basch, Nina Glick Schiller, and Christina Szanton Blanc (London: Routledge, 2003), p. 7.

5. Now that I have had a chance to travel in Europe, the United States, and many African countries, I have come to realize that each location has its own share of rich and poor people and that there are Kenyans who are wealthier than the majority of Europeans and Americans. However, in terms of relative wealth, Westerners are wealthier than Africans, and only a few Africans can afford to be tourists, even in their own countries.

6. Second-hand clothes were banned in Kenya until the early 1990s—a fact that may explain why this particular scholar found it particularly important to bring home some clothes from the United States. Despite the ban, however, second-hand clothes were available in Kenya from the 1970s, but illegally.

7. See Karen Tranberg Hansen's (2004) analysis of the transnational flow of second-hand clothes in Africa (and especially in countries like Kenya), which on the one hand imports used clothes and, on the other, exports new clothes to the American market under the quota system provided by the African Growth and Opportunity Act.

8. See Ferguson (2002).

9. Mwenda (2006:6).

10. Onyango-Ouma (2006) offers an intriguing discussion of the challenges he faced as an anthropologist conducting research in his own community. The social expectations bestowed upon him as an insider and his own desire to remain an outsider in order to stay true to his anthropological analysis led to a number of ethical challenges.

11. Anthropologically speaking, the matatu is a symbol of the transport industry in Kenya. With numerous residential areas coming up faster than the city authorities can plan for, the matatu has been brought in to fill the needs of a growing commuter base in a city with few commuter options or no public bus system. Indeed, the convenience of stopping anywhere and at any time, common with matatu, fits very well within an unplanned urban development phenomenon.

12. See Jennifer Hasty's (2005) discussion of corruption as a social rather than private phenomenon that occurs because of certain sociocultural contexts of power and privilege.

13. See, for example, Parikh (2007) for more on this phenomenon.

14. The term *Meru* stands for the people, the major city in the region, and an administrative district. The people are called the Ameru; the city, Meru Town; and the region, Meru District.

15. While I present this very positive attribute of the concept of *Harambee,* I might just note that at times the success of Harambee has meant that people have used it as private solutions to public problems and let the government off the hook in providing public resources to its citizens. In 2003 the government, under President Kibaki, weakened the Harambee movement by channeling development monies from the government to local communities through what became the Constituency Development Fund (CDF). This redirection of public funds through the CDF has meant that politicians cannot use their participation in public fundraising as an indication of their leadership credibility.

16. In 2003, the government, through the ministry of Transport and Communication, streamlined the matatu industry, and now the vehicles are not overloaded as they were in the 1990s.

17. For some examples of how anthropologists use the concept of imagination to explain various cultural phenomena, see Abu-Lughod (1997), Comaroff and Comaroff (1999), and Weiss (2002).

18. See Ntarangwi, Mills, and Babiker (2006).

19. While I am especially familiar with institutions in Zimbabwe, Uganda, Kenya, Tanzania, Ghana, South Africa, and Botswana, a review of African universities on

the Web (http://library.stanford.edu/depts/ssrg/africa/africaneducation/african-universities.html) confirms this fact.

20. Obbo (2006:159).

21. Quoted in Amuyunzu-Nyamongo (2006:245).

22. See Onyango-Ouma (2006).

23. Onyango-Ouma (2006:253).

24. Onyango-Ouma (2006:254).

25. Obbo (2006:158).

26. See Ntarangwi (2003a) and Obbo (2006) for some examples of this argument.

27. Today, almost twenty years after that summer I returned from Kenya, communication in the United States has turned more to electronic media, but there still is substantial use of paper for flyers on college campuses.

28. According to Timothy Jones (2006:3), on average American households waste food worth $43 billion annually.

Chapter 5: Mega-Anthropology

1. See Holmes and Marcus (2005, 2006). The argument of these two authors mirrors that put forth by some elite Africans (see Christine Obbo [2006]) who feel there is no need to engage the rural populace in any research because they assume they can represent the views of these less sophisticated people.

2. Lanthrop (2006:18).

3. Restrepo and Escobar (2005:100).

4. Degregori (2006:466).

5. See Ntarangwi, Mills, and Babiker (2006), especially the book's introductory chapter, for a critical analysis of the practice of anthropology in Africa today.

6. A commentary on this special meeting is reported by Kofi Akosah-Sarpong in a story titled "Awakening the Sleeping Ghana via Its Elites" (available online at http://www.ghanadot.com/commentary.akosah.maxwell.082508.html).

7. Turner (2005:6).

8. De Castro (2002:307).

9. See De Castro (2002:306).

10. Quoted in Graff (2003:145).

11. Graff (2003:146).

12. "Executive Board Motions Regarding Meeting Locations," American Anthropological Association, http://www.aaanet.org/meetings/loc_policies.cfm.

13. Harrison (2008:25).

14. See Ntarangwi, Mills, and Babiker (2006).

15. This use of anthropology as a toolkit for servicing other disciplines is not limited to Africa . In my current institution in the United States, I teach an introductory course in cultural anthropology for general education requirements. My institution, Calvin College, does not have a major or minor in anthropology.

16. "What We Do," Jacobs Strategies, http://www.jacobsstrategies.com/services
.php#Ethnographic%20Studies/.

17. "Short History of ASA," Association of Social Anthropologists of the UK and
Commonwealth, http://www.theasa.org/history.htm.

18. "Membership & Donations," American Anthropological Association, http://
www.theasa.org/rulesproc.htm.

19. "Short History of ASA" (see note 17, above).

20. "Membership Categories," American Anthropological Association, http://dev
.aaanet.org/membership/popupprofessionaleligibility.cfm.

Chapter 6: A New Paradigm for
Twenty-First-Century Anthropology?

1. Harrison (2008:2).

2. "Institute Of Anthropology, Gender & African Studies [sic]," "History Of The
Institute," University of Nairobi, http://www.uonbi.ac.ke/faculties/?fac_code=48.

3. In the United States, the field of African studies was greatly shaped by the work
of anthropologists—a fact that has been discussed by many scholars, including Southall (1983), Guyer (1996), and Moore (1994). In Kenya, however, anthropology as a
major was instrumentally initiated by presidential decree in the 1980s, as I discuss
in Ntarangwi (2008).

4. Wallerstein (1983:155).

5. Robinson (2003:7).

6. Title VI of the Civil Rights Act of 1964 protects against discrimination based on
race, religion, or nationality and is connected to the National Defense Educational
Act, which developed foreign language and area studies centers in major universities in the United States. From these two federal acts the African Studies Centers
emerged.

7. Gershenhorn (2004:xii).

8. Martin and West (1999:88), quoting from Kenneth Robert Janken's *Rayford W.
Logan and the Dilemma of the African-American Intellectual* (Amherst: University
of Massachusetts Press, 1993), p. 95.

9. See Rothstein (2008).

10. See Baba (1998:315).

11. World Anthropologies Network Collective (2006:9).

12. Stocking (1982:180).

13. See Ntarangwi (2008).

14. Marcus (2008:202).

15. See the further discussion of this reality in Ntarangwi, Mills, and Babiker
(2006).

16. See Ribeiro (2005).

17. See "World Anthropologies: Strengthening the International Organization and

Effectiveness of the Profession," Pan African Anthropological Association, http://www.upe.ac.za/paaa/world_council.htm.

18. Valenzuela and Molina (2007).

19. Ribeiro (2005:5).

20. Hannerz (2008:220).

21. Hannerz (2008:226).

22. Gledhill (2005:6).

23. See Ntarangwi (2007).

24. Low (2008:67).

25. Miller (2007:22).

26. Bourgois (2002a:417).

27. See the discussion of this reality in Udvardy, Giles, and Mitsanze (2003).

28. "Kenyans Fete Repatriated Relics," by Odiambo Joseph (BBC News, Chalani, Kenya, June 22, 2007), available online at http://news.bbc.co.uk/2/hi/africa/6231134.stm. See also Udvardy (1990, 1992, 2001) and Giles (1987, 1989, 1995, 1999).

29. See Gottlieb and Graham (1994) and Clark and Manuh (1991).

30. See Haraway (1988:581).

31. Clark (2009:7).

32. See B. Smith (1984), Reagon (1983), Harrison (1991), Page (1988), Ulysse (2002), and D'Amico-Samuels (1991).

33. See Southall (1983).

34. See Mills (2006).

35. Clark (2005).

36. See Ntarangwi, Mills, and Babiker (2006).

37. In the summer of 2008, I conducted research that yielded the following figures for the year 2006: in the United States, 885 PhDs were awarded in anthropology, as compared to 2,967 in sociology; 620 of those 885 degrees (65 percent) in anthropology were specifically awarded in cultural anthropology.

38. See Ntarangwi (2008).

39. "What Is Anthropology?" Department of Anthropology, Howard College Campus, University of KwaZulu-Natal, http://www.ukzn.ac.za/department/default.asp?dept=anthround.

40. See Ntarangwi (2008).

41. Sichone (2001:370; emphasis added).

42. See Obbo (2006).

43. See Sichone (2001).

44. See Spiro (1996).

45. Olaniyan (2003:40).

46. I use the term *perceived* here to show that anthropology and anthropologists were not always intimately connected to colonialism because at times anthropology was quite opposed to colonialism and colonial administrators disliked anthropologists. See Mills (2006) for specific examples of this phenomenon.

47. Mafeje (1998a:3).
48. Wallerstein (1983:155).
49. McGrane (1989:77).
50. Katongole (2000:240).
51. Eriksen (2006:25–26).
52. Marcelo M. Suarez-Orozco, "Terror at the Fin de Siecle: The Systematization of Hatred in a Paranoid Era" (unpublished manuscript, 1994); cited in Spiro (1996:776).
53. In no way am I minimizing the value of focusing on the production of anthropological knowledge; I am only highlighting the real demands for not only anthropology but many other disciplines in Africa today.
54. Zeleza (1997:iv).
55. Olaniyan (2003:42).
56. Ibid.

Bibliography

Abu-Lughod, L. 1991. "Writing against Culture." In R. G. Fox, ed., *Recapturing Anthropology: Working in the Present*, pp. 137–62. Santa Fe, N.Mex.: School of American Research Press.

———. 1997. "The Interpretation of Culture after Television." *Representations* 59: 109–34.

Amuyunzu-Nyamongo, M. 2006. "Challenges and Prospects for Anthropology in Kenya." In Ntarangwi, Mills, and Babiker, *African Anthropologies*, pp. 237–49.

Anderson, E. 1992. *Streetwise: Race, Class, and Change in an Urban Community*. Chicago: University of Chicago Press.

Appadurai, A. 1996. *Modernity at Large: Cultural Dimensions of Globalization*. Minneapolis: University of Minnesota Press.

Asad, T. 1975. *Anthropology and the Colonial Encounter*. London: Ithaca Press.

Baba, M. L. 1998. "Creating a Global Community of Practicing Anthropologists." *Human Organization* 57(3): 315—18.

Baer, Hans A. 1995. "Commentary: Elitism and Discrimination within Anthropology." *Practicing Anthropology* 17(1–2): 42–43.

Baudrillard, J. 1994. *Simulacra and Simulation* (S. F. Glaser, trans.). Ann Arbor: Michigan University Press.

Behar, R., and Gordon, D. A., eds. 1995. *Women Writing Culture*. Berkeley: University of California Press.

Beidelman, T. O. 1997. *The Cool Knife: Imagery of Gender, Sexuality, and Moral Education in Kaguru*. Washington, D.C.: Smithsonian Institution Press.

Bošković, A., ed. *Other People's Anthropologies: Ethnographic Practice on the Margins*. New York: Berghahn Books.

Bourgois, P. I. 2002a. "Ethnography's Troubles and the Reproduction of Academic Habitus." *International Journal of Qualitative Studies in Education* 15(4): 417–20.

———. 2002b. *In Search of Respect: Selling Crack in El Barrio.* Cambridge: Cambridge University Press.

Bruner, E. M. 2005. *Culture on Tour: Ethnographies of Travel.* Chicago: University of Chicago Press.

———.1991. "The Transformation of Self in Tourism." *Annals of Tourism Research* 18(2): 238–50.

———, ed. 1984. *Text, Play, and Story: The Construction and Reconstruction of Self and Society.* Prospect Heights, Ill.: Wavelength Press.

Buck, P. D. 2001. *Worked to the Bone: Race, Class, Power, and Privilege in Kentucky.* New York: Monthly Review Press.

Caplan, P. 1997. *African Voices, African Lives: Personal Narratives from a Swahili Village.* London: Routledge.

Carroll, R. 1987. *Cultural Misunderstandings: The French-American Experience* (C. Volk, trans.) Chicago: University of Chicago Press.

Chilungu, S. 1976. "Issues in the Ethics of Research Method: an Interpretation of Anglo-American Perspective." *Current Anthropology* 17(3): 457–81.

Clark, G. 2009. *African Market Women: Seven Life Stories from Ghana.* Bloomington: Indiana University Press.

———. 2005. "Accountability and Authority in Africanist Anthropology." Unpublished paper presented at the annual meeting of the American Anthropological Association, Washington, D.C.

Clark, G., and Manuh, T. 1991. "Women Traders in Ghana and the Structural Adjustment Program." In C. Gladwin, ed., *Structural Adjustment and African Women Farmers,* pp. 217–38. Gainesville: University of Florida Press.

Clifford, J. 1988. *The Predicament of Culture: Twentieth-Century Ethnography, Literature, and Art.* Cambridge, Mass.: Harvard University Press.

‣ Clifford, J., and Marcus, G. E., eds. 1986. *Writing Culture: The Poetics and Politics of Ethnography.* Berkeley: University of California Press.

Comaroff, J. L., and Comaroff, J., eds. 1999. *Civil Society and the Political Imagination in Africa.* Chicago: University of Chicago Press.

Combs-Schilling, M. E. 1989. *Sacred Performance: Islam, Sexuality, and Sacrifice.* New York: Columbia University Press.

Cornwell, G. 2005. "Cultivating Intentionality in Student Learning." Unpublished paper presented at May Faculty College, St. Lawrence University, Canton, N.Y.

D'Alisera, J. 1999. "Field of Dreams: The Anthropologist Far Away at Home." *Anthropology and Humanism* 24(1): 5–19. Available online at http://www.projectpast.org/jcbrandon/courses/1023H/readings/DAlisera99.pdf.

———. 1997. "The Transnational Search for Muslim Identity: Sierra Leoneans in America's Capital." Unpublished PhD dissertation, University of Illinois at Urbana-Champaign.

D'Amico-Samuels, D. 1991. "Undoing Fieldwork: Personal, Political, Theoretical and Methodological Implications." In F. V. Harrison, ed., *Decolonizing Anthropology:*

Moving Further toward an Anthropology for Liberation, pp. 68–87. Washington, D.C.: American Anthropological Association.

Davies, C. A. 1999. *Reflexive Ethnography: A Guide to Researching Selves and Others.* London: Routledge.

De Castro, E. D. 2002. "Cosmological Deixis and Amerindian Perspectivism." In M. Lambek, ed., *A Reader in the Anthropology of Religion*, pp. 307–26. Malden, Mass.: Blackwell.

Degregori, C. I. 2006. "Responses to '"Other Anthropologies and Anthropology Otherwise"': Steps to a World Anthropologies Framework' by Eduardo Restrepo and Arturo Escobar (June, 2005)." *Critique of Anthropology* 26(4): 463–88.

· Dettwyler, K. 1994. *Dancing Skeletons: Life and Death in West Africa.* Prospect Heights, Ill.: Waveland Press.

DeVita, P. R., and Armstrong, J. D., eds. 2002. *Distant Mirrors: America as a Foreign Culture.* Belmont, Calif.: Wadsworth/Thomson Learning.

➤ Di Leonardo, M. 2009. "The Trope of the Pith Helmet: America's Anthropology, Anthropology's America." In A. Waterston and M. D. Vesperi, eds., *Anthropology off the Shelf: Anthropologists on Writing*, pp. 160–71. Malden, Mass.: Wiley-Blackwell.

———. 1998. *Exotics at Home: Anthropologies, Others, American Modernity.* Chicago: University of Chicago Press.

———. 1984. *Varieties of Ethnic Experience: Kinship, Class, and Gender among California Italian-Americans.* Ithaca, N.Y.: Cornell University Press.

Dominguez, V. R. 1986. *White by Definition: Social Classification in Creole Louisiana.* New Brunswick, N.J.: Rutgers University Press.

· Drake, S. C. 1990. *Black Folk Here and There: An Essay in History of Anthropology.* Vol. 2. Los Angeles: Center for Afro-American Studies, University of California.

———. 1987. *Black Folk Here and There: An Essay in History of Anthropology.* Vol. 1. Los Angeles: Center for Afro-American Studies, University of California.

· ———. 1980. "Anthropology and the Black Experience." *Black Scholar* 11(7): 2–31.

· ———. 1978. "Reflections on Anthropology and the Black Experience." *Anthropology & Education Quarterly* 9(2): 85–109.

Du Bois, C. 1955. "The Dominant Value Profile of American Culture." *American Anthropologist* 57(6): 1232–39.

Edmond, A., Jr. 1993. "Blacks Enraged by Monkey Business at AT&T—Public Outrage over Monkey Illustration Used to Represent Africans in Corporate Newsletter, Focus." *Black Enterprise* (December), pp. 4–5.

Ember, C., and Ember, M. 1985. *Cultural Anthropology.* Englewood Cliffs, N.J.: Prentice-Hall.

Eriksen, T. H. 2006. *Engaging Anthropology: The Case for a Public Presence.* Oxford: Berg.

Fabian, J. 1983. *Time and the Other: How Anthropology Makes Its Object.* New York: Columbia University Press.

Ferguson, J. 2002. "Of Mimicry and Membership: Africans and the 'New World Society.'" *Cultural Anthropology* 17(4): 551–69. Available online at http://wayneandwax. com/pdfs/ferguson_mimicry.pdf.

- Frankenberg, R. 1993. *White Women Race Matters: The Social Construction of Whiteness.* Minneapolis: University of Minnesota Press.

Frankfurt, H. G. 2005. *On Bullshit.* Princeton, N.J.: Princeton University Press.

Gans, H. J. 1999. *Making Sense of America: Sociological Analyses and Essays.* Oxford: Rowman & Littlefield.

Geertz, C. 2000. *Available Light: Anthropological Reflections on Philosophical Topics.* Princeton, N.J.: Princeton University Press.

———. 1985. "Waddling In." *Times Literary Supplement* (June 7), pp. 623–24.

———. 1983. *Local Knowledge: Further Essays in Interpretive Anthropology.* New York: Basic Books.

———, ed. 1974. *Myth, Symbol, and Culture.* New York: W. W. Norton.

———. 1973. *The Interpretation of Cultures.* New York: Basic Books.

Gershenhorn, J. 2004. Series Editors' Introduction [unsigned]. *Melville J. Herskovits and the Racial Politics of Knowledge,* pp. i–xiv. Lincoln: University of Nebraska Press.

Giles, L. 1999. "Spirit Possession and the Symbolic Construction of Swahili Society." In H. Behrend and U. Luig, eds., *Spirit Possession, Modernity, and Power in Africa,* pp. 142–64. Madison: University of Wisconsin Press.

———. 1995. "Sociocultural Change and Spirit Possession on the Swahili Coast of East Africa." *Anthropological Quarterly* 68(2): 89–106.

———. 1989. "Spirit Possession on the Swahili Coast: Peripheral Cults or Primary Texts?" Unpublished PhD dissertation, University of Texas at Austin.

———. 1987. "Possession Cults on the Swahili Coast: A Re-Examination of Theories of Marginality." *Africa: Journal of the International African Institute* 57(2): 234–58.

Gledhill, J. 2005. "Reinventing Anthropology, Anew." *Anthropology News* (October), pp. 6–7.

Goddard, D. 1972. *Anthropology: the Limits of Functionalism. Ideology in the Social Sciences.* New York: Vintage Books.

Goffman, E. 1989. "On Fieldwork." *Journal of Contemporary Ethnography.* 18(2): 123–32.

Gottlieb, A. 2004. *The Afterlife Is Where We Come From: The Culture of Infancy in West Africa.* Chicago: University of Chicago Press.

———. 1992. *Under the Kapok Tree: Identity and Difference in Beng Thought.* Chicago: University of Chicago Press.

———. 1982. "Americans' Vacations." *Annals of Tourism Research* 9(2): 165–87.

Gottlieb, A., and Graham, P. 1994 [1993]. *Parallel Worlds: An Anthropologist and a Writer Encounter Africa.* Chicago: University of Chicago Press.

Graff, G. 2003. *Clueless in Academe: How Schooling Obscures the Life of the Mind.* New Haven, Conn.: Yale University Press.

Grinker, R. R., and Steiner, C. B., eds. 1997. *Perspectives on Africa: A Reader in Culture, History, and Representation.* Cambridge, Mass.: Blackwell.

Gupta, A., and Ferguson, J., eds. 1997a. *Anthropological Locations: Boundaries and Grounds of a Field Science.* Berkeley: University of California Press.

———. 1997b. *Culture, Power, and Place: Explorations in Cultural Anthropology.* Durham, N.C.: Duke University Press.

Guyer, J. 1996. *African Studies in the United States: A Perspective.* Atlanta, Ga.: African Studies Association Press.

Hannerz, U. 2008. "Afterword: Anthropology's Global Ecumene." In Bošković, *Other People's Anthropologies,* pp. 215–30.

Haraway, D. 1988. "Situated Knowledges: The Science Question in Feminism and the Privilege of Partial Perspective." *Feminist Studies* 14(3): 575–99. Available online at http://www.staff.amu.edu.pl/~ewa/Haraway,%20Situated%20Knowledges.pdf.

Harrison, F. V. 2009. "Reworking African(ist) Archaeology in the Postcolonial Period: A Structural Anthropologist's Perspective." In P. R. Schmidt, ed., *Postcolonial Archaeologies in Africa,* 231–41. Santa Fe, N.Mex.: School for Advanced Research Press.

———. 2008. *Outsider Within: Reworking Anthropology in the Global Age.* Urbana: University of Illinois Press.

———. 2000. Foreword. In B. Medicine, *Learning to Be an Anthropologist and Remaining "Native": Selected Writings,* pp. xiii–xviii. Urbana: University of Illinois Press.

———. 1997. "Anthropology as an Agent of Transformation: Introductory Comments and Querries." In F. V. Harrison, ed., *Decolonizing Anthropology: Moving Further toward an Anthropology for Liberation,* pp. 1–14. Washington, D.C.: American Anthropological Association.

———. 1995. "The Persistent Power of "Race" in the Cultural and Political Economy of Racism." *Annual Review of Anthropology* 24: 47–74.

———. 1992. "The Du Boisian Legacy in Anthropology." *Critique of Anthropology* 12(3): 229–37.

———. 1991. "Ethnography as Politics." In F. V. Harrison, ed., *Decolonizing Anthropology: Moving Further toward an Anthropology for Liberation,* pp. 88–109. Washington, D.C.: American Anthropological Association.

Hartigan, J. 2005. *Odd Tribes: Toward a Cultural Analysis of White People.* Durham, N.C.: Duke University Press.

Hasty, J. 2005. "The Pleasures of Corruption: Desire and Discipline in Ghanaian Political Culture." *Cultural Anthropology* 20(2): 271–301.

Holmes, D. R., and Marcus, G. E. 2006. "Fast Capitalism: Para-Ethnography and the Rise of the Symbolic Analyst." In M. S. Fisher and G. Downey, eds., *Frontiers of Capital: Ethnographic Reflections on the New Economy,* pp. 33–57. Durham, N.C.: Duke University Press.

———. 2005. "Cultures of Expertise and the Management of Globalization: Toward the Re-Functioning of Ethnography." In A. Ong and S. J. Collier, eds., *Global As-*

semblages: Technology, Politics, and Ethics as Anthropological Problems, pp. 235–52. Malden, Mass.: Blackwell.

hooks, b. 1994. *Teaching to Transgress: Education as the Practice of Freedom.* New York: Routledge.

Hymes, D., ed. 1972. *Reinventing Anthropology.* New York: Random House.

Jackson, M. 1999. *Paths toward a Clearing: Radical Empiricism and Ethnographic Inquiry.* Bloomington: Indiana University Press.

Jones, T. W. 2006. "Using Contemporary Archaeology and Applied Anthropology to Understand Food Loss in the American Food System." Bureau of Applied Research in Anthropology, University of Arizona. Available online at http://www .communitycompost.org/info/usafood.pdf.

Katongole, E. 2000. "Postmodern Illusions and the Challenges of African Theology: The Ecclesial Tactics of Resistance." *Modern Theology* 16(2): 237–54.

Kim, C. S. 1977. *An Asian Anthropologist in the South: Field Experiences with Blacks, Indians, and Whites.* Knoxville: University of Tennessee Press.

Landman, R. H. 1978. "Applied Anthropology in Post-colonial Britain." *Human Organization* 37(3): 323–27.

Lanthrop, S. 2006. "2005 Annual Meeting the Largest in AAA History." *Anthropology News* (February), pp. 18–19.

• Lewis, D. 1973. "Anthropology and Colonialism." *Current Anthropology* 14(5): 581–602.

Lewis, H. 1999. "The Misrepresentation of Anthropology and Its Consequences." *American Anthropologist* 100(3): 716–31.

Löfgren, O. 1989. "Anthropologizing America." *American Ethnologist* 16(2): 366–74.

Low, S. 2008. "Pursuing an International Initiative: Report from the World Council of Anthropological Associations." *Anthropology News* (October), p. 67. Available online at http://www.aaanet.org/about/Governance/Leadership/Past-President-Setha-Low.cfm.

Lutz, C. 1995. "The Gender Theory." In R. Behar and D. A. Gordon, eds., *Women Writing Culture,* pp. 249–66. Berkeley: University of California Press.

MacClancy, J. 2002. *Exotic No More: Anthropology on the Frontlines.* Chicago: University of Chicago Press.

MacLaren, P. L. 1987. "The Anthropological Roots of Pedagogy: The Teacher as Liminal Servant." *Anthropology & Humanism Quarterly* 12(3–4): 75–85.

Mafeje, A. 1998a. "Anthropology and Independent Africans: Suicide or End of an Era?" *African Sociological Review* 2(1): 1–43.

———. 1998b. "Conversations and Confrontations with My Reviewers." *African Sociological Review* 2(2): 95–107.

———. 1997. "Who Are the Makers and Objects of Anthropology? A Critical Comment on Sally Falk Moore's Anthropology and Africa." *African Sociological Review* 1(1): 1–15.

———. 1996. "A Commentary on Anthropology and Africa." *CODESRIA Bulletin* 2: 12–34.

Magubane, B. 1973. "The Xhosa in Town, Revised Urban Social Anthropology: a Failure of Method." *American Anthropologist* 75(5): 1701–15.

———. 1971. "A Critical Look at Indices Used in the Study of Social Change in Colonial Africa." *Current Anthropology* 12(4–5): 419–45.

Malinowski, B. 1938. Introduction. In J. Kenyatta, ed., *Facing Mount Kenya: The Tribal Life of the Gikuyu*, pp. vii–xiv. London: Secker and Warburg.

Marcus, G. E. 2008. "Postscript: Developments in US Anthropology Since the 1980s, a Supplement: The Reality of Center-Margin Relations, to Be Sure, But Changing (and Hopeful) Affinities in These Relations." In BoBošković, *Other People's Anthropologies*, pp. 199–214.

———. 1998. *Ethnography through Thick and Thin.* Princeton, N.J.: Princeton University Press.

———, ed. 1992. *Reading Cultural Anthropology.* Durham, N.C.: Duke University Press.

Marcus, G. E., and Fischer, M. M. J. 1986. *Anthropology as Cultural Critique: An Experimental Moment in the Human Sciences.* Chicago: University of Chicago Press.

Martin, W. G., and West, M. O. 1999. "The Ascent, Triumph, and Disintegration of the African Enterprise, USA." In W. G. Martin and M. O. West, eds., *Out of One Many Africas: Reconstructing the Study and Meaning of Africa*, pp. 85–108. Urbana: University of Illinois Press.

McAlister, E. 2002. *Rara! Vodou, Power, and Performance in Haiti and Its Diaspora.* Berkeley: University of California Press.

McCurdy, D. 2006. "Using Anthropology." In J. Spradley and D. McCurdy, eds., *Conformity and Conflict: Readings in Cultural Anthropology* (12th edition), pp. 422–35. New York: Pearson.

McGrane, B. 1989. *Beyond Anthropology: Society and the Other.* New York: Columbia University Press.

• Medicine, B. 2001. *Learning to Be an Anthropologist and Remaining "Native": Selected Writings.* Urbana: University of Illinois Press.

Miller, J. C. 2007. "Life Begins at Fifty: African Studies Enters Its Age of Awareness." *African Studies Review* 50(2): 1–35.

Mills, D. 2006. "How Not to Be a 'Government House Pet': Audrey Richards and the East African Institute for Social Research." In Ntarangwi, Mills, and Babiker, *African Anthropologies*, pp. 76–98.

Miner, H. 1956. "Body Ritual among the Nacirema." *American Anthropologist* 58(3): 503–7.

Monzo, L., and Rueda, R. 2009. "Passing for English Fluent: Latino Immigrant Children Masking Language Proficiency." *Anthropology & Education Quarterly* 40(1): 20–40.

Moore, S. F. 1998. "Archie Mafeje's Prescriptions for the Academic Future." *African Sociological Review* 2(1): 50–56.

———. 1994. *Anthropology and Africa: Changing Perspectives on a Changing Scene.* Charlottesville: University Press of Virginia.

Mudimbe, V. Y. 1994. *The Idea of Africa.* Bloomington: Indiana University Press.

———. 1988. *The Invention of Africa: Gnosis, Philosophy, and the Order of Knowledge.* Bloomington: Indiana University Press.

Mwenda, A. 2006. "Taking Time to Contemplate." *Daily Monitor* (August 18), pp. 4–5.

Nachbar, J., and Lause, K., eds. 1992. *Popular Culture: An Introductory Text.* Bowling Green, Ohio: Bowling Green State University Popular Press.

• Nader, L. 1969. "Up the Anthropologist—Perspectives Gained from Studying Up." In D. H. Hymes, ed., *Reinventing Anthropology,* pp. 284–311. New York: Pantheon Books.

Narayan, K. 1991. "Ethnography and Fiction: Where Is the Border?" *Anthropology and Humanism* 24(2): 134–47.

Nathan, R. 2005. *My Freshman Year: What a Professor Learned by Becoming a Student.* Ithaca, N.Y.: University of Cornell Press.

Newman, K. 1988. *Falling from Grace: The Experience of Downward Mobility in the American Middle Class.* New York: Vintage Press.

Ntarangwi, M. 2009. *East African Hip Hop: Youth Culture and Globalization.* Urbana: University of Illinois Press.

———. 2008. "Refacing Mt. Kenya or Excavating the Rift Valley? Anthropology in Kenya and the Question of Tradition." In Bošković, *Other People's Anthropologies,* pp. 83–95.

———. 2007. "Emerging from Shadows of Colonialism: Anthropology as a Collaborative Project in Post-Colonial Africa." Unpublished paper presented at the annual meeting of the American Anthropological Association, Washington, D.C.

———. 2006. "Reflections on the Challenges of Teaching Anthropology to American Students in Post-Colonial Kenya." In Ntarangwi, Mills, and Babiker, *African Anthropologies,* pp. 214–36.

———. 2003a. "The Challenges of Education and Development in Post-Colonial Kenya." *Africa Development* 28(3–4): 211–28.

———. 2003b. *Gender Identity and Performance: Understanding Swahili Cultural Realities through Songs.* Trenton, N.J.: Africa World Press.

Ntarangwi, M., Mills, D., and Babiker, M., eds. 2006. *African Anthropologies: History, Practice, and Critique.* London: Zed Books.

Nzimiro, I. 1979. "Anthropologists and Their Terminologies: A Critical Review." In Gerrit, H., and Mannheim, B., eds. *The Politics of Anthropology: from Colonialism and Sexism toward a View from Below,* pp. 67–83. The Hague: Mouton.

Obbo, C. 2006. "But We Know It All! Africa Perspectives on Anthropological Knowledge." In Ntarangwi, Mills, and Babiker, *African Anthropologies,* pp. 154–69.

———. 1990. "Adventures with Fieldnotes." In R. Sanjek, ed., *Fieldnotes: The Makings of Anthropology*, pp. 290–302. Ithaca, N.Y.: Cornell University Press.

Ogbu, J. U. 2003. *Black American Students in an Affluent Suburb: A Study of Academic Disengagement*. Mahwah, N.J.: L. Erlbaum Associates.

———. 1978. *Minority Education and Caste: The American System in Cross-Cultural Perspective*. New York: Academic Press.

———. 1974. *Next Generation: An Ethnography of Education in an Urban Neighborhood*. New York: Academic Press.

Olaniyan, T. 2003. "Postmodernity, Postcoloniality, and African Studies." In Z. Magubane, ed., *Postmodernism, Postcoloniality, and African Studies*, pp. 39–60. Trenton, N.J.: Africa World Press.

Onyango-Ouma, W. 2006. "Practising Anthropology at Home: Challenges of Ethical Dilemmas." In Ntarangwi, Mills, and Babiker, *African Anthropologies*, pp. 250–66.

Ortner, S. B. 2006. *Anthropology and Social Theory: Culture, Power, and the Acting Subject*. Durham, N.C.: Duke University Press.

———. 2005. "Subjectivity and Cultural Critique." *Anthropological Theory* 5(1): 31–52.

———. 2003. *New Jersey Dreaming: Capital, Culture, and the Class of '58*. Durham, N.C.: Duke University Press.

———, ed. 1999. *The Fate of "Culture": Geertz and Beyond*. Berkeley: University of California Press.

———. 1997. "Fieldwork in the Postcommunity." *Anthropology and Humanism* 22(1): 61–80.

———. 1984. "Theory in Anthropology since the Sixties." *Comparative Studies in Society and History* 26(1): 126–66.

Owusu, M. 1986. "An Ethnography of Ethnographers and Ethnography: Theory and Practice in Socio-cultural Anthropology, a Reconsideration." In M. D. Zamora and B. B. Erring, eds., *Human Intervention: Fieldwork in Cultural Anthropology*, pp. 47–85. Trondheim, Norway: Association of Third World Anthropologists and Department of Social Anthropology, University of Trondheim.

———. 1979. "Colonial and Postcolonial Anthropology in Africa: Scholarship or Sentiment?" In H. Gerrit and B. Mannheim, eds., *The Politics of Anthropology: From Colonialism and Sexism toward a View from Below*, pp. 145–60. The Hague: Mouton.

———. 1978. "Ethnography of Africa: the Usefulness of the Useless." *American Anthropologist* 80: 310–34.

Page, H. 1988. "Dialogic Principles of Interactive Learning in the Ethnographic Relationship." *Journal of Anthropological Research* 44(2): 163–81.

Parikh, S. 2007. "The Political Economy of Marriage and HIV: The ABC Approach, the "Safe" Infidelity, and Managing Moral Risk in Uganda." *American Journal of Public Health* 97(7): 1198–208.

Rabinow, P. 1986. "Representations are Social Facts: Modernity and Post-Modernity in Anthropology." In J. Clifford and G. E. Marcus, eds., *Writing Culture: The Poetics and Politics of Ethnography*, pp. 234–61. Berkeley: University of California Press.

Ramos, A. R. 1992. "Reflecting on the Yanomami: Ethnographic Images and the Pursuit of the Exotic." In G. E. Marcus, ed., *Rereading Cultural Anthropology*, pp. 48–68. Durham, N.C.: Duke University Press.

Reagon, B. J. 1983. "Coalition Politics: Turning the Century." In B. Smith, ed., *Home Girls: A Black Feminist Anthology*, pp. 356–68. New York: Kitchen Table Press.

Restrepo, E., and Escobar, A. 2005. "Other Anthropologies and Anthropology Otherwise: Steps to a World Anthropologies Framework." *Critique of Anthropology* 25(2): 99–129.

Ribeiro, G. L. 2005. "Formation of the World Council of Anthropological Associations." *Anthropology News* (October), pp. 5–6.

Rigby, P. 1996. *African Images, Racism and the End of Anthropology*. Oxford: Berg.

Robinson, P. T. 2003. "Area Studies in Search of Africa." Global, Area, and International Archive, http://escholarship.org/uc/item/36s7z124.

Rothstein, F. 2008. "New Commission on World Anthropologies." *Anthropology News* (March), p. 17. Available online at http://www.aaanet.org/PDF/upload/CWA-Column-Mar08.PDF.

Sacks, K. 1974. *All Our Kin: Strategies and Survival in a Black Community*. New York: Harper and Row.

Said, E. 1978. *Orientalism*. New York: Vintage Books

Schneider, L. 2006. "The Maasai's New Clothes: A Developmentalist Modernity and Its Exclusions." *Africa Today* 53(1): 101–29.

Sichone, O. 2001. "Pure Anthropology in a Highly Indebted Poor Country." *Journal of Southern African Studies* 27(2): 369–79.

Smith, B. 1984. "Between a Rock and a Hard Place: Relationships Between Black and Jewish Women." In E. Bulkin, M. B. Pratt, and B. Smith, eds., *Yours in Struggle: Three Feminist Perspectives on Anti-Semitism and Racism*, pp. 65–87. Brooklyn, N.Y.: Long Haul Press.

Smith, R. T. 1984. "Anthropology and the Concept of Social Class." *Annual Review of Anthropology* 13: 467–94.

Southall, A. 1983. "The Contribution of Anthropology to African Studies." *African Studies Review* 26(3–4): 63–76.

Spencer, J. 1996. "Symbolic Anthropology." In A. Barnard, and J. Spencer, eds., *Encyclopedia of Social and Cultural Anthropology*, pp. 535–39. London: Routledge.

Spiro, M. E. 1996. "Postmodernist Anthropology, Subjectivity, and Science: A Modernist Critique." *Comparative Studies in Society and History* 38(4): 759–80. Available online at http://www.unl.edu/rhames/courses/current/readings/spiro-anti-pomo.pdf.

Spivak, G. C. 1988. "Can the Subaltern Speak?" In C. Nelson and L. Grossberg, eds.,

Marxism and the Interpretation of Culture, pp. 271–313. Urbana: University of Illinois Press.

Sterk, C. 2000. *Tricking and Tripping: Prostitution in the Era of AIDS*. New York: Social Change Press.

Stocking, G. 1995. *After Tylor: British Social Anthropology, 1888–1951*. Madison: University of Wisconsin Press.

———. 1982. "Afterword: A View from the Center." *Ethnos* 47(1–2): 172–86.

Stoller, P. 2004. *Stranger in the Village of the Sick: A Memoir of Cancer, Sorcery, and Healing*. Boston: Beacon Press.

———. 2002. *Money Has No Smell: The Africanization of New York City*. Chicago: University of Chicago Press.

———. 1999. *Jaguar: A Story of Africans in America*. Chicago: University of Chicago Press.

———. 1997. *Fusion of the Worlds: An Ethnography of Possession among the Songhay of Niger*. Chicago: University of Chicago Press.

———. 1995. *Embodying Colonial Memories: Spirit Possession, Power, and the Hauka in West Africa*. New York: Routledge.

Thornton, R. J. 1988. "The Rhetoric of Ethnographic Holism." *Cultural Anthropology* 3(3): 285–303.

Turner, E. 2005. "Changes in the Writing of Anthropology." *Anthropology News* (May), p. 6.

———, ed. 1985. *On the Edge of the Bush: Anthropology as Experience*. Tucson, Ariz.: University of Arizona Press.

Turner, V. W. 1980. "Social Dramas and Stories about Them." *Critical Inquiry* 7: 141–68.

———. 1974. *Dramas, Fields, and Metaphors: Symbolic Action in Human Society*. Ithaca, N.Y.: Cornell University Press.

———. 1967. *The Forest of Symbols: Aspects of Ndembu Ritual*. Ithaca, N.Y.: Cornell University Press.

Udvardy, M. 2001. "The Involuntary Voyage of Katana's Vigango (Part 1): Kenyan Giriama Memorial Statues and the Global Market in African Art." Unpublished paper presented at the Triennial Symposium on African Art, ACASA, St. Thomas, U.S. Virgin Islands.

———. 1992. "The Fertility of the Post-Fertile: Concepts of Gender, Aging and Reproductive Health among the Giriama of Kenya." *Journal of Cross-Cultural Gerontology* 7(4): 289–306.

———. 1990. "Gender and the Culture of Fertility Cult among the Giriama of Kenya." Unpublished PhD dissertation, Uppsala University, Uppsala, Sweden.

Udvardy, M. L., Giles, L. L., and Mitsanze, J. B. 2003. "The Transatlantic Trade in African Ancestors: Mijikenda Memorial Statues (Vigango) and the Ethics of Collecting and Curating Non-Western Cultural Property." *American Anthropologist* 105(3): 566–80.

Ulysse, G. 2002. "Conquering Duppies in Kingston: Miss Tiny and Me, Fieldwork

Conflicts, and Being Loved and Rescued." *Anthropology and Humanism* 27(1): 10–26. Available online at https://segue.southwestern.edu/userfiles/ANT3596401-w09/Ulysse%20Duppies.pdf.

Valenzuela, H., and Molina, J. 2007. "Spanish Professional Anthropology Outside of Academia? A Case Study." Unpublished paper presented at the annual meeting of the American Anthropological Association, Washington, D.C.

Van Maanen, J. 1988. *Tales of the Field: On Writing Ethnography.* Chicago: University of Chicago Press.

• Visweswaran, K. 1998. "Race and the Culture of Anthropology." *American Anthropologist* 100(1): 70–83.

Wallerstein, I. 1983. "The Evolving Role of the African Scholar in African Studies." *African Studies Review* 26(3–4): 155–61.

World Anthropologies Network Collective. 2006. "Establishing Dialogue among International Anthropological Communities." *Journal of the World Anthropology Network* 1(2): 9–11. Available online at http://www.ram-wan.net/documents/05_e_Journal/journal-2/2.wancollective.pdf.

———. 2003. "A Conversation about a World Anthropologies Network." *Social Anthropology* 11(2): 265–69. Available online at http://www.ram-wan.net/documents/06_documents/wan_2003_a_conversation_about_a_world_anthropologies_network.pdf.

Yu, P.-L. 1997. *Hungry Lightning: Notes of a Woman Anthropologist in Venezuela.* Albuquerque: University of New Mexico Press.

Zeleza, P. T. 1997. *Manufacturing African Studies and Crises.* Dakar: CODESRIA.

Index

Abu-Lughod, Lila, and writing against culture, 36

Addis Ababa (headquarters of Organization of Social Science Research in Eastern and Southern Africa), 7

African American: disturbing mainstream anthropology, 16; experiences in anthropology, 17, 55, 128, 129; and the L.A. riots, 26; males as "endangered species," 32; and marginalization in anthropology, 17; in media images, 26; perceptions of race, 32; relations with Africans, 38, 128, 129; as scholars studying race, 27; as subjects of community research project, 25, 28, 30, 33, 35, 37, 45–47; as working-class, 65; working in a hotel in Washington D.C., 113. *See also* anthropology

African anthropology: conditions for growth, 150; relationship to postmodernism, 147, 149

Africana studies (combining African and African American studies), 129

African Diaspora, linking to African studies, 129

Africanist: as an academic identity, 130; call to emulate anthropology, 139, 140; training at Northwestern University, 130; White gatekeepers, 128

Africanist anthropologist: identifying as, 126, 140; responding to Mafeje's challenges, 77

Africanist anthropology: as dead, 76; as represented by Herskovits, 129

Africanity, as a shared identity for Africans, 3

African Sociological Review, and debate between Archie Mafeje and Sally Falk Moore, 77

African studies: in America, 128; as an area of research interest, 115, 126, 129; as dominated by White anthropologists, 128; and relationship to anthropology, 130; at the University of Nairobi, 127. *See also* Herskovits, Melville

African Studies Association: conference in Chicago, 107; meeting in San Francisco, 139

African Studies Center: at Northwestern University, 129; in Title VI universities, 130

alterity: Africans and, 72; anthropology's focus and fixation with, x, xii, 52, 74; as anthropology's undoing, 74; as the basis for nonscientific worldview, 149; as defining anthropology, 131, 148; as framed by Western scholarship of Africa, 148; Western notions and, 3, 148; why anthropologists pursue it, 70

American Anthropological Association (AAA): attempts to connect with global applied anthropology associations, 132; relationship to Society for Applied Anthropology, 64; as source of ethnographic data, xii, 101

American Anthropologist, as flagship journal, 123

American Ethnologist, as flagship journal, 123

Amuyunzu-Nyamongo, Mary, and view of anthropology as marginalized, 95

Anglo-French Axis, dominant Western anthropological practice as, xi, 153n5

annual meetings: AAA relationship to SfAA and, 64; book exhibits and, 114, 115; hosted in Africa by ASA, 124; job hunters and, 115, 116; membership, 125; as networking sites, 113–14; in New Orleans, 104, 115; PAAA and, 103, 106, 107; participants at, 125; as strategies for world anthropologists to collaborate, 138–39; as symbolic sites for studying anthropologists, xii, 81, 121; in Washington D.C., 111, 112, 136, 141

anthropological authority, weakening position of discipline through turn to poetics, 147

anthropology: in action, xi; of anthropology, 4; applied, 64, 99; Black experience and, 17; critiques of and, 14, 77; cultural Critique and, 100; dual identity and, 141, 142; ethnography of and, xi, 2; marginal and, 94–97, 141, 144–47; native perspectives and, viii; pure, 64; pursuit of the Other and, 70; racist label of, vii, 55–57; reflexive, xi, 1, 123; "soft science" and, 95; symbolic and interpretive, 12; toolkit for other disciplines and, 118, 161n15; Uganda and, 96; Western, viii, 2, 19, 22, 33, 78; World, 102

Anthropology News: announcing Commission for World Anthropologies, 131; announcing World Anthropology Network, 132; column on world anthropologies, 138

Arusha: ASA meeting in, 124; meeting Johannes Fabian in, 76. *See also* Association for Social Anthropology in the UK and Commonwealth

Association for Africanist Anthropology (AfAA), membership in, 112

Association for Social Anthropology in the UK and Commonwealth (ASA): in contrast with AAA, 103, 123; history of, 124;

meeting in Arusha, 124–25; meeting in London, 125; meetings in Africa, 124

AT&T, representing Africa with a monkey, 57

Baker, Lee, creating alternative epistemologies in anthropology, 15

Basso, Keith, working with Nyaigotti-Chacha at Yale, 4

Baudrillard, Jean, critiquing American culture, 50, 63

BBC (British Broadcasting Corporation), as source of alternative news in Kenya, 89

Beidelman, Tom O., recycling field notes, 75

Benedict, Ruth, engaging subjectivity in ethnography, 147

Boas, Franz: African American anthropologists and, 128, 129; as antiracist, 57; Elliott Skinner as Boas Chair at Columbia, 16; reputation in anthropology compared to Black anthropologists, 109

Britain: as anthropology center, 136; hegemonic centers of anthropology, 130, 136; as less racist than America, 16–17; production of intellectuals, 63

British social anthropology, functionalist approach, viii, 64

Bruner, Edward, and symbolic interpretive approach, 11

Buck, Pem Davidson, transcending nativization and Othering in anthropology, 15

capitalism: shaping liberal arts education, 66; shaping postmodern responses in anthropology, 18–19

Caplan, Pat, on informants writing ethnography, 75

Carroll, Raymonde, on the challenges of writing ethnographies, 22

Chicago School, and sociologists conducting ethnographic research, 144

Clark, Gracia, and ethnography as relational, 143–44

Clifford, James, and ethnography as fiction, viii

Cole, Johnnetta B. (AAA distinguished lecturer), 16

collaboration: American and other anthropologies and, 97; with local interlocutors, 19; signaling attempts to transcend national anthropology hegemonies, 132; theme of AAA annual meeting, 111

Combs-Schilling, Elaine, on images as powerful symbols, 54

Commission on World Anthropologies (CWA): in *Anthropology News*, 131; as opportunity for world anthropologies collaboration, 133–34; plans for improving collaboration among world anthropologists, 138; process of formation, 132

"communitas": research group dynamics and, 35; responding to critiques of concept of culture, 12

constructivism, shift in social reality and, 14

Cornwell, Grant, on consumerism in higher education, 66

corporatization, higher education and, 62, 66

corruption: endemic in Kenya, 88; as social phenomenon, 160n12

crisis: precursor to reflexive ethnography, xi; Western anthropology and, 19

D'Alisera, JoAnn, on switching field sites but studying same subject, 71–74

demonology, as precedent for anthropology in constructing Otherness, 148–49

Diasporic Africanists, as different approach to Africa compared to Herskovits, 129

Di Leonardo, Michaela, transcending nativization and Othering in anthropology, 15

Dominguez, Virginia (AAA president, 2009–11), 16, 138; transcending nativization and Othering in anthropology, 15

downward mobility, elite Africans in America and, 80

Drake, St. Clair: Black experiences in anthropology, 17; critiques of anthropology, 4; finding a home in sociology, 15; marginalization in anthropology, 16

Du Bois, Cora, and role of higher education in America, 62, 63

Du Bois, W. E. B., and opposition from Herskovits, 130

East Africa: culture of conferences, 107; music with social message, 5; return of community artifacts, 141–42; site for ethnographic research, 75, 92; studying the Swahili x; urban societies, 7

Ecuador, as exotic field site, 53

Egerton University: academic collaboration, 81; comparative analysis of utilizing teaching resources, 97; limited teaching resources, 87

empiricism, 14

endogamy, academic hiring and, 18

epistemology: critiques of Western worldview, 148; example of obscure writing, 110; regard for non-Western Other, 149

Escobar, Arturo: different anthropological paradigms, 102; formation of World Anthropology Network, 132; imbalance of power in anthropology, 102; personal networks, 136; World anthropologies symposium in Italy, 133, 136

Ethiopia, and anthropologists removing local artifacts, 141–42

ethnographer: advantages of being a foreigner, 39; commitment to local sociopolitical issues, 75; interpersonal connections, 143; power over informants, 20; promoting a cultural industry, 13; reflexivity and, xi; research and personal agendas, 144; serial informants, 118–21

ethnographic research: anthropology as toolkit, 140; evidence for defending repatriation of local artifacts, 141; other disciplines appropriating anthropological tools, 144; relationality and anthropology, 142–43

ethnography: of anthropology, 2; Chicago School, 144; end of, 118–22; as fiction, 1, 36, 153n2; mini-, 47; para-, 101; poetics of, 147–50; pseudo-, 118; quick and dirty, 118; reflexive, 33

European Association of Social Anthropology (EASA), anthropological kinship and, 137

European Other, construction of, 149

Evans-Pritchard, Edward, founding of ASA, 124

exotic: Africans as, 72; anthropology's distinctive identity and, 70; anthropology's fixation on, x, 14, 71; in contrast with para-ethnography, 101; learning about self and, ix

exoticism, anthropology and, 53

expressive culture, as sphere for analyzing construction of culture concept, 12

Fabian, Johannes, recycling field notes, 76
Facing Mount Kenya, as first Kenyan ethnography, vii
family values, and change in African American social practices, 30
feminism, as challenge to Western cultural hegemony, 19
Ferguson, James, on mimicry, 82
field notes: anxiety of studying up, 42; recycling and, 74–76, 109, 120
field site: Africans as quintessential Other, 71–74; relationship to fiction, 122; symbolized through cultural artifacts, 104
fieldwork: critiques of positivism, 134; interactions with interlocutors, 140; local expectations, 141–42; uncertainty of findings, 122–23, 143
Fischer, Michael, and anthropology as cultural critique, 21
Frankenberg, Ruth: Black-White relationships, 26; discussing race in the classroom, 49–50
Frankfurt, Harry, on obscure academic writing, 60

Gans, Herbert, on social class analysis, 67
gatekeepers: anthropology ownership and, 131; White anthropologists as, 128
gaze: cross-cultural experiences and, 11, 21; and cultural critique, 42; power relations and, 13; production of anthropological knowledge, x; reworking anthropology, 4
Geertz, Clifford: and concept of culture, 11–12; crisis in Western anthropology, 19; ethnography as fiction, 36; holistic study of culture, 8; model for Africanists, 140; symbolic and interpretive analysis, 2, 11; thick description of culture, 118, 150
gender: evading critical analysis of, 64; identity and, 16–18; perceptions of segregation and, 27; public norms and expectations and, 90; relationship to social inequalities and, 6; Swahili popular music and, 103
Gershenhorn, Jerry, on Herskovits's relationship to African Americans, 130
Giles, Linda, repatriating local artifacts, 141
Gledhill, John, practicing anthropology abroad, 137–38

globalization: anthropological traditions and, 133; future of anthropology and, 126
Gottlieb, Alma, and symbolic and interpretive anthropology, 11
Graduate Anthropology Student Association (GASA), symbolic representation of race, 52
Graff, Gerald, and obscure academic writing, 61, 110

Harambee, and spirit of community development in Kenya, 92, 160n15
Haraway, Donna, and ethnographic knowledge as relational, 142
Harnez, Ulf, on anthropological kinship, 137
Harrison, Faye: and American anthropology's relationship with other anthropologies, 126; and creating alternative spaces in anthropology, 112; mainstream anthropology tradition, 153n5
Hartigan, John, on transcending nativization and Othering in anthropology, 15
hegemony: middle-class cultural values and, 69; postcolonial corporate culture, 65; postmodernism as response to, 18–19
Herskovits, Melville: establishing African Studies at Northwestern, 129–30; relations with African Americans, 128–31
hierarchy: in anthropology, 16, 17, 134; anthropology on the margins and, 64; commoditization of higher education and, 66, 113; in the field, 25; as symbolizing racial differences, 57
HIV/AIDS: gendered identity and, 90; targets of applied anthropology, 145
Holmes, Douglas, on para-ethnography, 101
hooks, bell: on social class and money, 69; verbal prowess and social class, 65

immigrants, 14; African, 71, 72; Sierra Leonean, 74
individualism, 92
informants, 29, 33, 43, 73, 75, 118–22
Institute of African Studies, 94, 127
interdisciplinarity, 8
International Union of Anthropological and Ethnological Sciences (IUAES), as forum for international anthropologist to interact, 132, 139

Islam, as topic of ethnographic research, 72

Jordan, Glen, and African American anthropology, 16
Jordan, Michael, as symbolic representation of race, 53

Katongole, Emmanuel, and postmodernism and Africa, 149
Kenyan anthropology, as reflecting diverse traditions, 133
Kenyatta, Jomo: dictatorial rule, 89; writing ethnography, vii–ix

Lause, Kevin, and American anti-intellectualism, 63
Lewis, Diane, and anthropology's commitment to the local, 64
liberal arts college: social class and, 65; student entitlement, 66
Löfgren, Orvar, and challenges of studying up, 71, 73
Low, Setha (AAA president, 2007–9), 138
Lutz, Catherine, and abstruse language and anthropological theory, 61

Maasai: "Operation Dress Up," 13; resistance to Westernization, 159n2; Western gaze and, 15
MacLaren, Peter, on classroom reflection of social reality, 69
Mafeje, Archie: on African anthropology, 76–77, 148; on anthropology as racist, 24
Magubane, Ben, 15; relationship to sociology, 15, 16
malaria: collaborative anthropology and, 96; practicing anthropology in Africa, 145
Malinowski, Branislow, on need for "native" anthropology, viii, ix
Marcus, George: on anthropology as cultural critique, 21; on para-ethnography, 101, 161n1; world anthropologies, 134
Matatu: flouting traffic laws, 92, 93; as purveyors of popular culture, 87–89; symbolic representation of society, 160n11, 160n16
Matrioshka doll, as symbolizing anthropological practices, 136
Mazrui, Ali A., conscientious writing of, 20

McAlister, Elizabeth, on transmigrants, 80
McGrane, Bernard, and foundations of postmodernism, 148
Mead, Margaret, culture and personality, school, and, 147
medical anthropology, practice of anthropology in Kenya, 99, 145
Medicine, Beatrice (Native American anthropologist), 22, 56
Meru: cross-cultural experiences, 90–92; multiple meanings, 160n14
modernity: colonial and, 97; Western education and, 79; Western gaze and, 13
Mohammed, Malika (taarab musician), 7
Mohanty, Chandra, challenging Western feminism, viii
Moi University, African Studies at, 94
Mombasa, field site, 92–93
monkeys: representation of Africans as, 52, 53, 55, 57
Moore, Sally Falk, exchange with Archie Mafeje, 76, 77
Moses, Yolanda T. (AAA president, 1995–97), 16
Mudimbe, Valentine Y.: constructing the idea of Africa, 14; impenetrable books on Africa, 61
multiculturalism, and anthropology and study of race, 57–58
multivocality, representing field experiences, 11
music: gender and, 103; representations of women, 90; study of Muslim culture, 92
Muslim: popular music and, 92; transnational identity, 72
Mwenda, Andrew, on peasant culture, 82–83

Nachbar, Jack, and American anti-intellectualism, 63
Nacirema, and reflexive anthropology, 42
neoliberal model: AAA guidelines for hosting annual meetings, 112; African anthropology and, 139; role of anthropology and, 125–26
Newman, Katherine, and downward mobility, 80
Nyaigotti-Chacha, Chacha, and introduction to anthropology, 4
Nyerere, Julius, and alternative political ideology, 148

Obbo, Christine: place of anthropology in Uganda, 95–96; studying western anthropologists, 42

Ogbu, John: minority students in higher education, 158n21; place of foreigners in fieldwork, 39; studies of race and access in higher education, 15

Olaniyan, Tejumola, on postmodernism and Africa, 150

Ongala, Remmy, and music and social consciousness, 5

Onyango-Ouma, Washington, on anthropology and the question of its scientific identity, 95–96, 160n10

Organization for Social Science Research in Eastern and Southern Africa (OSSREA), support for research, 7

Ortner, Sherry: on anthropology and study of race, 67; defining culture, 12; on social class, 69; on studying up, 159n39; on symbolic and interpretive anthropology, 11

Owusu, Maxwell: alternative epistemologies in anthropology, 15; challenging African scholars, 108; position in mainstream anthropology, 16

Pan African Anthropological Association (PAAA): absence in World Anthropology Network, 135; symbolizing economic differences in practicing anthropology, 107

participant observation: among anthropologists, 98–99; in suburban America, 158n38; in Western American society, 71

postmodernism: abstruse language and, 150; Africa and, 149; anthropology and, 149; subjectivity in anthropology and, 147; Western male hegemony, 18

power: admission decisions in department and, 99; field relations and, 33; race and, 49; studying own culture and, 25; studying up and, 42

Rabinow, Paul, and anthropologizing the West, ix

race: and anthropology, 17, 23, 25; and gender, 16, 17; production of underlying epistemologies, 16–17; project on, 26–28, 38, 45–48; as topic of classroom discussion, 49–51

racism: attraction into anthropology, 56;

framework for anthropology, 24, 77; Franz Boas and, 57; intention and, 49; new anthropological discussions of, 157n7; physical anthropology and, 57

Ramos, Alcida, pursuit of the Other, 70

representation: of Africans in popular media, 57; anthropological writing styles and, 3; Eurocentricism and, 14; politics of, 13; using locally derived objects, 11; vulnerable self in ethnography, 2

Ribeiro, Gustavo Lins, on world anthropologies, 132, 133, 134

Robinson, Pearl, on Herskovits and Africans, 128

Rothstein, Frances, on Committee of World Anthropologies, 131

Sacks, Karen, transcending nativization and Othering in anthropology, 15

Secular Missionary Syndrome, anthropology and, 56

Sichone, Owen, on anthropology's tarnished name, 146

Skinner, Elliott, 15, 16, 112, 129

social class: in the classroom, 65–68; frame for understanding American culture, 64; sociologists and, 67; Whiteness and, 70

Society for Applied Anthropology (SfAA), relationship to AAA, 64

Society for Humanistic Anthropology, obscure writing in anthropology, 110

Society for the Anthropology of North America (SANA), studying American cultures, 15

studying down, power differences and, 3

studying up, problem of, 41–43, 71, 72

Swaleh, Zuhura (taarab musician), 7

taarab, as research topic, 7

Tanzania: ASA meeting in, 124; Maasai in, 159n2; participation in professional meetings, 107

Taylor, Edward B., and social Darwinism, 149

Torres, Lourdes, challenging Western feminism, viii

tourists: academic, 150; New Orleans and, 105, 106; representing Western culture, 81, 91

transmigrant, Africans as, 80

Turner, Edit: obscure writing in anthropology, 109, 110; symbolic and interpretive analysis, 11
Turner, Victor: defining culture, 12; and symbolic and interpretive analysis, 11

Udvardy, Monica, and repatriation of local artifacts, 141
Undergraduate Association for Student Anthropologists (UGASA), symbolizing race, 52–56
University of Nairobi, African Studies at, 93, 94, 127

Visweswaran, Kamala, and race and anthropology, 57, 157n7

Wallerstein, Immanuel, on academic division of labor, 127, 128, 148

Washington, D.C.: AAA annual meeting, 111; as a field site, 71, 74
Wenner-Gren Foundation for Anthropological Research, Inc., supporting world anthropologies, 132–35
White flight, desegregation and, 31
Whiteness: at AAA annual meeting, 113; discussions of race and, 50; social privilege, 70; in *Transforming Anthropology*, 157n6
Williams, Brett, transcending nativization and Othering in anthropology, 15
World Anthropology Network (WAN), expanding anthropological terrains, xiii, 132
World Council of Anthropological Associations (WCAA), creating spaces for collaboration, xiii, 102
writing against culture, ethnography and, 36

Zeleza, Paul T., and academic tourists, 150

MWENDA NTARANGWI is an associate professor of anthropology at Calvin College and the author of *East African Hip Hop: Youth Culture and Globalization* and *Gender Identity and Performance*.

The University of Illinois Press
is a founding member of the
Association of American University Presses.

University of Illinois Press
1325 South Oak Street
Champaign, IL 61820-6903
www.press.uillinois.edu

Printed by Printforce, United Kingdom